D(T)OXIC LANDSCAPES | Adrien Sina | born 1961, is an

Architect (UP1 Paris and AA London) and Theorist. Curator of the *Fugitive Fluctuations* and *Tragédies Charnelles* exhibitions

(published in *La Mazarine* #12, Paris, March 2000) and *Immanences Spatiales* (*La Mazarine* #13, June 2000). Residences:

Villa Médicis; New York; Tokyo, Villa Kujoyama, Kyoto; Art Center College of Design, Pasadena. Teaching initiative:

Multimedia performance and Cross-disciplinary Fusion. Other publications: Atlantica #23, Barcelona-Girona, and regularly

Inter Art Actuel, Québec. Virtual Urbanity: www.cicv.fr/virtual-urbanity. Virtual Parliament: www.cicv.fr/virtual-parliament

● AFTER AMNESIA | Nikos Papastergiadis | is the

Simon Research Fellow, University of Manchester. Recent books include: *The Turbulence of Migration* (Polity Press, 2000)

and editor of *What John Berger Saw* (Canberra School of Art Gallery, 2000).

● AN INTERVIEW WITH
BILL VIOLA | Stuart Morgan | ...is an art critic. His books include *What*

the Butler Saw: Selected Writings (1996) and *Inclinations* (a second selection of essays and interviews – forthcoming), both

from Durian Publications.

● INTERVENTIONS: AN INTERVIEW WITH ISAAC
JULIEN | Devin Anthony Orgeron | teaches film and film theory

at the University of Maryland. Recent publications include an article in Film Quarterly on Isaac Julien's *The Attendant*. An

article on the historical roots of the road film will appear in the second edition of *Travel Culture*, edited by Carol Williams.

| Marsha Gabrielle Orgeron | is completing her dissertation "Making Reputations:

Publicity and Representation in the Cinematic Era" at the University of Maryland. Recent and forthcoming articles can be

found in the *Quarterly Review of Film & Video*, *College Literature*, the *Canadian Review of American Studies* and

Enculturation.

● DOT.JP: A CURATOR'S TOUR | Barbara
London | is a curator and has created one of the first ongoing video exhibition programs in the world. At The

Museum of Modern Art, New York she has built an essential context, linking the electronic arts with the more traditional art

mediums, for the visionary statements being made internationally in media art by emerging talents and more established

artists such as Joan Jonas, Nam June Paik, Gary Hill, and Bill Viola. She has taught at New York University, the School of Visual

Arts, and has written and lectured extensively. Her web projects include: www.moma.org/stirfry, www.moma.org/internyet,

www.moma.org/dot.jp, and www.moma.org/rewind.

● **IN PLACE OF FIRE: INSECTS AND THE DEATH OF PAN** | | Nicky Coutts | is an artist and writer shortly

to complete a research degree on the appearance and significance of insects in art and literature at the RCA. Recent projects

include the co-founding of Prawn Publishing (prawn@food4u.com).

● **MOVING AN EDITION FOR COIL: LEAVING 25 BEDEFIELD CROMER ST. KINGS CROSS LONDON 1988–2000 COLOUR PHOTOGRAPH (SERIES OF 6) / QUOTE SONG OF SOLOMON / MUSIC CRYING ROY ORBISON / I'VE BEEN CRYING (1990 TEXT) / STILLS FROM THE 12 YEARS OF FILMS** | | Sarah Miles | is not sure about being a

writer/director or an artist/filmmaker. *MOVING* was made as a response to being transferred by Camden Council after 12

years living on a sink estate in Kings Cross. Currently in development: *there's no place like home*, an installation for the

Belfry St. Pancras Church and *2001 a family odyssey* for ACE.

● **HAMMER ON THE HEAD: THE LAST INTERVIEW OF DAVID WOJNAROWICZ** | | Sylvere Lotringer | editor of Semiotext(e), teaches French literature and philosophy at Columbia

University. He is generally credited for having introduced French Theory to America. He is presently editing a volume

of William Burroughs's interviews and a book around David Wojnarowicz's work. His essay on "Doing Theory" will be

published by Routledge in 2001.

● **LIFE IN MUSIC** | | Nelson Henricks | is a graduate of the Alberta College of Art (1986); he moved to Montréal in 1991, where he received a BFA from Concordia University (1994). Henricks continues to live and work in Montréal, where he teaches part-time at

Concordia University, the Université de Québec à Montréal and McGill University. A musician, writer, curator and artist,

Henricks is best known for his videotapes, which have been exhibited worldwide.

● JOHN LATHAM

Jurgen Harten ...... was

Director of the Städische Kunsthalle Düsseldorf when this article was first published in 1975.

● WHATEVER

1954: Point mark approach to form

THE INCIDENTAL PERSON | John Latham

HAPPENED..? |

breaches the disciplines to disclose principles of structure in events. In order... 1968 Book reliefs. 1961 Film. 1965 Paintings

for a turning cylinder. 1967 Event Structure board. 1972 Time-Base Roller. 1973 With Barbara Steveni and APG, formulated

Whitehall Treaty. 1992 Basic (T) diagram as flat time: Three time-related components only to constitute an inclusive

cosmology.

● JOHN CAGE'S EARLY WARNING SYSTEM |

Charlie Gere ...... is a lecturer in the School of History of Art, Film and Visual Media, Birkbeck College,

University of London. He is currently writing a book on Digital Culture for Polity Press.

● AN ENDLESS

INSURRECTION | Gilles Lazare ...... is a writer based in London, his

writings have appeared in Parallax (*Honour* issue 1999), Inventory, COIL and Errant Bodies *Flowers* (Los Angeles).

● UNWINDING COIL... | A.L. Rees ...... is Senior Research Fellow at

the Royal College of Art. His book, *A History of Experimental Film and Video* was published by BFI Publishing in 1999.

● GHOST LENS | Tina Keane ...... works with installation, Film, Video and the Digital Area. Has

shown in Galleries and Festivals world wide including one person British Council tours of Australia and Japan, as well as the

MOMA New York and the Hayward, Tate, Serpentine and ICA, London. She is a Professor and Research Fellow in Fine Art

Film and Video at Central Saint Martins College of Art and Design. Technology for Tina Keane is an active ingredient, the

process through which her work evolves and engages with a conceptual momentum.

Death 24 times a second:
the tension between movement and stillness in the cinema

Laura Mulvey

The cinema recently, in 1995, celebrated its 100th birthday and since then, like the rest of us has hurried towards another major temporal marker: the year 2000. These markers may be, and perhaps should be, simple celebrations of survival but they are also moments when the transitions, upheavals and profound changes that have overtaken the cinema in recent years acquire dramatic, public, visibility. Critics, theorists and even the public at large suddenly focus their attention on the current 'state of the cinema'. This essay belongs very much to that kind of flurry of speculative activity. However, it is not about the new image generating technologies that are enhancing the 'millennial effect' hanging over the cinema at the moment. It derives from the presence of these technologies, the concepts and different ways of seeing that they bring with them and the way they affect critical perspectives on the cinema. That is, it is more about different ways of thinking about the cinema *as it has been*, in the past, than about ways in which the cinema is or will be changed in the future. Such an altered perspective may, itself, be a by-product of electronic and digital technologies. Thomas Elsaesser sums up the paradox:

> **"[The cinema] will remain the same and it will be utterly different... For the digital is not only a new system of post-production work and a new delivery system, or storage medium, it is the new horizon for thinking about cinema, which also means that it gives a vantage point beyond the horizon, so that we can, as it were, try to look back to where we actually are and how we arrived there. The digital can thus function as a time machine, a conceptual boundary as well as its threshold."(1)**

...

Death and the cinema

...

With the actual passing of time and the sudden impact of the 'digital', the cinema, aged 105 in the year 2000, has assumed a new aura of 'oldness'. It is not simply this 'oldness' that has brought a sense of death to the cinema, although the passing of time has certainly brought the cinema/death relation into relief. As the cinema has always had the ability to capture the appearance of life and preserve it after death, it is perhaps only the ironies of this property that are now becoming more apparent, more visible or analysable. From this angle, tension between movement and stillness is essential to the cinema as a technology and as an illusion. But on another, more metaphoric, level the stillness/movement tension coincides with the cinema's capacity to create an illusion of life out of the presence of death. But there is another aspect to the stillness/movement tension that is not specific to the cinema. As a medium, which always has been, and still is, subject to the demands of storytelling, the cinema shares the tension between movement and stillness that is characteristic of narrative itself. Again, the present moment, with its attraction to endings, with the threat of 'ending' hanging over the cinema itself, brings with it an extra awareness of the death-like properties of narrative closure. Inevitably, such a conjuncture shifts the attention of the psychoanalytically influenced critic away from a preoccupation with the erotic as the propelling force of narrative towards death. The death drive, as a propelling force of narrative, starts to merge with the cinema's stillness, its own death-like properties. With the arrival of new technologies, new ways of consuming and perceiving the cinematic image have become available, giving new visibility to the cinema's inherent stillness. The individual frame, the projected film's best kept secret, can now be revealed, by anyone, at the simple touch of the relevant button.

...

These themes, stillness/movement in cinema and in narrative, the impact of new technologies, have combined to give (me, at least) an altered perspective on death, the cinema and Freud's concept of the death-drive. In this essay, I have selected only certain aspects of the issues at stake, concentrating on the death-drive in narrative structure to create a backdrop for my argument about death in the cinema as such. My main point of reference will be Hollywood's mode of storytelling during the studio system period. Hollywood managed to transcend movements and epochs to establish itself as the cinema, if only for a few decades, and it is probably the decay and diffusion (in the 60s) of its characteristic industrial system of production, distribution and exhibition that, in popular imagination, sounded the death-knell of the cinema. The studio system is synonymous with the star system, and the great stars who fronted for it, its icons and emblems, have themselves died only to be threatened with resurrection by computer generated simulation. I will end the essay with Marilyn Monroe, not only as an extreme example of the star system and its condensation with an emblematic femininity, but as a star whose actual death coincided with the death of the system that had made her a star.

...

Although new technologies figure as a starting point for this essay, most of it consists of two detours, returning to their impact on the perception and consumption of cinema at the very end.

The first detour

...

1 Stillness becomes movement: cinema and narrative

...

As everyone knows, the cinema consists of a series of still frames, in sequence, on a strip of celluloid. When actions are filmed and then projected at the speed of 24 (give or take) frames per second, they then give the spectating eye an illusion of natural movement. This paradox lies at the heart of many debates about the cinema's ontology and carries over into its specificity as a narrative form.

...

The excitement of 'the movies' extends into a chain reaction out of this initial animation of the still frame. Once the picture comes alive, the illusory movement of the frames merges into the movements inside the shot. Concentrated very often, especially in stories, into the movement of its human characters, movements accumulate from shot to shot, merging into sequences and scenes. These movements, from shot to shot and from scene to scene, may then merge with the overall movement of narrative itself. The frame, the cinema's latent stillness, is mobilised and woven into the sequence of shots, the chain-like structure characteristic of narrativity attaches itself easily to the cinema's affinity with sequence. And a particular story, its fiction and its characters, then makes up its own movement, with excitements, suspense, drive etc., animating what would otherwise be an interesting, but inert, pattern.

...

Of course, narrative, its characteristic movements and its varying patterns, exists in its own right, outside the cinema, pre-existing the cinema. Peter Brooks, in his analysis of narrative movement and stillness, makes a distinction between its serial nature, its chain-like formation, and its movement, which, he suggests, is activated by desire:

> **"The description of narrative needs metonymy (the figure of contiguity, combination and the syntagmatic relation) the figure of linkage in the signifying chain: precedence and consequence, the movement from one detail to another, the movement towards totalisation under the mandate of desire."(2)**

And he locates this, activating, element of narrativity within a psycho-analytic dimension, also restoring the temporal dimension to narrative structure that tended to disappear in structuralist distrust of linearity:

> **"Lacan helps us to understand how the aims and imaginings of desire move us from the realm of basic drives to highly elaborated fictions. Desire necessarily becomes textual by way of a specifically narrative impulse, since desire is metonymy, a forward drive in the signifying chain, an insistence on meaning towards the occulted objects of desire."(3)**

Although, the drive forward towards meaning and the resolution of desire are key elements in plotting narrative, stillness is its essential counterpoint. In the simplest terms, now a cliché of basic narrative theory, an initial point of stasis is activated into a process of movement and change which returns to a same yet different stasis at the end. However slight, compared to the length and events of the story as a whole those points of stasis may be, they still mark out, or book-end, the space of change and transformation. For instance, in traditional folk-tales, the two points of stasis may be literally rendered by:

a) The home, static like the beginning of the story itself, that the hero leaves

And:

c) The new, grander, home the hero establishes with the princess which 'settles' both his movement and that of the story

While the movement between the two is marked by:

b) The path of his journey from one to another, the road along which he travels which literally figures the process of narrative change and transformation.

...

Closure, the final stasis, is realised as 'wedding' and the subsequent establishment of a new home and a new family. This is the kind of story analysed by Vladimir Propp in his *Morphology of the Folk Tale*. And although its 'rite of passage' narrative may not be relevant to the urbanised twentieth century, the power of its structure and the importance of marking 'The End' as (sexual) stasis has been passed on, like a family legacy, to twentieth century popular cinema. But the 'happy end' with which this story comes to rest is built on top of the villain's grave. His death, the resolution of the story's mobilisation as conflict, prefigures the hero's wedding so that both 'death' and 'wedding' realise the abstract necessity of narrative closure.

...

2 Movement becomes stillness: narrative and the 'death drive'

...

When considering the term 'death drive', it is important to remember that James Strachey chose to translate Freud's concept *Trieb* into English as 'instinct' in preference to 'drive' which had been used previously. In his 1920 essay *Beyond the Pleasure Principle*, Freud discusses the instinct which overwhelms the pleasure principle, seeking to find a way back to "an earlier state of things" to the inorganic and ultimately, he argues, to death. Throughout the essay, the stimulation to movement, inherent in the instinct, jostles with its aim to return, to rediscover the stillness from which it originally departed. Reading the essay, especially in the context of its relevance to narrative, the old term 'drive' takes on an extra resonance. Peter Brooks has described Freud's concept of the death instinct (drive) as his "master plot" and has used it to analyse the problem of narrative's own drive to find a return to stillness and the inorganic after its initial animation under the aegis of desire. Freud's own use of metaphor provides another dimension to the 'plotting' of the death instinct across narrative event and narrative pattern. As these instincts are always striving to return to a previous state and are fundamentally conservative in nature, they assume, as a disguise, the appearance of movement, of progress and change:

> **"Conservative instincts are therefore bound to give a deceptive appearance of being forces towards change and progress, whilst in fact they are merely seeking to reach an ancient goal by paths alike old and new...it would be a contradiction to the conservative nature of the instincts if the goal of life were a state of things which had never yet been attained. On the contrary, it must be an old state of things, an initial state**

> **from which the living entity has at on time or other departed and to which it is striving to return by the circuitous paths along which its development leads." (4)**

In this paragraph, Freud's use of metaphor, invoking 'paths' and 'departure' alongside 'return' and 'initial state', resonates with the topographies of narrative, suggesting that life itself is subject to similar patterns. These are the elements that allow Peter Brooks to perceive a 'master plot' at stake:

> **"We emerge from reading Beyond the Pleasure Principle with a dynamic model that structures ends (death, quiescence, non-narratability) against beginnings (Eros, stimulation into tension, the desire of narrative) in a manner that necessitates the middle as a detour, as struggle toward the end under the compulsion of imposed delay, as an arabesque in the dilatory space of the text." (5)**

The type of narrative that ends with marriage, with the hero's foundation of a new home symmetrical to the one he left, evokes stasis through its topography: the home as 'journey's end'. The movement of adventure etc. has returned to stillness and, in some sense, there is a metaphoric aspect to the story's depiction of its ending. But, as Peter Brooks points out, with the end of a story realised as death, the metonymy of the narrative chain, of its journey through the space of telling, finds a vivid realisation in metaphor. Narrative end and human end coalesce. He points out that narrative 'ending' not only implies the silence and stillness associated with death, but that this death-like property of 'the end' may well literally be figured by a final death in the narrative. He says:

> **"The more we inquire into the problem of ends, the more it seems to compel an inquiry into its relation to the human end."(6)**

In *Beyond the Pleasure Principle*, Freud gives a considerable amount of attention to the difficulty of relating the death drive to the pleasure principle, particularly, of course, the sexual instincts. His final opposition is not, as previously, between ego-instincts and sexual instincts but between life and death instincts. This tension recurs with the problem of endings. For instance, Hollywood has been derided throughout its history for following the convention of the 'happy end', marked, at least in popular imagination, by a final kiss which fades out to 'The End'. But some darker genres, particularly gangster pictures and film-noir, could mark 'The End' by death. However, there is also, obviously, room for an attraction between the two, which allows the sexual drive and the death drive to form a narrative alliance in the 'dying together' ending. For instance, in King Vidor's melodramatic Western *Duel in the Sun*, the doomed lovers (Gregory Peck and Jennifer Jones) having shot each other, kiss before dying in each others arms. And the movie ends.

The second detour

...

1 Stillness in movement: time and the cinema.

...

As everyone knows, the cinema consists of a series of still frames, in sequence, on a strip of celluloid. When actions are filmed and then projected at the speed of 24 (give or take) frames per second, they then give the spectating eye an illusion of natural movement. This paradox lies at the heart of many debates about the cinema's ontology and carries over into its specificity as a narrative form.

...

I argued, in the previous section, that cinema's objective alliance with narrativity absorbed and concealed its essential stillness, its existence as a series of still frames (photogrammes) on a strip of celluloid. Here lies an important difference between the movement of narrative as such and that specific to cinematic narrative. The cinema can only maintain its illusion of mobility by suppressing its inherent stillness. As a medium for storytelling, it is vulnerable to the tension between its material base and the drive of narrative. Stillness becomes its secret, its repressed and then comes to present a trouble, a difficulty, for film theory that I will return to later. On the other hand, avant-garde film has consistently exposed cinema's stillness and given visibility to the frame, taking pleasure in the fact that there is more to cinema than movement, or, indeed, narrativity. As Peter Kubelka said in an interview with Jonas Mekas:

"Cinema is not movement. This is the first thing. Cinema is not movement. Cinema is a projection of stills ñ which means images which do not move ñ in a quick rhythm. And you give the illusion of movement, of course, but this is only a special case."(7)

But, of course, for most people, this is not a special case. Cinema as illusion of movement is the primary, often the only, way in which it is experienced. For most people, cinema is the movies, in which the excitement of the moving image merges with the excitement of the visualised story, literally moving along, unfolding on the screen across time and space. For this sense of excitement, the eruption of stillness is anathema.

Duel in the Sun (King Vidor, 1946 b/w125 mins)

In the first instance, the collapse of the illusion of movement may simply be that: a breakdown of the cinema as a story-telling device. But narrative cinema, unlike written or oral narratives, has a double time structure. Conflicting temporalities lie at the heart of cinema creating a contradiction or a fundamental duality:

There is the moment of registration, the moment when the image was inscribed by light onto photosensitive material passing in front of the lens. This is the indexical aspect of the cinematic sign and, in common, of course, with the still photograph, represents a 'there-and-then-ness'.

Just as the still frame has to be absorbed into the movement of narrative, so does the moment of registration have to lose itself in the temporality of the narrative and its fiction. There is a presence, a 'here-and-now-ness' in cinema's storytelling.

Narrative asserts its own temporality. But the cinema does not have the complexity or flexibility of language and its grammar. Its preferred temporalities are sequentiality or simultaneity and its here-and-now-ness, its immediacy, is part of its appeal. The difficulty that the moving image has with tense, its clumsy flashback devices or calendar leaves flipping forward, are familiar to all moviegoers. Sometimes the ambiguities of tense may be exploited for aesthetic purposes, for instance, in *Last Year at Marienbad*. But these devices represent uncertainty about the status of time within the story and, however sophisticated it might be, the there-and-then-ness of the film's original moment, its moment of registration, stays hidden.

Jean Epstein, avant-garde filmmaker and early theorist of the cinema, evolved the concept of photogenie as the essence of the cinema. While he argues that cinema's essence is in keeping with the essential mobility of time, "only the mobile aspect of things, beings and souls can be photogenic" he also draws attention to the cinema's double temporality: "On screen, we re-see what the cinema has already seen". But the irony is that the cinema can only record "the mobile apex of things", and re-present them to us projected on the screen, by means of a sequence of still images with spaces between them.

Epstein's Soviet contemporary, Dziga Vertov, made *The Man with the Movie Camera* in 1929. Among the many beautiful and interesting devices in this documentary record of filming everyday life in Moscow, one stands out in the context of this argument. The man with the movie camera is filming a white horse as it draws a carriage of new arrivals from the station to their hotel. The horse is moving briskly, at a canter. Suddenly, at a moment when the horse fills the frame and its movement is, in a sense, the subject of the image, the film comes to a halt. The horse seems to shift in time into the 'there-and-then-ness' of the still photograph. This frozen image is more magical, it suddenly seems, than the illusion of movement itself. The spectators' look, one moment casually following the horse's movement, is, the next moment, arrested. The bustle of the city, its continuity and presence, falls away. Vertov then takes the film out of the street, and re-locates it in the editing room where it becomes a simple strip of frames in Elisaveta Svilova's hands.

Man With A Movie Camera (Dziga Vertov, 1929 b/w 137 mins)

2 Stillness in the moving image: death in and of the cinema.

...

In his book *Camera Lucida*, Roland Barthes discusses the still photograph's relation to time. As the photographic image embalms a moment of time, it also embalms an image of life, which will eventually become an image of life after death. In numerous passages he associates the photographic image with death.

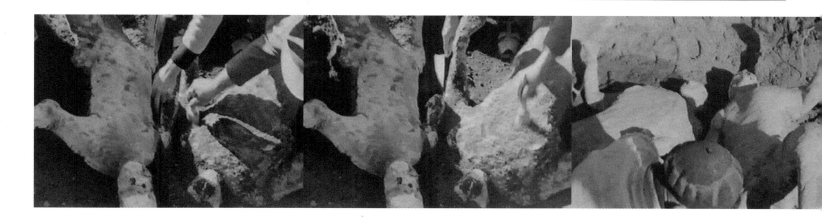

"Whether or not the subject is already dead, every photograph is this catastrophe." (8)

But he doubts that cinema can generate such an inexorable feeling of 'that has been'. It loses its relation to time, to the inscribed presence of the past; movement and fiction disguise the presence of the past. Christian Metz also argues that the immobility and silence of the still photograph, with its associated connotation of death, disappears in the moving image.

...

Raymond Bellour paraphrases Roland Barthes' distinction between the photograph and the cinema saying:

Voyage to Italy (Roberto Rossellini, 1953 b/w 80 mins)

"On one side there is movement, the present, presence; on the other, immobility, the past, a certain absence. On one side, the consent of illusion; on the other a quest for hallucination. Here a fleeting image, one that seizes us in flight; there a completely still image that cannot be fully grasped. On this side, time doubles life; on that, time returns to us brushed by death." (9)

Again following Barthes, he points out that the spectator cannot halt time in the cinema. But he goes on to discuss the effect that the appearance of a still photograph, within a fiction film, might have:

"What happens when the spectator of a film is confronted with a photograph? Without ceasing to advance its own rhythm, the film seems to freeze, to suspend itself, inspiring in the spectator a recoil from the image that goes hand in hand with a growing fascination." (10)

And he then ends by saying:

"As soon as you stop the film, you begin to find time to add to the image. You start to reflect differently on film, on cinema. You are led towards the photogram which is itself a step further in the direction of the photograph. In the frozen film (or photogram), the presence of the photograph burst forth, while other means exploited by the mise-en-scene to work against time tend to vanish. The photo thus becomes a stop within a stop, a freeze frame within a freeze frame; between it and the film from which it emerges, two kinds of time blend together, always inextricable but without becoming confused. In this the photograph enjoys a privilege over all other effects that make the spectator, this hurried spectator, a pensive one as well."(11)

According to Bellour, although a photograph in a cinematic fiction allows the space for "the pensive spectator" to come into being, its presence directs thought at the nature of the cinema itself. It does not allow space for the photograph to generate a punctum (the photograph's power to move its spectator through a detail, unintentional and inexplicable). Garrett Stewart, writing in the same (On Film and Photography) issue of Wide Angle, follows a similar line of argument, suggesting that the presence of a photograph does tend to conjure up consciousness of the cinema's materiality:

"Does photographic stasis within film inevitably reinforce the power of motion in screened pictures or can it sometimes dynamite and anatomize that illusion of movement? Doesn't the held image occasionally remind us that the stillness of photography, its halt and its hush, is never entirely shaken loose by sequential movement in and as film but merely lost to our notice? If and when this founding stillness is called to view may it not be understood a sign of death?"(12)

He concludes however that the

"death work stays in the main hidden, glimpsed only in local ruptures of a film's duration."

Garrett Stewart suggests that cinema tolerates stillness more easily when the photograph or freeze frame has a particular narrative significance, for instance, a death; "Death within the plot tends to thematise – and so to absorb – the disruptive potential that could otherwise sabotage the technological deceptions of the cinematic continuum." He points out that if a death coincides with an ending, it is quite frequently rendered with stillness, freeze-frame or photograph, Here, Peter Brooks' comments on the way 'The End' may be literally realised as death, the point at which metonymy shifts to metaphor, finds a further extension in the cinema. Just as narrative's return to stasis may be marked by the death of its protagonist, the movement of film halts, marking both narrative stasis and the death of its protagonist with a rare acknowledgement of is own stillness. Narrative stasis, death and the photogramme coincide to return the animate to the inanimate, the organic to the inorganic, at 'The End', with the further implication a point 'beyond narratability' has been reached. The silence of the ending is that of death and also its ultimate 'beyond-ness'. When the cinematic repressed, its stillness, does achieve some kind of visibility it is also naturalised through the power of metaphor.

…

Michael Powell's *Peeping Tom* (1960) tells the story of a young photog-

rapher whose aesthetic, and indeed perverse, aim is to capture not only the moment of death, but also the moment of terror at the moment of death, on the moving image. To this end, he murders three young women in the course of the story but cannot capture the perfect image he has in mind. The film ends with his suicide, a performance implying that his aesthetic aim, to capture the image of death on film, had always been impossible. He captures the image of his own death with still cameras, each one triggered by a trip wire as he runs past, like a Muybridge experiment. The still thus represents a return to the inanimate, to the 'inorganic' perhaps, at any rate to the 'before' of cinema. More fancifully, to paraphrase Freud, Mark with his suicide recorded by a series of still photographs, returns the cinema to its old state of things, in this case its proto-cinematic state or "the initial state from which the living entity has at one time or other departed...".

. . .

Animating the inanimate

...

I have been working through a series of homologies that link the Freudian concept of the death drive, the end in narrative structure, the fictional protagonists' death and the freezing of the moving image. Ending, death and stasis seem to converge or condense in an aesthetically satisfying manner. The year before he wrote *Beyond the Pleasure Principle*, Freud wrote *The Uncanny*. The Uncanny is also concerned with relations between the living and the dead, the organic and the inorganic, the animate and the inanimate. Freud used Ernst Jentsch's original article on the topic (published in 1906) as his starting point. Jentsch had noted the sense of uncanniness aroused by an apparent blurring of boundaries between the animate and the inanimate particularly in relation to representations of the human body. Having noted the uncanny impression caused by wax-works, he goes on to say:

Peeping Tom (Michael Powell, 1960 b/w 101 mins)

"**This peculiar effect makes its appearance even more clearly when imitations of the human form not only reach one's perception, but when on top of everything else they appear to be united with certain bodily or mental functions...for example life size automata that perform complicated tasks, blow trumpets, dance and so forth very easily give one a feeling of unease. The finer the mechanism and the truer to nature the formal reproduction, the more strongly will the special effect also make its appearance.**"(13)

And he goes on to comment on ETA Hoffman's story *The Sandman* which Freud, of course, takes up and expands in his essay. As Jentsch unfolds his argument he discusses the way inorganic objects may suddenly take on anthropomorphic features and how this phenomenon condenses with belief in ghosts, animistic spirits etc. all of which belong to a category "intellectual uncertainty". In Freud's most interesting reflection on Jentsch's essay, he points out the particular "intellectual uncertainty" with which the human mind, even the most scientific, faces, or rather fails to face, death.

…

Here there is perhaps another set of homologies that are relevant to the cinema. The cinema literally transforms the living human body into its inorganic replica. Once projected, these static images then become animated reproducing the living actions once recorded by the camera. In keeping with the double temporality discussed earlier, there is, there-fore, also another doubling: the recording of life on inanimate celluloid and the illusion of life recreated on the cinema screen. And the homologies extend: from inorganic to inanimate to still to death and from organic to animate to moving to alive. When blurred, these boundaries start to affect each other with uncanniness. The cinema has, or course, by and large worked hard to suppress spectator consciousness of this phenomenon. But a sudden sense of the uncanny may occur incidentally, or accidentally, half glimpsed with a particularly striking close-up or gesture of a favourite star now long dead. The screen image turns into a perfectly preserved death mask or veronica. Barthes, in *Camera Lucida*, acknowledges this sensation and cites it as one of the rare, if not the only occasion, in which the cinema can, for him, have the still photograph's power to reproduce death in life.

…

At this point, there is a divergence between questions affecting the cinema as such, the problem of the end, and questions for the cinema arising from the Jentsch/Freud concept of the uncanny. This aspect of the uncanny is to do with the human body and its life-like representations that Freud discusses in his detailed analysis of *The Sandman*. In the story, the hero falls in love with the beautiful automaton Coppelia. This figure, mechanical, technically perfect, fascinating, is exactly like but unlike the living human body. In her analysis of Villiers de l'Isle Adam's *On the Eve of the Future*, a novel about an exquisite automaton created by a fictionalised Thomas Edison, Annette Michelson suggests an analogy between the cinema and the beautiful automaton. Hadaly the mechanical woman with whom the hero falls in love is, as she puts it, "the phantasmatical ground of the cinema itself". Hadaly creates a transition from the fantasy of the beautiful automaton to the beautiful women featured in the magic shows of Georges Melies, living but subject to the mechanical tricks of the cinema. This is not woman as an object of cinematic iconography, but the female body "in an ultimate, phantasmatic mode of representation as cinema."

…

The Hollywood film industry perfected an image of stylised femininity, highly produced, by the most consummate artifice. Every aspect of performance, movement, gesture, look and so on, had to have an appearance of the natural and spontaneous which concealed timing and rhythm that suited the cinematic spectacle. (This may have been true also for male stars but their style tended to be more underplayed and more naturalised.) The female star may thus be, on the one hand, close to the uncaniness of the beautiful automaton: she merges with the stillness of the cinema, its essential stasis. On the other hand, her beauty and fascination distract the viewer from thinking about the actual mechanics of the cinema, about its essential stillness. All human movement recorded on camera may be compared, when animated by the projector, to the movement of the automaton, but the great female movie icons add the final veneer of fetishistic glamour to the illusion of movement.

…

Back to the future

…

Nowadays, the cinema is more likely to be viewed electronically than on celluloid. Does the cinema's new relationship with electronic and digital technologies affect modes of spectatorship? The viewer can now control the unfolding of the cinematic spectacle, fragment the story, breakdown the shots, fetishise a sequence with endless repetition, slow down a gesture or a look and perhaps discover, hidden behind the coherent flow of images another relationship to the figures performing, now, on the small screen.

…

Thomas Elsaesser discussing the aesthetic breaks between the digital and the cinematic makes the following point. He says:

> **"Roland Barthes in Camera Lucida, speaks of the way a photograph involves the viewer in a certain kind of presence and absence, what he named the sense of 'having been there'. The sense as he analyses it is also a tense, joining a perfectum with a present, in a conjunction mark of place and time."(14)**

Elsaesser then comments on cinema's double temporality "the tense structure in which (the cinema) holds the viewer, a 'here and now' which is always already a 'there and then". New technologies create new possibilities of time/space relation, a new consciousness of the deitic, between viewer and image. Although Elsaesser is reflecting primarily on digitally composed images, his emphasis on tense and new possibilities of perceiving complex temporalities is relevant to my argument here. With the electronic or even more, the digitialised versions of old films something happens which works to break down Barthes' insistence that the cinema can have no presence or punctum. ("Do I add images to the movies? I think not. I don't have time.") And gives a new significance to his single reference to Bazin in *Camera Lucida*:

> **"The screen as Bazin has remarked is not a frame but a hideout; the man or woman who emerges, emerges living";**

juxtaposed with his reflection that

> **"there is always something of the Resurrection about the photograph."(15)**

Paradoxically, these attributes of the hidden, secret, material base of the moving image, its animation out of the inanimate stillness of the photograph is easily accessible through digital and electronic technology. As the great days of the star system are long gone and the stars are now dead, their artificial, stylised performances, have now, literally become ghostly. Watching these movies now is to feel the reality of Jean Luc Godard's answer to the question: What is cinema?

> **"Cinema is death 24 times a second."**

…

Notes

1 Thomas Elsaesser: 'Digital Cinema: Delivery, Event, Time' in Elsaesser and Hoffmann (eds.): *Cinema Futures: Cain, Able or Cable? The Screen Arts in the Digital Age.* Amsterdam University Press, Amsterdam,1998, p204-5

2 Peter Brooks: *Reading for the Plot. Design and Intention in Narrative,* Vintage New York, 1985, p91

3 ibid. p105

4 Sigmund Freud: 'Beyond the Pleasure Principle' (1920) in *Standard Edition of the Complete Psychological Works of Sigmund Freud* Volume XVIII, The Hogarth Press, London, 1954-74, p38

5 Brooks op.cit. p103

6 ibid. p95

7 Jonas Mekas; 'Interview with Peter Kubelka' in P.A.Sitney (ed.) *Film Culture Reader* Praeger Publishers, New York, 1970

8 Roland Barthes: *Camera Lucida,* Vintage Press, London, 1993, p96

9 Raymond Bellour: 'The Pensive Spectator' in *Wide Angle,* Volume 9 number 1

10 ibid.

11 ibid.

12 Garrett Stewart: 'Photogravure: Death Photography and Film Narrative' ibid. p13

13 Ernst Jentsch: 'On the Psychology of the Uncanny' Angelaki 2:1

14 Elsaesser op.cit p208

15 Barthes op.cit. p55

The Search for 𝕶

Nick Norton

I'm the King of the Castle
And you're a Dirty Rascal

Across Vauxhall Bridge from the Tate Gallery, facing the river, its back up against Albert Embankment, there is a strange folly built on the site of a distillery. As a home for M**, it does not exist; as home for a branch of Britain's secret services, Terry Farrell's post modern architecture is suitably castle-like. But it is a castle of a child over disciplined in all things anal and so, although all the turrets are smartly, correctly aligned, still they carry an air of the modular. They could be neatly returned to the original packaging — instructions carefully filed, file double locked, coded and then, to preserve secrecy, carefully lost. This does not really exist as a building. Yes — and of course the client wanted it exactly so: for all its cost and ostentation the building is a nomadic tent, a vanishing act. (1)

· · ·

Temporality is the fate of all castles and all fortresses. After the battle, after the siege, the ramparts are allowed to disappear. If they do not then they change: the crenellations become tokens of pomp and splendour, the castle a glorified manor house; they become tourist attractions or bureaucratic centres — which is, in effect, a re-entrenchment of at least one part of their original function. The Vauxhall site seems to combine all three attributes — a persisting as well as disappearing castle.

· · ·

"By definition, the castle is the private stronghold of a feudal lord. (…) feudalism was a product of weak government, [a] compromise by delegating to the great local magnates many of the functions proper to a central government." (2)

· · ·

During the period of Stephen's reign, prior to and through the War of the Roses, the role of a lord's retainers first developed into one of infamy. It was a period of every landlord for himself, 'bastard feudalism' (3), and many castles were built without licence from the King. Soldiers, returning from long senseless wars in France, were willing to be hired into private armies. They bullied and subverted courts, they kidnapped and tortured with impunity.

· · ·

I hesitate to draw any parallels whatsoever between such anarchy and those modern day retainers which the state now chooses to house in their own special fiefdoms.

· · ·

In the Tate Gallery there is a painting by René Magritte. Bald head on pillow, blanket pulled up to the nose, this uncertainly sexed figure sleeps in a shallow wooden oblong. The box bears an obvious similarity to a coffin except that, jammed into the top third of the canvas, it is held above a sky by the picture's confines. A plastic, amorphous mass pushes up the picture plane before the sky. Embedded in it are various objects. Normal things. A hat, an apple, a ribbon tied in a bow, mirror, pigeon and a lit candle. The figure appears dead at first, it looks far too calm for such a claustrophobic space. But then we recall the title, *The Reckless Sleeper*. Is this then a Houdini act? Or does recklessness simply denote the perversity of sleeping, of allowing oneself to be helpless, especially in so odd a space? But the turn of the blanket suggests instead a

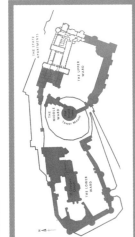

Windsor Castle

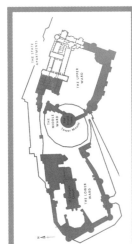

dreamer, the half twist and pillow rub of a body whose subconscious is rolling forth grand narratives and epic wonderments.

· · ·

Are we then to see a brief ossification of this dream in the blob below? Is it a statue, a plinth? Are we meant to combine the objects to make a narrative model for the dream? Or do these objects themselves represent keys, decisive clues by which to unlock the dream? If so then this is a dream that nonetheless remains closed to us. Here are the keys to the castle, where is the castle?

· · ·

A castle before whose door one may stand. And stand. As in Kafka's parable, Before the Law. A parable Orson Welles used twice in his filming of *The Trial*, once at the very beginning and then again quoted by the Advocate (played by Welles); "I've heard it all before." K. (Anthony Perkins) rudely retorts, "We've all heard it."

· · ·

When offered an opportunity to film Kafka, Orson Welles at first chose *The Castle*, and was denied. His backers insisted on the better known title. This castle, in the unfilmed book, is undoubtedly a bureaucratic rather than military strong-hold, although one will never know for sure. Its defences are far more sophisticated than curtain walls, gate house, tower and portcullis. K. cannot even make it to the approach road proper as he is wholly distracted by the officials, pretend officials, hirelings and vassals who gather in the village. Village life is entirely dominated by that of the castle and yet nothing for sure can ever be discovered of life in the castle. K., in this narrative, is even further removed from the door through which the narration would have him compelled to pass than that of the man who, in the parable, wished only to know the Law. Both passages, it is suggested, are equally impossible. Neither character can accept or understand this.

· · ·

"There is an end," writes Kafka, "but no way; what we call the way is shilly-shallying." The question, then, is how to find the end? Of course we may presume that the end will find us but, even in death, nothing is certain.

· · ·

The revelations of attics. An on-going process of retirements and deaths coupled to the end of litigation. A pause in litigation at least: through the pauses and breaths of debates about laws and lies and territory and possession; after the stuttering of grief — slowly — an artist's legacy is revealed. It appears that some mourn still, their attics locked tight. Legal manoeuvres continue, or so it is rumoured. Shh, let us not mention such things.

· · ·

One can imagine Orson Welles drawn to film *The Castle* for many reasons. There is however a particular resonance with an earlier subject, another great study of failure, *Citizen Kane*. Failure however is too simple a term. It is little more than a side effect of success, in Kane's story, and incompletion in K.'s. Interestingly, David Thomson suggests that Kane's dynamics were based closely on the twenty four year old Welles. Only the career belonged to Randolph William Hearst, who is more normally accounted for as

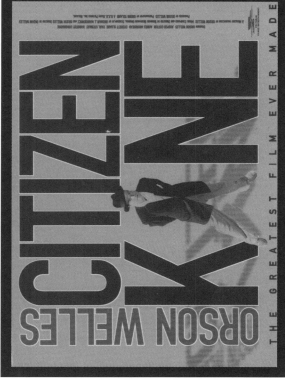

the film's model. That this pattern may have continued gives his move from Kane to K. An interesting significance. And then there is the resonance of the castle itself. Macbeth's castle, Xanadu in *Citizen Kane*, and the architecture of Hearst's own baronial ambitions.

· · ·

"𝔓𝔥𝔬𝔢𝔟𝔢 𝔥𝔢𝔞𝔯𝔰𝔱 [𝔚𝔦𝔩𝔩𝔦𝔞𝔪'𝔰 𝔪𝔬𝔱𝔥𝔢𝔯] 𝔱𝔬𝔬𝔨 𝔚𝔦𝔩𝔩𝔦𝔞𝔪 𝔱𝔬 𝔈𝔲𝔯𝔬𝔭𝔢, 𝔴𝔦𝔱𝔥 𝔞 𝔱𝔲𝔱𝔬𝔯, 𝔴𝔥𝔢𝔫 𝔥𝔢 𝔴𝔞𝔰 𝔢𝔩𝔢𝔳𝔢𝔫. 𝔒𝔫 𝔳𝔦𝔰𝔦𝔱𝔦𝔫𝔤 𝔱𝔥𝔢 𝔏𝔬𝔲𝔳𝔯𝔢 𝔥𝔢 𝔞𝔰𝔨𝔢𝔡 𝔥𝔦𝔰 𝔪𝔬𝔱𝔥𝔢𝔯 𝔱𝔬 𝔟𝔲𝔶 𝔦𝔱. 𝔅𝔲𝔱 𝔬𝔫 𝔰𝔢𝔢𝔦𝔫𝔤 𝔚𝔦𝔫𝔡𝔰𝔬𝔯 𝔠𝔞𝔰𝔱𝔩𝔢 𝔥𝔢 𝔰𝔞𝔦𝔡 𝔥𝔢 𝔴𝔞𝔫𝔱𝔢𝔡 𝔱𝔬 𝔩𝔦𝔳𝔢 𝔦𝔫 𝔦𝔱." (4)

· · ·

San Simeon in California, the undoubted model for Xanadu, is a false mountain with bits of real castle built into newer materials. Not at all unlike the construction of most other castles that we might naively call more 'genuine', with the exception of a time frame spanning years rather than generations. But, compounding our suspicion that the newspaper baron desired and indeed did act more like a feudal lord, Hearst also bought himself 'the genuine article'.

· · ·

Windsor, in occupation since William the Conqueror first built on the site, never came onto the market. Hearst did however get St. Donats, near Llantwit Major, Wales, overlooking the Severn Estuary. What made San Simeon and Xanadu a fantasy was their lack of life, or life recorded; history. Like K., Hearst wanted to get on the inside. But this was a man who would never allow himself kinship with one such as K. So, his version of doing was; Buy It. And then he sent in the interior decorators with the command, "we need ancient atmosphere". (5) He also wanted running water and to be connected for electricity. All of which he duly got. Here he entertained in grand fashion; his retainers were on occasion to dress in Medieval costumes, with harpists playing in the background, there was roast boar and peacock on the menu. However, in all, Hearst hardly spent any time at St. Donat's.

· · ·

By 1937 the castle was costing $11,400 a day to maintain.

Hearst himself was in debt and no one in Britain had money enough to buy the castle at worth. Ironically, there was serious talk of it being sold for use as a royal residence. Hearst might never have got on the inside but his cast-offs were worthy of consideration. One then wonders if such institutions as the Royal Family really are 'the inside'. Was the play acting of Hearst's guests and retainers any less an indication of power, worthy to be deemed 'a centre', than the longer standing rituals of Windsor? It is all a very touch matter of perceptions wherein the notion of 'belonging' becomes an ever receding will-o'-the-wisp.

· · ·

Hearst has of course gone now, his empire dissipated, bought up, like history. *Citizen Kane* remains, the royal family continue to reside at Windsor, St. Donat's was bought for the nation, and *The Trial* also remains — the book and the film. It would be correctly liberal, and generally hopeful, to say that art persists. It does. But ritual and tradition are equally tenacious. And furthermore, although the Hearst newspaper empire no longer exists, this is a very

long way from saying that his influence on world media, on the very matter of our daily diet, cannot still be felt. There are new magnates, we could all name some of them, whose fortunes make Hearst's money look like toffee wrappers.

...

Orson Welles in his lifetime was charismatic enough a person to inspire great friendships, powerful love, admiration, and by turns dismay, censure and abhorrence. He has been described as "a dog who has broken loose from his chain and gone to sleep on the flower bed." (6) I am of an age able to say that I first discovered his charms through voice-overs for sherry and lager adverts and even in this debased, senseless medium, one remembers a lingering gravitas, a suspicion of greatness. One had an impression that — through simply being on this advert — Orson Welles could subvert it, that he was somehow pulling off a trick while still allowing the listener in on it: Buy sherry, perhaps, but there is art beyond.

...

His profession as an actor is by repute the one trade he possessed which he believed fitted badly. The one art he tried to move away from although, in the end, it was the only one to provide any income and thus it stayed. Except for conjuring, he was always a magician.

...

Can we call that a trade? Rather not a calling which fed into all his other trades? Nonetheless, the trick of advertising is to allow the audience to believe that they are in on something. But sherry, surely, but know that on the way one carries the gravid potential of a masterful artist. And in the end, it is almost too much of a cliché but still we must remind ourselves of the presumption, in the end Orson's most enduring role was that of himself. This is the most terrible role for anyone, *to be yourself*; how much more so when one is hired to go on chat shows?

...

Those who loved Orson, loved him and worked with him and denounced those who thwarted him, even if those denounced also loved Orson and also worked with him, or tried to work with him. How many producers, I wonder, have counted the years lost to Orson Welles' projects? Time taken in trying to pin down the man with one hand, the bank with another, a crew, a cast, a script, a location, and Orson again and by this point they had long run out of limbs — and cash.

...

Eventually it looked as if only those who loved Orson were working with him, working on his personal portfolio of unfinished film projects. But in America, in Hollywood, working for nothing is a crime; to work for love is folly. (While, on the other hand, The Folly is at the heart of film making. Flat fronted ghost towns and papier-mâché towers, the essence of a studio based cinema.) for the unmade films of Welles and against the American system the retort is scathing and not a little idealistic; but perhaps idealistic is simply how one has to pitch these things: while the producer may be out of pocket, Orson Welles has lost another dream.

...

For sure, Orson always gave the impression that he had

dreams to spare but one wonders how true this can be. If each dream is thwarted then does one begin to build disaster in from the start? Do you dream thwarted dreams? Yet Orson Welles was a genius! This part of his image was stored up and secure with him barely out of his teens. So much so that while the Mercury Theatre productions were affecting New York and their radio broadcasts were syndicated across America, before he had even entered Tinsel Town a jealous storm was being cooked up for the Boy Wonder to walk into. Territory was to be protected. While dining in a restaurant an actor hacked off Welles' tie with a knife. Pauline Kael, in *Raising Kane*, duly notes the Freudian nature of this prank assault. (7)

・・・

Orson Welles' first cinematic production was to be an adaptation of Joseph Conrad's *Heart of Darkness*. The work must have been alive in the young man's mind, and the script cannot have been far off, as Mercury had just produced it as a radio drama. Welles was to play both Marlow, the book's narrator, and Kurtz. Scenes were shot in test, proving

to RKO's satisfaction that the production costs would be too great and thus *Heart of Darkness* became Orson's first unmade film.

・・・

"A voice! A voice! It rang deep to the very last. It survived his strength to hide in the magnificent folds of eloquence the barren darkness of his heart." (8)

・・・

John Houseman, while recalling the writing of Citizen Kane — he was the editor/personal manager of Herman Mankiewicz for the duration — describes Orson as the "Dog Faced Boy". (9) In the insult there is a slippage: Welles the original, larger than life, larger than human, made animal also. In this dream, this psychosexual drama, Welles becomes Seth, a dog faced Egyptian god. Horus and Seth fight. Seth rips out Horus' eye, Horus tears off Seth's testicles. Summaries of Seth are ambivalent: brother and murderer of Osiris, he is also seen in a rite of reconciliation with Horus. He does not easily fit into a schema of simplified

archetypes. Although in these stories 'inauspicious', Seth is not simply Darkness. He might be Desert, or Storm, although Sexuality is another option. Also some say his dog-like features are more camel-like, ass-like, jerboa, hog, boar, long-snouted mouse, fennec, oryx, or giraffe-like.

・・・

It is said that Herman Mankiewicz picked up *Rosebud* from a no doubt sloshed confession that became rumour, has become legend, that Marion Davies' clitoris was adored by her lover, William Randolph Hearst, by this name. Welles himself has dismissed (or deliberately talked down) this 'MacGuffin', *Rosebud*, as cheapskate Freudian. Hollywood Freud is rarely anything else. Freudian Freud could be described thus, while economic would be a kinder term, for once brought into play Freud's ideas — or versions of his ideas — usually provide considerable mileage. And *Rosebud* is a fine example of this. Who, otherwise, would step onto the slippery slopes of a clitoris married to a sledge? Of course if the story of the source of *Rosebud*, which is the

William Randolph Hearst

source that allows us to explore the story of Kane, is true — then the story of Hearts's persecution of the film and Mankiewicz in particular becomes entirely understandable. Marion Davies and William Randolph Heart's was an enduring love, unlike that of Charles Foster Kane.

· · ·

'The horror! The horror!' 'Rosebud!'

· · ·

Stripped naked a rose is all genital, Georges Bataille would have us tremble at the confrontation. (10) Nonetheless a rose is rude for more complex reasons than this confusion of botany and human anatomy. A rose's scent and pollen and attraction rely on a slow unfurling in the presence of wind and rain and sun while its copulation requires the dance of bees. A rosebud is a pursed kiss anticipating its own despoliation. We cannot avoid the anthropomorphic and yet stripping back the metaphor to a pornographic core does not necessarily engender a shock of recognition. Given recognition, this will remain ambiguous because the uncanny is a slower, more cultured effect.

· · ·

In the introduction to *Amerika* (which was also the original title for *Citizen Kane*) Edwin Muir writes of Kafka: "He sees everything solidly and ambiguously at the same time; and the more visually exact he succeeds in making things, the more questionable they become." (11)

· · ·

If a life is lived in deeds then telling stories of that life should be enough to understand it. In theory; 'they did this, because of this, that led to that'. However if a life is lived even partially in dreams, and it always is; counting on dreams, concocting dreams, creating and hoping for dreams; then after this recounting deeds alone become akin to watching a puppet show. The strings, the hand up the puppet's rear, convention alone has it that these enjoiners are ignored.

· · ·

Orson Welles really was great on *The Muppet Show*.

· · ·

Kafkaesque: adj. (or situation, atmosphere, etc.) impenetrably oppressive, nightmarish, in a manner characteristic of the fictional world of Franz Kafka., German speaking novelist. (d.1924.) (12)

· · ·

How can a noun become an adjective? How can an end be a beginning? The end of ending?

· · ·

Kafkaesque came after death. After the death of the German speaking novelist, certainly. After World War Two probably. What was written that would become Kafkaesque when taken away from itself was written at the end of empire(s). A period of endings no less grandiose in demise than the supposed End of History. The first made visible (and then blinded) in trench warfare, the other marked succinctly — if glibly — as a hammer blow on the Berlin Wall. It was not written so, not written there or then — but, yes, Kafkaesque was perhaps born with The Wall. Invented for Cold War, espionage, 'a wilderness of mirrors' (such as that seen in the climatic shoot-out of *The Lady From Shanghai*).

· · ·

Marion Davies

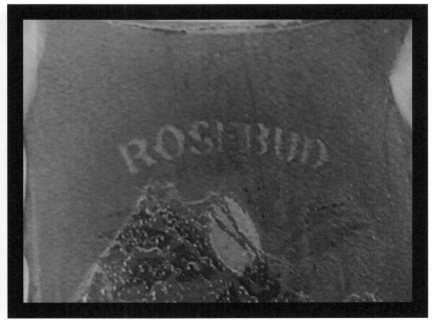

Still from *Citizen Kane*

From the intimate terrors of mistaken identity we slide nauseously through the Final Solution and into the bright dawn of nuclear paranoia. Already we have approached end of speaking; that we cannot; and still cannot allow ourselves silence because that is the silence of Death Camps. That is factory work.

· · ·

"𝔗he criterion for representing the 𝔥olocaust cannot just be propriety or awe, as would be appropriate in the face of a 'cult object'. 𝔖entimental angst is to be avoided, remembering should negate the 'traumatic ossification' of a 'melancholic fixation.'" (13)

· · ·

"𝔗he whole of 𝔎afka's art consists in compelling the reader to re-read him." (14)

· · ·

K.'s wall is the Great Wall of China; the four wall's of

Gregor's room that, in *Metamorphosis*, he is forced to study after his transformation into a large brown bug. On any scale, this architecture is too close and simultaneously too infinite. (The dying Emperor has a message specifically for you, whispered in the ear of a most trusted messenger. A message for you from the dying Emperor. His bedroom walls have been removed to accommodate the crush of great princes around his bed. The messenger struggles to push through this mighty crowd. It is barely conceivable that he will ever reach the palace's stairs and after the stairs the court and then "if at last he should burst through the outer-most gate — but never, never can that happen — the imperial capital would lie before him..." (15)

· · ·

K., because of this architecture, because of the specificity of his descriptions, because of how he and with him we — his characters — occupy these spaces; this literature will not translate into film *Impenetrable oppressive*, suggest that dictionary definition, despite the fact that we have already penetrated far enough to use such a description. Something

is so, so we say so, we say so because we feel ourselves surrounded.

· · ·

1920, Prague, and cinema must close by. The camera is here. A camera in a studio for which a young, refined man, at the start of a career, foot on the ladder — an insurance clerk maybe — poses with his bride to be, or not to be, a reliable, capable looking woman... Although there are other reasons, surely, for the palpable loss of the Yiddish Theatre in Prague. Not just the camera.

· · ·

Has cinema only ever occupied emptied ground? As its architecture is vacated to be occupied by Bingo Halls and as the Bingo Halls are drained by the supershed entertainment complexes so is the left over space of cinema again made available for new entertainment? Does this remain the very same sort of space that was once occupied by, for example, Yiddish theatre?

· · ·

As a language, for Franz, Yiddish is already faltering. He

takes lessons in it, as do other young intellectuals of his milieu. I am not certain but it would appear that his family, with its powerful aspirations, avoid this 'old' language: German was the language of ambition and commerce and this was the language they chose. It was also the language in which Franz Kafka wrote. He was never quite convinced, it seems, by his friend's Zionist hopes. This not through want of sympathy and despite hoping to be convinced. Nonetheless; impossible. Too much is escaping, changing, too much cannot be said: will not be said despite always being with us, always present and unchanging. Like the Law. Or his father. Or desire, which is however continuously changing. So Franz writes in German and thus overwrites his father's chosen language. In the language of commerce and certainty; commerce made doubtful, a disappearing chased, convulsed, ever so quietly.

...

Impossible to film, so obviously the director of choice is Orson Welles. An impossible man for an impossible task. And knowing the scale of his dreams oblates both his own girth and his backer's all too shaky, snaky, mist like resources then Orson will fall back on what he knows best; sleight of hand. David Thomson writes:

> "He felt bound to make Joseph K less passive – 'To interest me, the character must do something.'"

He also proposed, Thomson continues:

> "that, had Kafka been writing after the Holocaust, he would not have endured this own book's ending and the resignation with which Joseph accepts his fate and death. That seems not just poor literary criticism but a sign that Welles was never a searching reader." (16)

...

Everything after the Holocaust is different. We believe that it is different, hope that it must be, and it is different in that we are now scared that in fact nothing is different: that the Death Factory will not be shut down, that once it has been cranked up it has wheels and will trundle around in the night to one day sit in Rwanda, the next in Serbia, and maybe one day we will wake up to find in parked on our own street.

...

However, less portentously, we may talk about cinema. There is a need to film K. Orson Welles had to find a way to film. Famously his backers failed to find money for sets, famously Orson saw two moons at night; Gare d'Orsay, an abandoned railway depot, perfect — and perfect for the "kind of sorrow that accumulates in a railway station where people wait". It seems he was hoping to capture an emotional residue, something physically absent but left over, in terms of psyche, like the glistening weave of dry snail trails.

...

Also, remember, Orson preferred *The Castle* to *The Trial*: while Thomson's criticisms hold for Joseph K., who although not passive does at times demonstrate a strange, languorous anxiety; in *The Castle*, K. in fact cannot do anything for doing. Throughout the book he is trying,

Stills from *Citizen Kane*

demanding, going to see people (missing them inevitably), plotting, forcing others to intrigue with him; not listening but doing. A sort of doing imbued with an agony and nervousness that Anthony Perkins does. Maybe Orson Welles did also, in a less skeletal form.

...

So Orson had played a trick on us here, putting a character from one book in the lead role of the film of another. Not an outrageous trick. It is the gift of filmmaking, the function of the edit, the structure of the splice to tie together different times, spaces, characters, rhythms and events.

...

David Thomson says that Orson Welles, "missed Kafka's humour", whereas in Peter Bogdanovich's book of interviews with Welles (17) we have the director laughing out loud, and being hushed for it, at a Parisian screening of *The Trial*. Yes, Kafka is funny, he tells Pete (PB is duly in awe of OW). Admittedly Orson might have been laughing at his own rather than K.'s humour. Perhaps he was enjoying the paradoxical state of being revered in his lifetime (was he filming *F for Fake* at the time, I wonder?) and simultaneously being told to hush at one of his own screenings.

...

If one does not think of Franz Kafka as a humourist then likewise *Rosebud* might be viewed as a rather suspicious punchline. It does not help that it is told at the start and we need to sit through the entire film to know this. Although to be fair, like all good conjuring, it is all up there for us to see. *Citizen Kane* most certainly does have an End, it ends with death like a real true story, except that this end is at the beginning. The director/ writer/ stage magician has diverted our gaze and we will follow the 'wrong' cup through the rest of the act. The cup is not actually 'wrong', it simply does not conceal anything. Nonetheless, a trick with just one cup concealing one ball is incomplete. It needs the double orbits of at least two empty cups. And again, the trick, the 'magic', is still elsewhere: in the commanding voice, perhaps, the lighting, the presence (the absences), in our ability or desire to believe.

...

When *Citizen Kane* was first released, the studios knew they had to squash it. The film had to disappear before Hearst's lawyers made them disappear — or at least a considerable chunk of their income. Therefore the studio dumped their much-touted 'boy wonder'. The Dog Faced One had his leash yanked, as quietly as possible (remember, Seth pokes out Horus' eye, Horus tears off Seth's testicles). Orson's incredible contract was, as if by magic, transformed into confetti. This was a contract that reputedly gave Welles complete control, complete freedom, the keys to the castle. Rather more a ball and chain by which he would be allowed to sink; ballast overboard; save the studio. What did the poster for *Citizen Kane's* first release proclaim? "It's Terrific" And a picture of some men sitting round a table. Pathetic. Now we have: "The Greatest Film Ever Made" and the young Welles, as the dynamic young Kane, photographed to look like a dapper exclamation mark. Yes, NOW we want to believe. Now we are ready to enter Xanadu.

...

Hearst Castle

" – and now as all the electric light went out too – for who should they remain on? – and only up above the slit in the wooden gallery still remained bright, holding one's wandering gaze for a little, it seemed to K. as if at last those people had broken off all relations with him, and as if now in reality, he were freer than he had ever been, and at liberty to wait here in this place usually forbidden to him as long as he desired, and had won a freedom such as hardly anybody else had ever succeeded in winning, and as if nobody could dare touch him or drive him away, or even speak to him; but – this conviction was at least equally strong – as if at the same time there was nothing more senseless, nothing more hopeless, than this freedom, this waiting, this inviolability." (18)

...

Notes

1 'It was the largest pre-cast concrete cladding contract to date in the UK. The building is utterly impermeable — the façade allows no insight into the human activities inside. These appearances are by no means deceptive: built into the concrete framework is a 'Faraday Cage' — a mesh which prevents electro-magnetic information from passing in and out of the building. An anonymous site had gained a theatrically ominous building — apt that its neighbour to the west should be the Nine Elms Cold Store.' *A Guide to Recent Architecture*, Samantha Hardingham, London, Artemis, 1994

2 *Castles in England and Wales*, W. Douglas Simpson, B.T. Batsford, 1969

3 op. cit.

4 *Hearst's Other Castles*, Enfys McMurray, Seren, 1999

5 op. cit.

6 'Raising Kane', *The Citizen Kane Book*, attributed to Jean Cocteau: Pauline Kael, Paladin, 1974

7 op. cit.

8 *The Heart of Darkness*, Joseph Conrad, Penguin Books, 1989

9 'Raising Kane', *The Citizen Kane Book*, Pauline Kael, Paladin, 1974

10 The most ideal is rapidly reduced to a tatter of aerial manure' 'The Language of Flowers' in *Selected Writings*, Georges Bataille, Minnesota Press, 1984

11 'Introduction', Edwin Muir, in Franz Kafka, *Amerika*, Penguin Books, 1988

12 *Oxford Concise Dictionary*

13 'Monument and Memory in a Postmodern Age', *The Art of Memory, Holocaust Memorials in History*, Andreas Hussen, James E. Young (ed.), Prestel, 1994

14 'Postscript', attributed to Albert Camus: Nahum N. Glatzer, *Collected Short Stories*, Nahum N. Glatzer (ed.), Franz Kafka, Penguin, 1988

15 'An Imperial Message', *Collected Short Stories*, Franz Kafka, in op. cit.

16 *Rosebud*, David Thomson, Abacus, 1997

17 *This is Orson Welles*, Peter Bogdanovich, HarperCollins, 1992

18 *The Castle*, Franz Kafka, Penguin Books, 1979

Windsor Castle

Life in Space

When I was four years old my parents bought a climbing frame for my brother and I. It was a wooden space frame of rods and posts which divided up about a five foot cube of space. I loved climbing about on it, being able to move in any direction, figuring out little journeys through it and hanging upside-down. I enjoyed the new perspectives it gave me, the spatial freedom and the vivid pattern of lines marking out this lump of space.

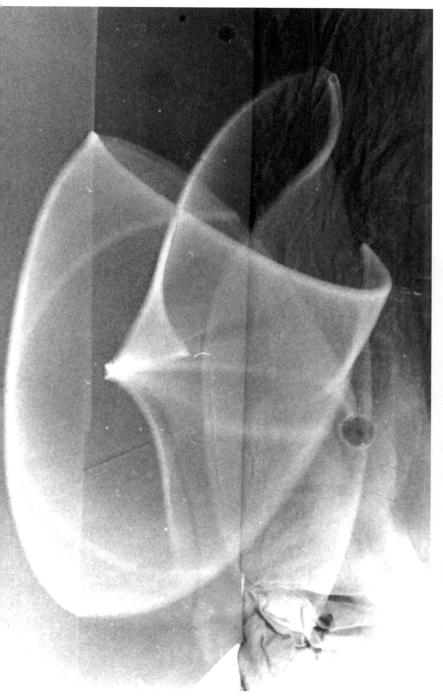

Circles have no way up

As a student of architecture and later of sculpture my obsessions with space, geometry and orientation were re-kindled by the influence of Buckminster Fuller, the inventor of geodesic domes, tensegrity structures and space frames, and by Keith Critchlow, a geometer and lecturer at the Architectural Association School of Architecture. I spent hours doodling with geometric ideas and making little models to try them out. Circular structures, circular movements and circular images often found their way into my work. I developed variations on a shape I called the ORBAL, which rolls along with an unusual motion...

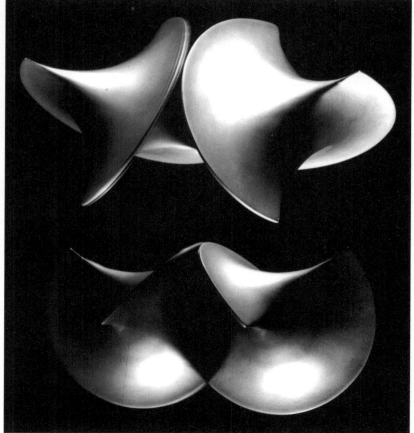

I just like to make things

I am always making things, usually things that have
not been made before like a falling-over-slowly machine,
a parachute tent and numerous devices for filming...

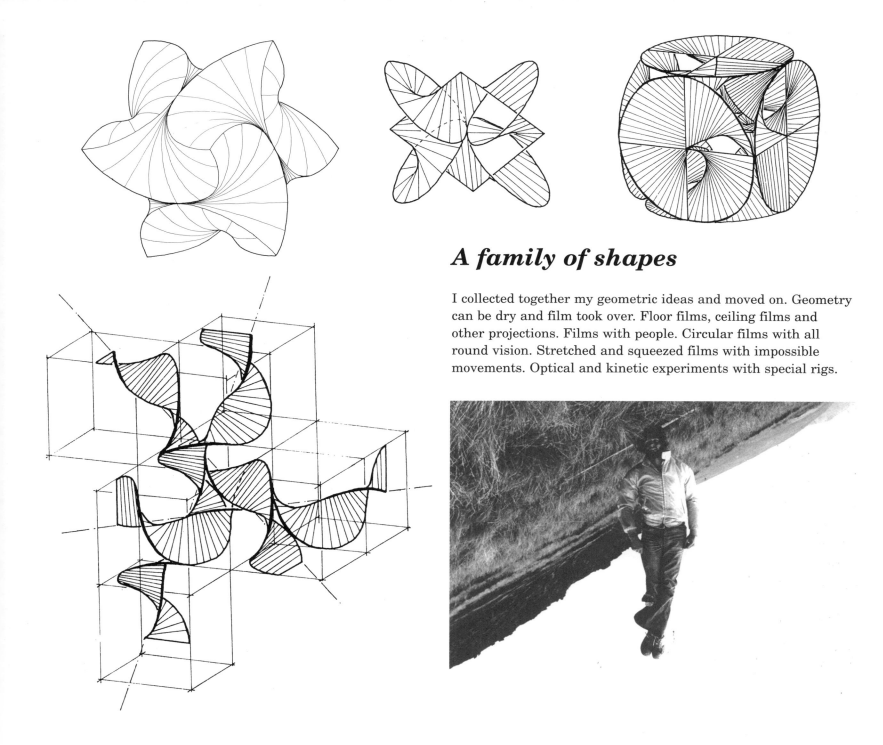

A family of shapes

I collected together my geometric ideas and moved on. Geometry can be dry and film took over. Floor films, ceiling films and other projections. Films with people. Circular films with all round vision. Stretched and squeezed films with impossible movements. Optical and kinetic experiments with special rigs.

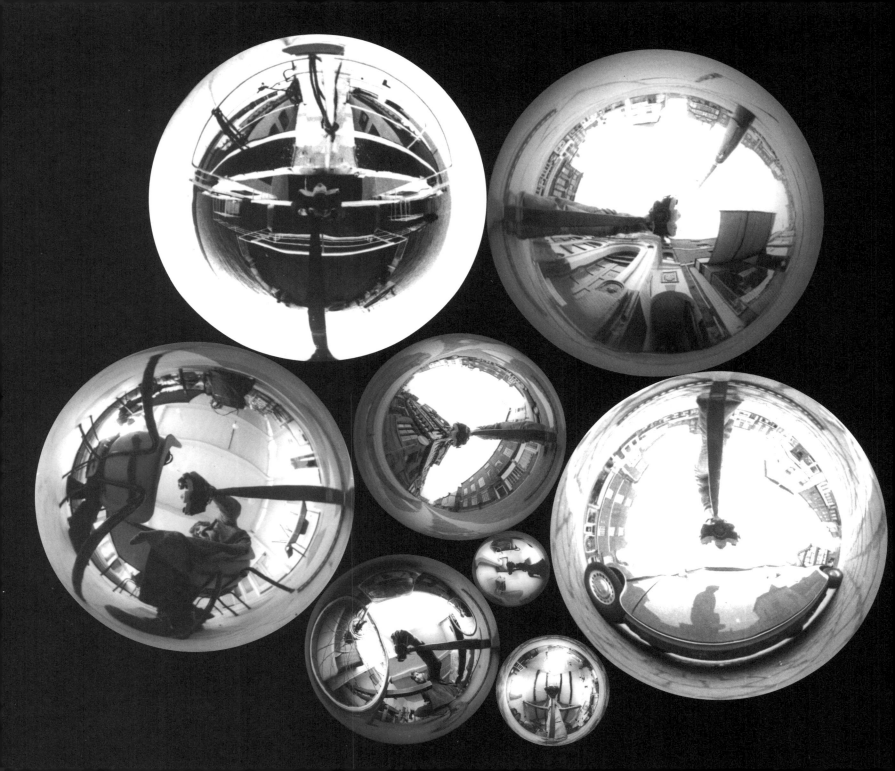

Darkness and silence

Faint muffled sound of children playing and people talking

Very gently and slowly the camera rises up through the earth and grass and out of the ground.

In the moments of light appearing the sound reaches its normal level and clarity

A child, close up, spins a toy that optically puts a bird in its cage.

Adults are talking, it's a picnic scene, a field with tall trees beyond, birds singing.

Children play gymnastic games, standing on their head, cartwheels, leagfrog, etc.

The camera is all the while slowly rising and tipping forwards in a circular arc, the ground slowly tilting up.

Food leftovers are spread about, adults are drinking wine, some sitting, others lying down.

A man is speaking:

"... I was staying at my brother's place out at Chingford. Sometimes at night I would go for a walk on the golf course. One night it was very clear, there was no moon and the stars were very bright. I walked up to the highest point and lay down on my back looking up. After a while I began to feel like I was a fly stuck to a huge ball. I lay like this..."

He lies on his back and spreads his arms and legs.

"... and I had the whole world behind me, nothing in front of me, only space. I felt that any moment gravity would stop and I'd fall off..."

The camera is now directly overhead looking down on the group with the spreadeagled man centre frame and almost upright.

The camera continues its slow, inevitable movement apeing the daily track of the sun.

Somehow the people are now upside-down, stuck on a ceiling of grass. Cows can be seen in the distance.

A dandelion seed floats by close to the camera.

A clicking sound can be heard.

The camera is now approaching the ground. A young boy's head enters the top of the frame. The camera reveals that he is playing with a small wooden puzzle that clicks as he moves it. His feet pass by and the camera slowly enters the ground.

Birdsong and clicking fade rapidly.

And so it goes...

TONY HILL

Film Video TV (1)
Nicky Hamlyn

This essay explores the work of three artists; the film-maker Guy Sherwin, video-maker David Larcher, and David Hall, who has used both media to make public interventions into the TV experience.

In recent years there have been arguments, more or less interesting, about the respective merits of video and film. For Peter Wollen the relevance of these debates has already been eclipsed by the widespread presence of hybrid forms — videos shot on film, films cut on tape — a tendency he notes in his introduction to the *Arrows of Desire* show held at the ICA in 1992 **(2)**. At the same time though, Wollen has protested loudly at plans by the BFI to distribute on video films that were hitherto available as 16mm prints. Wollen's stance epitomises the state of the debate: on the one hand film, video and digital are all current moving image media, all equally viable and in some respects interchangeable. On the other, it is important to respect the integrity of a work's original medium: there are still significant differences between these media in terms of how they are experienced. Top quality video projection (with added digital grain and flicker!) may soon appear indistinguishable from the 16mm equivalent. However, a gallery full of projectors running film loops could not be more different from a multi-monitor video installation. Film projectors in galleries inevitably draw attention to themselves. The best work made for this format plays on the contrast between the sculptural/mechanical presence of the projector, the filmstrip, and the projected image itself. Video projectors are relatively self-effacing machines, whose noiseless operation facilitates the direction of the viewer's attention to the image. **(3)**

The dramatic differences in cost and working practice at different stages in the production process have affected the way different media are approached. Guy Sherwin has made an explicit commitment to film, arguing for its strong ontological links to the profilmic. The cheapness and mutability of video has allowed David Larcher to assemble large-scale, improvisatory works that would be considered extravagant, not to say impossible, had they been created on film. David Hall has stated that his work is not necessarily media specific, but that he has used available moving image media to mount a sustained investigation into the ideologies and phenomena of broadcast TV **(4)**.

Like Larcher, his earlier works were made on film, the later ones on tape.

In 1971, David Hall made ten *TV Interruptions* for Scottish TV, which were broadcast, unannounced, in August and September of that year (a selection of seven of the ten was later issued as *7 TV Pieces*). These, his first works for television, are examples of what *Television Interventions*, as they came to be known, can be. Although a number of such interventions have subsequently been made by various artists, the *7 TV Pieces* have not been surpassed, except by Hall himself in *This is a Television Receiver* (1975) and *Stooky Bill TV* (1990). The *Pieces* were shot on film, partly because union problems prevented the use of videotape, but in some ways this was appropriate, since a lot of TV in those days was either shot on film or took the form of live broadcast. **(5)**

In the opening work we see a time-lapsed scene of a TV cabinet burning in a landscape. Periodically, the screen goes black and

a voice calls out: "interruption". There is a play here on the idea of the landscape as a formerly romantic retreat, now sullied by commercial exploitation: a suggestion that TV is everywhere, omnivorous and insatiable in its quest for subject matter. At the same time there is the implication that a burning TV makes better television than most of the output to which we are subjected. The work also sets out the iconoclastic tone of those to follow.

In the second, a shot of the sky is vertically bisected by the edge of a steel-framed window and its handle. Clouds drift through the frame. This is followed by a high angle view of open countryside with fast-moving cloud shadows, then a similar angle on a quadrangle with a wind-blown tree and a rectangular shadow on the grass cast by buildings behind the camera. Thus the work sets out a number of framing implications. In the first shot it is as if the real window frame is intrusive, spoiling the view. Yet the TV frame (TV Set), which of course we do not really notice, is the real culprit here, since it cuts out what we may not see and forces us to see what 'it' wants us to see. The window frame also stresses the picture plane, seeming to connect the top and bottom of the TV. In the shot of open country we enjoy an illusory freedom, before the final view of the quadrangle. Here the shots jump through time so that the cast shadow from the buildings behind changes position and finally disappears. The presence of shadow combined with the absence of its cause reminds us again of the fundamentally manipulative nature of most moving-image

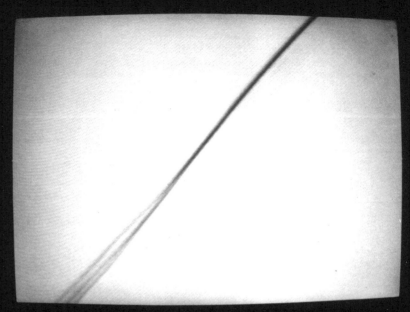

production, but especially of TV. Why especially TV? Perhaps because the cinema experience trades heavily on off-screen space. There we can project imaginatively into the adjacent darkness (6) in a way that is precluded in the TV experience where the box, which is always visible, functions to contain and inwardly direct the gaze. Designers have tried to make the set less visible by replacing varnished wood with darker, less reflective materials, but in any case TVs are invariably watched in un-darkened rooms.

The idea of the TV as a container is neatly explored in *Tap*, the third and probably most well-known of the *7 TV Pieces*. Unseen hands place a tap inside a glass tank, framed so that the tank's edges coincide with the sides of the TV. The tap is turned on, filling the space with water until it itself is submerged. The tank continues to fill until the meniscus — the surface line of the water — rises out of view. The tap is withdrawn and turned off, leaving that most forbidden of things, a blank, silent screen. After a pause of several seconds the plug is pulled and the tank empties, now with the meniscus cutting across the screen at a 45° angle. Beyond the reference to the box as glass-fronted container, the piece serves to demonstrate how framing is crucial in determining how we understand an image, and hence how meaning is created, not just by what framing includes, but also in the sense of the editorial function that it performs. This leads to a wider reading of the work as a critique of the largely invisible editorial practices of programme makers and indeed the TV institutions. Dziga Vertov, in the

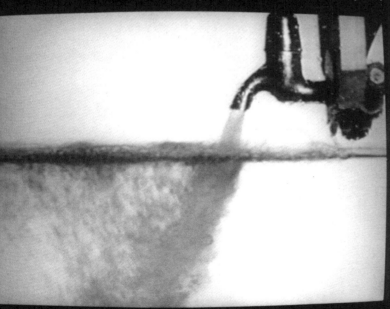

1920s, held that all stages of film production were editorial, but TV, with its impression of live, unmediated presence, can appear to bypass that truth. By making the framing of an object coincide not just with the shape and size of the TV screen, but also with the physical properties of the set, Hall foregrounds the constructedness of these processes. The concealed reorientation of the camera before the plug is pulled adds to this. The meniscus no longer appears as such, but looks more like a waving line cutting through the void. Its disorientation causes ours: we read it before as a meniscus, not because we could see the water under it, but because of its horizontality and its coincidence with the gushing of the tap. Now, through the act of re-framing, and in the absence of these associated cues, we no longer see it in the same way at all. The effect is reminiscent of the end of Bruce Baillie's short film *All My Life* which ends with a slow tilt up into the sky across a telephone wire. Once the shot clears the ground, it is the wire which appears to move, not the camera.

The fourth piece is a time-lapse of a number of people watching TV — wheat threshing, a western, folk singers — in a large room. After an abrupt pull-out at the beginning, there is a gradual zoom in to the TV set. The work wryly demonstrates that while watching TV may be engrossing, watching other people watch TV is a lot less so. This leads to the old, but none the less true conclusion that watching TV is antisocial, unless it is done purposefully and communally. **(7)** The screen within the screen re-emphasises the paucity of scale and scope that is in the nature of the medium. This is simultaneously conveyed in

the fact that the framing reproduces similar conditions to those under which the piece itself would have been seen when broadcast. There is also a play on diegetic/non diegetic sound, since it is difficult to tell if the increasingly strident movie soundtrack comes from the TV, from another part of the room, or has been dubbed-on.

In the fifth we pan from black across a TV-shaped opening through which can be glimpsed an Edinburgh street, shot from a fixed position. This shot structure is repeated ten times, each time with different vehicles and pedestrians in the frame. The soundtrack is in the form of a loop, so that the relationship between sound and picture shifts with each repeat, but all are plausibly synchronous. The work contradicts the normal state of affairs in which a camera pans across a scene, offering a seemingly open and unmediated panorama. Here the re-filming camera pans across the scene, but framed within the frame of the TV set. Instead of panoramic plenitude, we get only a frustrating limited view. The panning highlights how even the most seemingly open view is actually very restricted, partial, and centripetal.

In the sixth, three camera operators perform a live filming event at a busy town-centre road junction. The ultimate target of their cameras is a wooden TV cabinet with doors on the front (the same one that burns in *Interruption*?). A woman's voice calls out the shots' durations at five second intervals while the camera operators race to set-up the next shot. The shots are made in a chain so that each time we see a camera in one shot we see that camera's point of view in the next. Finally the doors of the TV cabinet are opened and in a zoom-in we see Hall himself filming through from the back of the empty cabinet, framed by its screen-shaped opening. Again, the richness of the film-work and the expansive complexity of the location contrast with the diminished final view seen through the constrictive rectangle of the opening in the cabinet. The presence of Hall's camera pointing directly back at us reminds us that every shot on TV is somebody's point of view, and not some disembodied omniscient perspective.

The last of the seven works presents us, in a single, unbroken shot, with the constituents of a television programme, but not the programme itself. A man wearing headphones sits, quite still and silent at a table, with his back to us — a familiar TV scenario reversed. Behind the table is a plain backdrop. This and the man are lit by two lamps and there is a Bolex cine-camera on the desk in front of him. After about one minute of stasis, another man enters the scene, in time lapse. He replaces the camera with a pile of straw, then reverses these actions, passing between the man and the camera filming him as he does so. Finally the seated man — Hall himself — stands up

David Hall, street piece from TV Interruptions (broadcast by Scottish Television, Aug-Sep 1971)

David Hall, two figures piece from TV Interruptions (broadcast by Scottish Television, Aug-Sep 1971)

a transparent point of view for the viewer. The seated man can be seen as a technician, who probably should be behind the camera, not in front of it. The TV set on which all this would have been seen is the only normal part of the experience, which must have seemed very strange, not to say baffling, in 1971.

After the *Interruptions*, Hall made a group of films with Tony Sinden which took an analytical approach to questions such as the picture plane, *This Surface* (1972-3); to depth, foreshortening and framing, *Edge* (1972-3); acting, *The Actor* (1972-3) and the projection event, *Between* (1972-3); and abstraction/ambiguity through framing, *View* (1972-3). *Between*, is one of the most media-specific of Hall's works. A cameraman walks backwards and forwards along the cone of light thrown by a film

David Hall, This is a Television Receiver (commissioned, produced & broadcast by BBC Television, 1976)

and removes the headphones, simultaneously revealing that they are not attached to anything. He then picks up the camera and walks out of frame. An electronic beep is heard at regular intervals throughout the piece. Thus a theme of negation and uncertainty runs through the work: the man never speaks and we don't see his face until the moment he leaves. The backdrop behind the desk is blank, rendering the lighting semi-redundant, and the only movement is the time lapsed section. Even here the second man is perceived to be not in motion, but in a series of static positions. This time lapsed section retrospectively renders the first part ambiguous, since there is no way of telling if that too was in time lapse, or in real-time. As well as stasis, real-time and time-lapse, clock-time is also present in the form of the regular beep.

If *Interruption* is literally iconoclastic in its physical destruction of that most familiar emblem of TV, the set itself, this last section adopts an attitude of quiet resistance to the paraphernalia of the TV studio, and by association, its institutions, since it is in such studios that programmes are produced and presented. Instead of designer desks, effusive anchormen, sparkling graphics and 'up' musical stings, we have in Hall's alternative an austere, silent space, a pine table and a mute, inanimate figure who has turned his back on the viewer. His headphones, normally a link to sound, here serve to isolate him from auditory stimuli. The moving man breaks what was certainly then a TV studio taboo by walking between the camera and its subject, disrupting the spatial unity by which the studio offers

projector, capturing his shadow as he walks towards the screen, and the light coming from the projector as he returns. At every turn we see a copy of the previous section, then a copy of the copy and so on, until the image has broken down into high-contrast grain patterns.

This technique was used again in what is Hall's most notorious work: *This is a Television Receiver*, which was broadcast unannounced at the opening of BBC2's Arena programme on March 10th, 1976. The then well-known newsreader Richard Baker reads a didactic text describing the physical features of a typical TV set. He goes on to explain that what looks like a man is not actually a man but the image of a man, and what sounds like a man's voice is in fact "vibrations on a cone". The two played together create the impression of a man talking, "but it is not a man". At the completion of Baker's speech we see a copy of it, made by re-shooting the original from the TV screen. This is followed by a copy of the copy and so on for three repeats.

Describing the work in this manner makes it seem almost absurdly banal and literal, a parody, perhaps, of some of the more heavy-handed structural film of the period. But within the context of broadcast TV the work is already subversive in a number of ways. Although they often become celebrities, newsreaders never draw attention to themselves, much less their function, in the way Richard Baker does here. TV personalities almost never discuss TV in a manner that calls into question its very nature and raison d'être: such debates, on programmes like *Points of View*, are usually over the content, costumes or performances in a programme, or are concerned with allegations of bias or imbalance within a programme or the institution as a whole. The unannounced insertion of an event like *This is a Television Receiver* throws into relief the character of most TV programming, hopefully giving the viewer pause for thought.

By the time we reach the final repeat the image and sound have deteriorated dramatically. The grossly distorted face now appears as a smear of coloured lines, which pulsate and flow around the hard edges of the screen. Landscape-like spaces can be read into what has become a mesmerising, ethereal image. The pleasure thus derived is in itself subversive, since it substitutes an anti-TV aesthetic of 'useless' pleasure for the dull instrumentalism of most output. Furthermore one can contemplate, in its unfolding, the widening gap between what one 'knows' one is watching and what is actually unfolding before the eyes: at a certain point one is obliged to recognise that the 'image of a man' can really no longer be so described, even though it is logically derived from that original image. The virtual space initially occupied by the talking head has been displaced by an abstract surface, whose rippling immateriality emphasises the constraining boxiness of the TV set.

The process of making a copy of the copy etc (8) uses a visible, material process to expose the nature of the video image, magnifying the stream of electronic pulses, RGB gun-firings and brief phosphor-glowings that create the illusion of an image. The noise in the (analogue) system which causes the deterioration from generation to generation increasingly becomes the subject of the work. This too is part of its subversiveness: the idea that an unwanted by-product of data transfer might displace the carefully engineered products of broadcast television to give the viewer something just as interesting, if not more so, to watch.

This approach, by which unwanted, intrusive or negative phenomena are positively embraced is reprised, digitally, by David Larcher in his tape *Videovøid* (1993) some of whose imagery is conjured from tape 'drop out'. Videovøid springs out of a negative paradox, tape drop-out being the trace (presence) of an absence, in this case the absence of magnetic coating from the tape's base material, resulting in the horizontal white lines familiar to viewers of rented videos.

Larcher has long been interested in the 'trace', a phenomenon that can be distinguished from the indexical sign by its immateriality. A footprint stands as evidence of a substantial event with physical consequences: the foot can be reconstructed as a plaster cast, for example. The trace, by contrast, exists only fleetingly, as a record of an event such as the passing of a bird, that might leave no more evidence than a momentary disturbance in the movement of the air. Some such phenomena, or epiphenomena, can only be caught, if at all, as a moving image.

Before he began working in video, Larcher made very long films; *Mare's Tail* (1969) 2 hours, *Monkey's Birthday* (1975) 6 hours. Both are notable for the extensive, laborious reworking that took place on the camera footage using an optical printer. Clearly video, with its flexibility and ease of use in post-production is a far more suitable medium for someone like

Larcher, who made immediate and effective use of it in *EETC.* (1988).

EETC. is a transitional, hybrid work that was shot on a mixture of film and tape. Post-production began on film, with optical printing at the London Film-makers' Co-op, and was completed on tape: "off off off lined at London Video Arts". Larcher's earlier films were assembled from accumulated quantities of footage gathered whilst travelling with his family in their

Mercedes lorry around various parts of the world. *EETC.* continues this trend of diary/home-movie making, except that now the footage is continuously reworked, re-examined according to the unifying idea of the 'trace'. The recurring image of a flock of birds flying in an E-shaped formation is eventually accompanied by words spoken on the soundtrack by the French painter Tal Coat:

> **"a flight is also nothing but a trace. A flight of birds...you see the flight...you no longer see the bird. When is the bird, when is the flight, when is the trace?"**

After a protracted 'title sequence' *EETC..* opens in a manner that looks 'backwards' to film even as it simultaneously

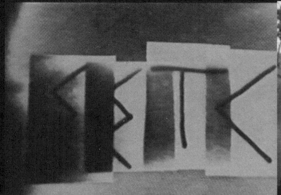

introduces a live matting and luma-key 'performance'. The camera points at a portable cinema screen set up in an open-air situation. Larcher enters the frame to put on a handclap sync-mark, a common practice amongst documentary film-makers when it is inconvenient to use a clapperboard. At about the same time a rectangular matte is superimposed on the screen, in such a way that when Larcher walks into shot he sometimes appears within the matted area, and sometimes outside it. There follows a series of variations on this set-up, during which the cinema screen is sprayed black. At one point Larcher removes a square of paper from the sprayed screen, creating a white square within the black one. This white square is then sprayed as well. The blackening of the screen renders it useless for purposes of projection (except metaphorically), but perfect for luma-keying.

This sequence establishes a number of things. First, we are posited as an audience, about to see a projection (fiction) on a screen which is bordered by the (real) world (which also has its own off-screen audience who are heard but not seen). But this distinction between fictive and real is broken-down, as soon as it is established, by the matting of new background images in place of the opening ones. The constant swapping

around of foreground and background breaks down the initially naturalistic space, replacing it with collaged images whose spatial relationships are unfixed or contradictory. The images contained within one or other of the rectangular mattes periodically bleed through into adjacent rectangles. When this happens the spatial recession implied by the array of frames within frames is undermined. Semantic relationships are also created between, for example, grain reticulation seen in close-up, (the micro-structure of the image) and its macro effect (the background landscape) and between grain and flower petals (both organic phenomena).

In both technological terms this sequence is the most interesting in the whole work. The manual creation of what are usually electronic procedures; sync marks, mattes, luma-key back-grounds, implies neither an anachronistic distrust of impersonal new technologies, nor a sentimental attachment to the craft ethos of film. Rather it should be seen as a way of taking control of those video processes which come pre-packaged and which are not yet fine-grained or adaptable enough that they don't impart a prefabricated, straight from the box look to the work. Larcher's actions serve to demystify these processes, which are commonly used in video and TV production, but which are either concealed or are, by their electronic nature, invisible.

At the end of this sequence edge fogging intrudes from the left hand side of the screen, adding yet another layer to the process, reminding the viewer that for all the elaborate and quite concrete-seeming on-screen activity of hand-clapping and spray painting, this is still in the end only a flimsy image born out of a highly refined controlling and channelling of light: light is both creator and destroyer of the image. As Tal Coat says: "the sky is everywhere".

At the end of *EETC.* the screen within a screen template remains, but we have left the hybrid, organic world behind and arrived at a wholly electronic space filled with skewed video colours and slow-motion scan lines.

Throughout the work analogies are drawn between the trace, film-making and cooking as processes. We see film of Larcher hand-processing film in a Morse tank, while on the soundtrack a voice describes the way that gelatine, the medium containing the silver halide crystals, is produced. We also see film cans being opened and closed and 16mm film being hung out to dry in a garden. We hear the 'music' of film rolls flapping around on a Steenbeck editing table, and in a scene where logs are thrown from one spot to another, the raw sound of the logs clonking against each other is sampled and 'cooked' into a set of musical phrases. This process precisely prefigures the major processes of *Ich Tank* (discussed below) whereby naturalistic sources are transformed into highly synthetic sequences. The multi dimensional spatialities of *Ich Tank* are also prefigured in *EETC.*, except here it is time that is so treated. When the 16mm film is hung out to dry in the garden, we see an image in the present of an event from the past. The 16mm film constitutes a future to that past image in that it will be seen — printed and projected, perhaps incorporated into *EETC.* — at some future date. Near the end of *EETC.*, we see a screen within a screen within a screen of Larcher watching himself watching himself knocking a hole in a wall, except that in the innermost screen — the hole knocking — the film is running backwards. Thus a void is being filled with a sledge hammer, and the time of the innermost screen is running backwards towards that of the outer ones.

As *EETC.* progresses the pace increases: photographs, movie footage and mattes are churned into an electronic flux of grain, colour, distortion and vestigial images. The representations of processes seen earlier in the work are themselves processed and incorporated into ever more complex collages. The difficulty of describing the work in conventional terms — there are no shots or scenes in the usual sense — is a function of its state of flux. Our language is based around a division of the world into objects which are located in a determinate time and space. *EETC.* breaks this structure down, questioning its adequacy to describe phenomena which are by their nature ongoing, mutable, evolving. This is a process eminently suited to video. Unlike film, video camera-footage can be effortlessly re-used, so that any event can be endlessly reworked, opening-up the idea of an inexhaustible reality. And the video image itself exists only as a dot traced horizontally, line by line, down the screen, fast enough so that the retina can retain the sum of the information as an image. Therefore the image does not exist in a determinate moment of time but is always a partial image that is being continuously updated.

The constantly evolving, unpredictable processes of *EETC.* are given a verbal expression near the end of the work where we hear again the voice of Tal Coat:

> "(Frans Hals) tried to do exactly what he saw but couldn't conceive of...and that is the great thing...no longer to conceive of things...to limit oneself to one's perceptions...but in such a way it implies the 'never seen'."

The 'never seen' is precisely the promise that video, as opposed to film, can deliver. Film's strength, or its weakness in this context, is its tie to the real. Digital media hold out the possibility of quite new and unimaginable images, synthetic images, in the same way that the birth of electronic music in the 1950s offered the prospect of completely new kinds of sound-worlds. The ambition to create the 'never seen' is taken much further

in Larcher's most recent work *Ich Tank* (1999). Where *EETC.* was organic, funky and anthropocentric, *Ich Tank* is crystalline, hi-tech and other worldly, despite the periodic presence of fish, birds and Larcher himself. The work opens with a slow-motion view through the bottom of a goldfish bowl which Larcher peers into and manipulates. This shot is distinguished from the rest of the work by its distortions and motion being manually created in a kind of biofeedback performance for camera. Eventually the image changes abruptly to a scene on a boat at sea. This shot is 'tiled' and these tiles are then reassembled into rectangular tunnel-like structures down which we travel. This sets the tone for the rest of the tape.

No sooner does a naturalistic image appear than it is replicated and repositioned to become a piece in a geometric construction. This construction may itself then form an element in a yet more complex construction. The work reaches a high point at the moment at which a 3D 'object', formed out of a shot of water, traces an upward spiral, leaving a continuous wake. The spiral flattens into a rectangle and a new spiral forms around the flattened one. This whole then tips through 90 to form the frame for an image of a bird tapping on a window.

The layering process — screens within screens — initiated in *EETC.* are taken to the multidimensional 'nth degree in *Ich Tank*. Images are the raw material out of which fractal-like multi-dimensional structures are compounded. Larcher goes about as far as possible in creating an artificial world of evolving, abstract kinetic shapes. Although abstracted from nature, the bits of reality from which these forms were derived survive only as texture or microscopic movements which animate the surfaces of the forms. Yet they gain much of their efficacy from their being occasionally intercut with shots of birds or fish, which, after the giddy complexity of the synthesised sequences, are startling in their concreteness.

The work is performative in two ways. Firstly there is Larcher's presence, manipulating the goldfish bowl at the beginning then later, naked, submerged in a large glass tank. Secondly, the construction of the work is a kind of digital editing performance, in that it continuously evolves, with new elements being added in, and new processes being applied, to create something akin to a large-scale improvised musical performance.

If Larcher's recent work demonstrates the power of digital editing to facilitate the total, bottom-up restructuring of a given image, Guy Sherwin's films demonstrate just as distinctively the importance of film for its indexical ties to the real. In a programme note to a screening of his films at the Lux Centre in London Sherwin wrote: "whatever advantages digital technology might have over film, its ontological link to the objective image-source is weaker than in film. In other words, digital imagery always appears synthetic in comparison to film, even if the image depicted has more detail. My black and white, silent, grainy films have a stronger sense of fidelity or connectedness to the reality 'out there' than their high-definition digital counterpart — and that film is the medium with the strongest link to its referent."[9]

It is important that Sherwin's argument rests not on the 'superior' picture quality of film but on the fundamental differences between the way film and video images are formed. [10]These differences may be summarised as follows: film's image, like photography with which it is identical in this respect, is formed directly by light falling on the film, whereas video images — or, strictly speaking, signals, since they are at any one moment almost entirely incomplete (see above) — are electronically reconstituted from a stream of voltages.

In a recent untitled film from the *Short Film Series* (B & W, silent, 3mins, 1975-1998), a single, three-minute shot of a tree-lined river is subjected to a simple procedure at the printing stage whereby the trees and their reflection in the river swap places. This is achieved by printing the film the right way up, then printing it again onto the same roll of print-stock, upside down. This means that the upside down superimposition also runs backwards. A consequence of this is that the film has a double palindrome or 'mirror fugue' structure. The resulting work asks us to reflect on how much an object can change before it becomes a different thing: at what point on a sliding scale does the change-over occur? Where, in other words, are the grey areas in our taxonomy of the world, and what do those areas tell us about that taxonomy's limitations?

The film is experimental in the sense that a number of effects are created which could not easily have been anticipated The ripples in the water appear to move in a downward sweep, but at the

Guy Sherwin, Short Film Series (1975-98)

Flight (B & W, sound, 4mins, 1998) is made from a tiny fragment of film of pigeons, semi-silhouetted in trees, shot with a
long lens. The imagery has been slowed-down and sometimes
stopped, using an optical printer to rework the original fragment. The effect of this is that a bird, frozen in the act of taking
off from a branch, disappears. This is nothing to do with cam-
ouflage, but is a function of the way a frozen blur of a bird

Guy Sherwin, Flight (1998)

mid-point of the film, where there is 50:50, trees/reflection
in both 'halves' of the picture, this movement appears as a
continuous flow from the top of the screen down through the
frame, not in contrary motion from the middle as one might
expect. A Coot which passes backwards through the frame
towards the end of the film appears the right way up, even
though one understands that it is really the reflection that
is the right way up.

It is important to the meaning of the film that the procedure
by which it is made is a material one, the result of setting-off
a visible procedure which is allowed to run its programmed,
mechanical course. The same effect could be achieved using
video/non-linear editing, but this would involve a rendering
process in which the two shots are mixed together through a
process of electronic reconstitution. Such a process, however,
would break the causal chain by which the work was produced
and thereby go against its raison d'être. The work's impact
comes from the dramatic gap between means; fixed, mechanical,
predictable, and the visible results; unpredictable images,

effectively becomes part of the surrounding foliage: what
appears are alterations to the foliage, not a frozen bird against
a frozen background. As movement is returned it is still unclear
whether one is seeing the bird's flapping wings or the wind in
the trees. Thus we are invited to consider how the visual field
may be full of such disappearances and ambiguities, spurious
phenomena to which we are generally blind because our world
is held together by an intuitive sense of the continuity and
completeness of vision.

As before, it is important for the efficacy of the work that the
problematic, to which the film gives rise, is generated from
re-ordered, as opposed to manipulated frames: the integrity

of the original imagery is clearly intact. If the work had been made in video and edited digitally, it is possible that the questions raised by the film version would not arise, because the viewer can assume they are witnessing sleights of hand attributable to digital trickery. (This relates to what is behind the underwhelming quality of so much special FX work in recent feature films.) **(11)**

Like the above two works, *Night Train* (B & W, optical sound, 2mins, 1979) may be seen as continuing the Vertovian tradition of employing film to reveal phenomena not normally visible to the naked eye. *Night Train* was shot from a moving train at night, using time exposures of half a second per frame. The camera records passing lights as traces, the nearer the objects to the train, the longer the trace. This results from the familiar travel experience whereby we appear to pass nearer objects faster than distant ones. Here, this translates into a black screen with abstract horizontal white lines, distant light sources making short feint lines, near ones long and bright. The judder of the train also affects the quality of the trace, imparting a zigzag which makes it look even more like an ECG scan. The lines draw themselves onto the celluloid, or rather the train draws itself across the light sources, making lines in the same way that a glacier acquires striations from the rocks it passes. Thus one can think of the film shooting itself, in the sense that it is the product of a procedure which is allowed to run its course unimpeded. The soundtrack is created by extending the image into the optical sound area at the edge of the film. The continuous flow pauses once or twice when the train stops at a station and a naturalistic image abruptly forms. The striking contrast between these two kinds of image forces us to rethink our experience of night travel. We conceive of the distant lights and the railway stations as roughly the same kinds of thing, yet the visual trace of these presents us with images so distinct as to seem almost mutually exclusive beyond the common denominator of light.

There is a precise technical sense in which this work could not have been made on video, that is in regard to time-exposure: it is possible to increase the shutter speed of a video camera, it cannot be decreased to below 1/25th of a second. But such technical distinctions between video and film cannot by themselves provide the basis for arguing for a medium-specific use of film, video and TV. Part of the motivation for writing this essay was that, as a film-maker, I feel inevitably under siege. I like working with film, have done so for twenty five years, and would like to continue to do so, for the old fashioned reasons to do with the fact that, like a painter, one develops a practice within the specifics of one's chosen medium. However, because of the growth of new moving image media this desire to continue with film demands some reasoning/ justification along the lines

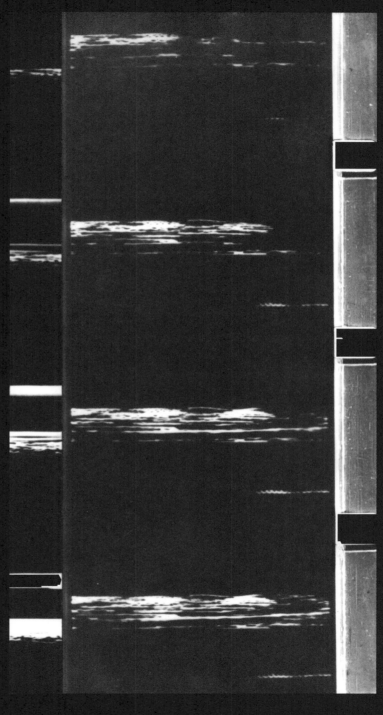

of medium specificity which can all too easily lead down the cul-de-sac of essentialism. How can one argue for film, as opposed to video, without seeming like an essentialist anachrophile? **(12)**

Perhaps I can only point to the difference in my experience of these different media. The difference in the strength of media specificity varies considerably between artists' work, but here are some comparisons. Guy Sherwin has stressed the importance of film for his work, but sometimes a film may be less film specific, yet informed in a significant way by a knowledge of the contours of film production and a training in its demanding disciplines. In a number of his films, notably *Downside Up* (1985, 16mm 17mins, colour) and *A Short History of the Wheel* (1992, 16mm, 1min, colour) an awareness of the cost of film-stock and the limitations at the editing stage have stimulated Tony Hill to develop and extend the possibilities of the shooting process by the invention of ingenious camera mountings which facilitate an economic shooting ratio but also, more importantly, allow us to see the world in novel ways. Hill's facility with engineering devices, indeed his whole approach must surely come out of his background in architecture and sculpture. In terms of technological requirements and, to a lesser extent, looks, much of his work could have been made on video. However his background in film arguably led to the development of aesthetic solutions which might not have occurred to a video artist for whom the editing suite is where the innovations take place.

One further example of a film which usefully highlights distinctions between the media is Rob Gawthrop's *Distancing* (1979, 16mm, 15mins, colour). The camera points out, from a fixed position, at a rain-spattered window, a head, a plant, the sea and the horizon. Gawthrop continuously pulls focus and aperture so that the picture-plane breaks down and the objects dissolve and reform in an ever-changing flux, "bringing into question the very act and accuracy of cinematic description" **(13)**. The effectiveness of this work depends very much on the image and the grain of the film being physically identical, in a way in which video images somehow are not. With film the image reforms and shifts, frame by frame, with every shift of the grain structure, so that it is fundamentally unstable. The beguiling mobility of the film image has a lot to do with this mobility of grain.

With video there is frame to frame stability, a quality of unmediated presence, nowness. But this stability is achieved at the cost of an apparent mismatch between the micro-structure of the image and the fixed array of RGB guns used to generate it. Film grain seems to hold out the promise of more detail at a greater level of magnification in a way that video does not.

With the latter one reaches a bedrock of the three pure colours generated from a more or less visible grid, beyond which nothing visible (meaningful?) exists. This should not be taken to imply that there is significance somehow beyond the grain in film, or at a greater degree of magnification. But because the spectator's eye cannot keep up with the speed of the grain's movement, there is a constant sense of things ungrasped within the image, things slipping by, even when there is very little movement in the profilmic.

Texture is not necessarily to do with the presence of grain, but is also a product of the resolving power of a given medium. Video recording is biased to the green and blue parts of the spectrum, the parts to which humans are most sensitive. This means that reddish images, such as faces, are less well recorded and hence less well textured. This lack of texture means a lack of differentiation within the image, which manifests as weaker three dimensional modelling and hence flatter-looking imagery. The importance of texture in the creation of convincing three-dimensional images is evidenced in the ubiquitous and often excessive use of texture mapping in 3D computer modelling. Video's tonal range too, is only a fraction of film's and the consequent lack of contrast within an image contributes to its lack of depth and dynamism. **(14)**. One has only to think of strong chiaroscuro painting to appreciate this. None of these remarks, however, should be seen as value laden: flat paintings can be just as exciting as ones which exhibit depth, and video, with its own potentialities, can offer experiences as rich as that of film.

The works discussed here are all effective advocates for the media with which they were made because all of them have expanded the aesthetic language of those media in exciting and distinctive ways. The artists are old fashioned 'adepts' in that their work is the result of ideas developed through a sustained engagement with a particular medium or, in Hall's case, with a set of institutional norms. This marks them out from many artists today who entrust the fabrication of their work to others, or whose use of film, video and TV is transitory or occasional. The consequent lack of awareness of the specificity and the history of the medium being used in such cases frequently leads to the creation of work which is inappropriate, naive or retrograde.

All images from Stooky Bill TV, David Hall, (1990)

Notes

1) I would like to thank A.L.Rees for his invaluable comments on earlier drafts of this essay.

2) Peter Wollen: catalogue essay, *Arrows of Desire*, ICA, London, 1992, p6-16

3) Anthony McCall's *Line Describing a Cone* (1973, 30minutes) and Dryden Goodwin's *1998 frames* (1998, indefinite) both make effective use of the contrast between the film image and the technology generating it. McCall's is a fixed duration gallery — or cinema space — work, incorporating the projector, the beam of light (enhanced with smoke) and a slowly evolving image. The image, the gradual 'drawing' of a white circle on a black background, simultaneously manifests as a growing arc of light in the beam. When the circle is complete the arc has become a palpable cone into which the spectator can move his head. Goodwin's film is a loop of 1984 frames, each one having a different image of a car on it. The film is 'driven' through the projector, the cars are driven under the bridge from which they were filmed. The film-strip moves through the projector, but the images of the cars are still images: non-sequential single frames.

The slight up and down movement of the film image — caused by each successive frame being inaccurately thrown onto the place of its predecessor — grain movement, the rattle of the projector and the visibility of its beam all contribute to the medium's imposing presence. By contrast, Bill Viola's installation *The Passing* would not work on film. The hushed ambience within which the image of the submerged man floats holographically in space is very much the product of video technology used in the most self-effacing possible way: noiseless, concealed projector, dim beam, stable image etc. Because the image is so dim, the relative contrast between it and the darkness of the room within which it is presented is slight. This helps to draw

attention away from the image's source, contributing to the sense of it being detached and immaterial, like an apparition. (Many of James Turrell's light installations similarly efface their technology by avoiding any strong or obviously directional light sources which would thereby draw attention to themselves.)

4) Interview with Steve Partridge in Transcript, Duncan of Jordanston College of Art, Dundee, 1999, vol. 3, issue 3, p40

5) Ibid. p34

6) Dolby Stereo, by concretising off-screen space through the placement of speakers which emit off-screen sound, has diminished this pleasure.

7) In her *Book of Cookery and Household Management*, Mrs Beaton gives guidelines for hosting a TV party. As well as catering suggestions, she gives tips on seating and lighting and on the desirability of allowing time to discuss the programmes! *Mrs. Beaton's Cookery and Household Management*, Ward Lock Ltd., 11th Edition, 1971, p108

8) The process of copying the copy is found in a number of art and sound works from around this time, including Steve Reich's *Come Out* (1966), Alvin Lucier's *I am sitting in a Room* (1970) and Art and Language's *Xerox Book* (1969).

9) Guy Sherwin: 'Chronology and Some Reasoning', programme notes to screening at the Lux Centre, London, 30th Jan, 1998

10) For an appraisal of the relative quality of film and video see 'Film Vs Video' by Thomas G Wallis, a technical director at Kodak, in Film Waves no 8, Summer 1999, p28, pub. Obraz Productions Ltd, London

11) For a discussion of the disappointments engendered by FX-laden movies, see Jonathon Romney: 'The Return of the Shadow', The Guardian G2, 22nd Sept, 1999, p16 Romney praises the horror film *Cat People* (1942, Jacques Tourneur) for its subtle understatedness and castigates Jan de Bont for replacing shadowy, suggestive mise-en-scène with computer generated monstrosities in his crass 1999 remake of the original 1963 version of *The Haunting* by Robert Wise.

12) At the time of writing, the facilities upon which film-makers depend are beginning to contract. The Lux is to dispose of its film processing machine and at least one London laboratory no longer makes 16mm answer prints, although large quantities of negative continue to be developed. Telecine has replaced the answer print since most work nowadays is destined for TV or video. The decline in commercial demand for 16mm prints therefore may eventually have a direct effect on the activities of film-makers. Artists working with commercial media in a rapidly changing environment are in a precarious position given that their chosen medium may only be available for as long as there is a commercial demand for it, unless facilities houses make a special effort to continue to provide services which in themselves may not be cost effective, or can cross-subsidise these services like Hendersons, the black and white-only lab in Norwood. Hendersons provide an excellent service from 16mm neg development through to show-prints, but their bread and butter is in archival printing and in the printing of 35mm optical soundtracks for use in the production of DVD transfers of old movies.

13) Rob Gawthrop, London Film-makers' Co-op catalogue, 1993, p48

14) Thomas G Wallis, op cit.

Crossing Parallels

Edwin Carels

Graphic Design – Raggi Aerts

In Chinese medicine there is a therapy that consists of a simple optical exercise:
fixating ones eyes on the flames of two parallel candles and trying to make them visually blend together.
If, in spite of the distance, such a virtual collision takes place, a vital energy spreads itself through
the eyes over the entire body…

> **" Something bulges outward, pushing against the house's skin. Out it pops in all**
> **its nineteenth-century ugliness and absurdity, a bay window with its scrollwork**
> **cornices, its latticed windows. It is the house's tumor, Adorno thinks. It is the underbelly**
> **of the prewar technorationalism, the unconscious of the modernist Sachlichkeit.**
> **It is surrealism, connecting us, through the irrational, with the other side of progress,**
> **with its flotsam, its discards, its rejects. Progress as obsolescence."**

Rosalind Krauss, *The Optical Unconscious* (p.34)

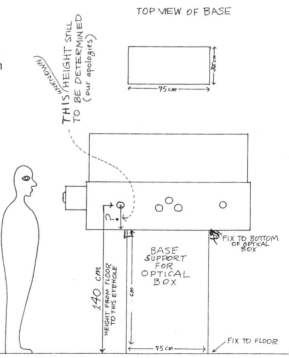

With each new animated film, The Brothers Quay have achieved a higher level of perfection in their animation technique and confirmed their unique style and vision. Their particular universe and idiosyncratic language has already, often been approached by writers, mostly in lyrical terms. But rarely has their particular position within the field of filmmaking been systematically analysed, and if so, mostly through analogies with literature or music. Are The Brothers Quay, then, really so unique that they defy any comparison? Of course not, they themselves even prefer to talk about much admired examples (such as Norstein, Tarkovskij, Borowczyk, Bunuel, Svankmajer, Paradzjanov and more, sometimes very eclectic names) rather than choose to expand upon their own ideas and choices.

Every alternation produces an alteration.

Rosalind Krauss, *The Optical Unconscious* (p.166)

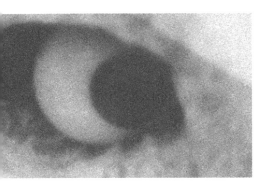

One alternative way of approaching their aesthetic universe could be via the perspective of the tradition of experimental film. Keith Griffiths, the longstanding producer and early collaborator of The Brothers Quay, has even made some documentaries on Len Lye, Andy Warhol and Abstract Cinema, during the years that The Brothers Quay were working on their own vocabulary. Frustrating the conventionalised patterns of expectations is a major strategy that The Brothers Quay have in common with classic works of experimental film. Each of their works not only suggests a fantastic story (and yet refuses to tell it), but also invites us to deconstruct the medium and become aware of our own glance.

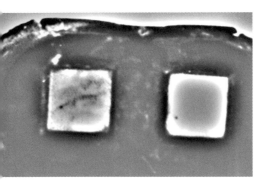

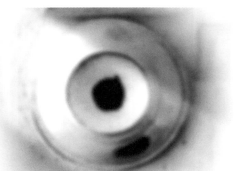

The camera never erases itself to place the viewer in the position of an ideal and unseen witness but functions as an active, participating character on the set. A typical Quay film is as confusing and complex as it is analytical and self-aware. The rhythmic movements of the camera, the elliptic editing and the flicker in the animation together induce a hypnotic (or for Stan Brakhage 'hypnagogic') effect. The restrained frenzy they produce in this way can best be compared with the rapid eye movements each sleeper makes during the dream-phases. Without qualms, The Brothers Quay celebrate the absolute relativity of time and space. A logical orientation through their sets is often impossible. They enjoy leaving the image blurred, which can prove a nightmare for projectionists. As they once described, their ideal set for a theatre piece or an opera could only be seen properly from one vantage point, one single chair in the audience. Always reserved by a mysterious person, of course. But that doesn't mean the viewer is totally disregarded by this hermetic play with parameters, quite the opposite. In each of their films, the screen undeniably radiates a particular sensuality, their ambition being apparently to transform the screen into a projected erogenous zone for the viewers eye. Our scopic drive is met with many free-floating, caressing puppet-hands that address our tactile senses more than they inform us on a strictly visual level. Whatever they install in front of their camera lens, The Brothers Quay essentially make their films for the voyeur that wants to become not only infatuated with, but also affected by the cinematographic image as such.

Another way to approach the paradigm that underlies the filmography of The Brothers Quay (and mutatis mutandis also in their graphic work, their design for theatre, opera etc) is to incorporate them into the current art-theoretical approaches that try to reintroduce some phenomenological ideas (cf Vivian Sobchack's *The Address of the Eye,* 1992) or stress the notion of a corporealised observer (cf Jonathan Crary's *Techniques of the Observer,* 1990) or try to connect physical, cerebral and physiological perception (cf *The Optical Unconscious* by Rosalind Krauss, 1993). It only seems natural to note that our viewing habits are not monocular, we normally watch with both eyes and the parallel perspectives we perceive are not processed immediately by our eyes but rather with our mind and with our whole body. Nevertheless, it is only a relatively recent phenomenon that the universal validity of the idealised, so called objective monocularity of the cinema apparatus (derived from the camera obscura) is put into question.

That the largely intuitive Brothers Quay are open to such a comparison can be proven by their collaboration with a project called **Loplop /re/presents: the im/pulse to see**, an exhibition-project in which the author of this text elaborated the ideas of Rosalind Krauss into a visual essay. For this exhibition, that drew largely from the collection of the Rotterdam Museum Boymans Van Beuningen but also included pre-cinema instruments as well as new media applications, The Brothers Quay created their first sculptural piece, specifically designed for a museum space. Conceived as a kind of prelude to the show, this homage resulted in a imaginary accommodation for Loplop, the birdlike alter ego of Max Ernst, which most often appeared in his collages. In her book, Rosalind Krauss accentuates precisely the collage-work of Max Ernst, and most particularly those in which he refers to pre-cinema toys. A crucial work (from the 1930 collage-novel *Rêve d'une petite fille qui voulut entrer au Carmel* – A little girl dreams of taking the veil) depicts a curious paradox: in the manipulated engraving we see a zoetrope (or magic drum), an instrument which demonstrates the effect of afterimages on the retina, as also used by Etienne-Jules Marey in his research which led to the invention of cinema. Normally the spectator is meant to look into the device from the outside, but Max Ernst places his personage in the very centre of the drum. A girl covers her eyes with one hand, stretching out the other as she gropes her way forward. White clay birds fly around her in a regular rhythm (cf Marey's scientific demonstration tool). Is the girl in her 'colombodrome' feeling dizzy? Can she see dancing dots of light now that she finds herself in the epicentre of an image machine? Besides the pretty much obvious allusion to sexual pleasure (cf the fluttering birds and the suggestive slits on the drum, normally used as peepholes), Max Ernst reverses the positions in such a way that the Alice-like girl is now standing inside the drum instead of observing it from outside, and she is experiencing the production of moving images with her body, rather than with her eyes. The passive observer has become an active participant.

The same goes for the optical box The Brothers Quay produced as a kind of metaphoric birds nest for
the mythical Loplop. The Brothers Quay already made references to this culture of optical toys (also called
philosophical toys, because they were meant to demonstrate a law of nature), most notably in the opening
sequence of *Street of Crocodiles* and in their documentary on anamorphosis, *De Artificiali Perspectiva –
Anamorphosis*. In each case they suggest an ironic commentary on the notion of 'true vision'. Their optical
box resembles a large peep show, which as such was a popular variation on the idea of the camera obscura
turned outside in. Only, instead of the standard singular viewpoint that reveals the interior of the box,
this peep show offers no less than twelve different openings, in different sizes and with different lenses
attached. And still it proves impossible to get a clear picture of what is inside the box. As in their films,
The Brothers Quay perform a game which involves a lot of blur, anamorphic distortion and a deliberately
crammed field of vision. The viewer has to move around the box and stretch and bend over in order to get
a glimpse of what's going on inside. And the narrow passage that locates the box, turns the viewer himself
into a spectacle of obstruction. It is the beholders curiosity and the scopic drive of the beholder that
is put on display here.

In their optical box The Brothers Quay have recycled some of the figures and motifs from their film *Rehearsals for Extinct Anatomies,* which was a variation on an etching derived from an original painting by Fragonard, *Le Verrou.* Apart from the constant perversions of a straight, single line, this film also challenges the viewer to keep track of the sightlines amongst a few very neurotic, restless puppets. Some of them are monocular, but then the image, as such, often consists of two layers that give the Marey-like illusion of seeing two stages of a movement at once. The trajectory of his gaze is like the rampant course of an eye-ball (the film features a lot of ping-pong balls as well). Not only during our sleep, but even more when we are awake, our eyes perform restless, jittery reactions to whatever comes into our sight. Scientists were able to record these so called 'saccadic' eye-movements, by which our eyes 'scan' the elements within a given frame, for instance a painting. It has also been proven that people from a different background (e.g. medical students compared with art students) create a different trajectory with their successive points of attention. All this happens unconsciously of course, but it illustrates the fact that our vision is never stable, but rather consists of a constant combining of viewpoints. What The Brothers Quay demonstrate with each film, technically as well as metaphorically, but most explicitly with their *Rehearsals for Extinct Anatomies,* is precisely this process of vision being driven (or animated) by our unconscious. Rosalind Krauss refers frequently to the classic novel by Georges Bataille, *The Story of the Eye (Histoire de l'Oeil),* in which the main character is not a person but a continuously morphing object. Krauss further expands on Bataille's notion of 'l'informe', a term he developed during his polemic with Andre Breton and the 'Official' Surrealist movement.

> **" The informe is a conceptual matter, the shattering of signifying boundaries, the undoing of categories. In order to knock meaning off its pedestal, to bring is down in the world, to deliver to it a low blow."**
> Rosalind Krauss, *The Optical Unconscious*

When Rosalind Krauss considers Surrealism as the most relevant art-historical movement of the twentieth century, it is precisely because it is the least easy to classify. In principle, everything remains dependent on the associative potential of the individual viewer.

Krauss uses an early collage by Max Ernst *The Master's Bedroom (it's worth spending a night there)* as an example of how Surrealism perverts traditional notions of orientation and perspective on a physical as well as a conceptual level. Now that the reality principle as an absolute given is being put into question on many different levels, by scientists as well as philosophers, it is only logical that the idea of the camera obscura, and along with that the analogue cinema, is being discarded in favour of the animated image. An animated film doesn't need to take into account a horizon or gravity as a given; and, within the chosen technological framework, it can explore any direction, and try out any definition. From the suggestive *Rotoreliefs* of Duchamp, to the digital morphs in recent music video's, *The Story of the Eye* dominates the art history of the twentieth century as a motor of transgression. The Brothers Quay have often been labelled as surrealist, if not Surrealists proper. In a less admiring way, they are considered as hopelessly outdated nostalgics or self-indulgent anachronisms. But regardless of the specific references they use to establish their favourite universe within each film, the operating force behind their decorative evocations is one that can be traced back to the actions of some of the most important artists of this century, as mentioned by Krauss.

> *" What I'd like to broach here is the issue of a rhythm, or beat, or pulse - a kind of throb or on/off on/off on/off - which, in itself, acts against the stability of visual space in a way that is destructive and devolutionary."*

Rosalind Krauss, *The im/pulse to see in the reader Vision and visuality,* Dia Art Foundation

Another contribution to the Loplop exhibition was the design The Brothers Quay made for the small captions, which featured literal/visual quotes from *The Optical Unconscious*. As an ornament, they came up with elegant 'brackets' that lie horizontally on top of and at the bottom of each quote, instead of standing at the usual left and right side. These plates, with a text far more philosophical and condensed than the usual information found on such a format, also forced the viewer to again move and bend and stretch a little because of their often awkward placing. For Rosalind Krauss, the importance of l'informe lies precisely in this willingness to always shift our position as viewer, to change our perspective and play with different focal points. But not only is l'informe about turning (the values of) the world topsy-turvy, it also implies an erotic activity, and this turning about of shapes is not only a matter of visual effects, but a formal strategy. As she suggests in the quote above (taken from an essay in which main ideas of *The Optical Unconscious* are already developed, 1988) Krauss finds action more important than definition. In other words, it is the animation that counts, the interaction between the images, rather than the images as such. In parallel to what Krauss describes about the effect of certain artworks, in cinema too this dynamic is essentially a false one, as film only gives the illusion of movement. The real movement happens within the mind of the beholder.

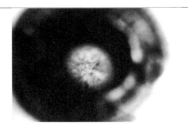

"Balls, says Lyotard, quoting Duchamp."

Rosalind Krauss, *The Optical Unconscious* (p.166)

The experience of moving images is thus primarily a physiological phenomenon, as Joseph Plateau demonstrated in 1832 with his turning wheel or phenakistiscope. Some film theoreticians (e.g. Noël Burch in his *Life to those Shadows*, 1990) have claimed that the unspoken ambition of cinema has always been to offer the public much more than a strictly audiovisual experience. It aimed at "building a haptic space", meaning, offering an all round illusion of space and materiality. The inventions that led to the cinema as an apparatus (e.g. the fantasmagorias and the panoramas) often met with this expectation more successfully than the actual projection of moving images onto a flat screen. Nevertheless, some filmmakers are better at creating an illusion of tangibility than others. Commercials and music videos in particular are aimed more at communicating a level of physical excitement, rather than being strictly visually informative. Although their narrative is so vague and the emotional build up of the film so unpredictable and hard to define, the films of The Brothers Quay nevertheless have a strong appeal to a considerable audience. The explanation of this lies in the instantaneous recognition of materials, movements and atmosphere. What these films address is in the first instance sensorial memory in the mind of each beholder. It is a common observation that the person who knows how to play a ball game such as tennis experiences more subtleties when watching the same sport on a screen than a person who is totally unfamiliar with the sensation of playing it. Like Marcel Proust who only needed a madeleine biscuit to relive an important part of his youth, the haptic experience of the viewer is being re-animated by The Brothers Quay through their delectation of sensual close-ups and movements. The flawlessly synchronised and extremely original choreography of objects, puppets, lights and camera functions like a massage for the eyes and the mind. This effect, together with the twins indulgence of double-imagery, almost resembles that of viewing photographs in a stereoscope. This ghostly paradox of tangibility, the illusion of being within reach of the tactile senses, the feeling of closeness between object and viewer, those were the most important impressions a stereographic image provoked. In combination with the realism of photography, this resulted in an enormous craze for stereographs in the mid-nineteenth century, with a significant quantity of nude poses involved, which only stresses the desire for intimate relationships with the image.

In *The Optical Unconscious* Krauss illustrates her chapter on Max Ernst with a scientific illustration that was repeatedly used by the artist in his collages. A simple black and white engraving demonstrates a hand with index and middle finger crossed, holding a little ball between them. Underneath there is the explicative text, "the illusion of touch". Krauss thus not only refers to one of the sources of Ernst's iconography (popular science books and manuals for conjurors), she also alludes to the notion of synaesthesia. In a further reflection she proposes that the masculine and the feminine constantly shift places in this image. What The Brothers Quay aim at in their films is the same atmosphere of ambivalence. Their sets are disorientating, the gender of their characters sometimes confusing *(The Comb)* their storylines hopelessly erratic, but their objects always stunningly present, in an almost tactile sense. If we really wanted to align the art of The Brothers Quay with a particular tradition, then perhaps the *Machines Célibataires* is most relevant. Marcel Duchamp certainly did not initiate this practice in contemporary art (which brought it to wider attention only in the mid-1970s with an exhibition curated by Harald Szeemann) but his *Large Glass* or *The Bride Stripped Bare by Her Bachelors, even, the Precision Optics, the Rotoreliefs* and *the Etant Données* can all be considered as playfully ironic, semi-scientific commentaries on scopic regimes, as many invitations to achieve erotic pleasure by means of subversion and/or sublimation of optical information. As chance would have it, all of these works by Marcel Duchamp are on permanent display in the Philadelphia Museum of Art close to where The Brothers Quay were born. The European artist found his place in the States, the American twins built their nest with twigs from all over Europe, but in their art they all aim for an imaginary constellation of sightlines, a polymorphous perverse paradise, where parallels cross and the viewer can achieve a sensuous satori.

Quotations: Rosalind E. Krauss: *The Optical Unconscious, An October Book,* The MIT Press, Massachusetts Institute of Technology, Cambridge, Massachusetts 1993.
Rosalind E. Krauss: *The im/pulse to see,* in *Vision and Visuality, Discussions in Contemporary Culture,* #2, Edited by H. Foster, Dia Art Foundation, Bay Press, Seattle 1988.

I WANTED TO TOUCH THE WORDS
THREE ARTWORKS AS DYNAMIC MATRIX OF INTERACTIVE EXPERIENCE
Miroslaw Rogala

I have a 25-year history of creating mixed media, video and multimedia installations that offer the viewer linear and non-linear experience with multiple levels of content. Due to their complexity, these works demand repeat viewing. Recent advances in technology allow a new type of media installation where the content is organized according to feedback and response from the viewer. The participant, viewer/user – (v)user – can create new experiences for every visit through the installation.

The central concept of the works presented is freedom of speech. My understanding of democracy is not only one of rights – the traditional definition in the USA – but of responsibilities. Interactive media not only give audiences the 'right' to work on the content and in certain circumstances even the form of the work; they also entail, in the shift of emphasis from author to (v)user, a shift of responsibility for the work to the (v)user. The (v)users interactions therefore become integral to the work to the extent that the (v)user takesup that responsibility, choosing the amount of time and involvement they care to give, and being rewarded accordingly. In this way creativity can be shared, and is integral to the work, but only when the (v)users learn, not just the interface mechanisms, but the principles of democratic responsibility for their actions.The three projects discussed here will outline creative possibilities for single- and multi-user interaction and opportunities to define a new aesthetic of artist/participant relationships.

Interactive media art relies on technology. Technology alters our experience of everyday life and applies as well to artistic expressions, behaviors, and practice. These have been undergoing a remarkable transformation, situated within a strong social and political context. In describing the relations between technology, digital media, and human relationships, Ihde (1990) refers to a "magnification-reduction structure" as an essential feature of instrumental mediation in aspects of experience through technological means. Audience reception, production means, creation, funding, survival, as well as a new definition of artist responsibility, and social and global awareness are all aspects being altered by the convergence or simultaneity of time, place, and gesture in both physical and digital realities.

Miroslaw Rogala *Gesture with Light* **1981**
Photography by John Boesche

In a variety of media and themes, my artwork addresses the issues of a boundaryless artistic space of relationships, poetics, individual and group interaction, intervention, technologies, open structures, large scale, immersiveness, and participation.

I will discuss my experience as an artist in designing, creating and producing artworks for single-user and multi-user interaction. I will also discuss how the contemporary artist is affected by complex changes in creating an artwork for multiple media and diverse use of physical and virtual place and space.

One has to address the issue: how much interaction can the interface handle? Can it be flexible enough to provide a powerful experience for the single user as well as crowds. The experiences of single users interacting with an artwork in a public space are not similar to multi-users interacting with the artwork and among themselves. As this experience is applied to large audiences, there is a built-in learning curve for understanding, appreciation, awareness, and interpretation of artwork. In this paper, I point out the difficulty and potential of building a vocabulary, creating an artwork, and producing it for flexible receptions, perceptions, and interactions.

Lovers Leap:
Scale, Hand and Body as Interface

I participated in an artist-in-residence program during 1994-1995 at the ZKM/Center for Art and Media, located in Karlsruhe, Germany, a cultural institution promoting new media and technology in the arts. ZKM offers artistic residencies, commissioning and producing artist media works in a variety of technology-based disciplines. During this residency, I created and produced Lovers Leap*, an interactive environment and artwork in multiple forms – as an interactive installation and simultaneously as a CD-ROM. This experience was indicative of future directions for artistic and (v)user flexibility and expressions in multiple forms, independent of art genres and technology. This work was produced in collaboration with Ford Oxaal (Minds-Eye-View Perspective software), and Ludger Hovestadt (12-D Authoring programming).*

Movement through space is a physical aspect. Movement through perspective is a mental construct – one that mirrors other jumps and disjunctive associations within the thought process. This movement is explored in an attempt to create a physical space that is a model of a mental process. When viewers enter the space they become aware that their movements or actions are changing the view but doesn't necessarily realize how. This means that the viewers are not really in control, but simply aware of their complicity. Control strategies assume either dominant or submissive roles.

Miroslaw Rogala *Lovers Leap* **1995**

Description: The participant entering into the public installation of Lovers Leap *stands in a 15 x 12 meter area between two 7 x 5 meter screens of double human size. Through the participant's wearing of a headset, his or her position in space is determined by a nearby receiver attached to a PC computer. As the participant walks closer to either of the screens, the image appears to zoom in.*

Following is one viewer's comments: "If you're exactly between the two screens, yikes! You'll see eerie fish-eye images that look like a ball with buildings growing out of them (Fig. 2). Then, without warning you leap to Jamaica, in the middle of a Third World culture where wood is chopped with a crude ax, not sliced and diced with an electric band saw. Then, as quickly as it came, the QuickTime clip (of which there are 50) vanishes and you're back on that bridge in Chicago. All the while, you're surrounded with first-rate sound, from Chicago street noises to the gentle whooshing of Jamaica's cool blue surf." (White, 1995).

The installation is cited as offering "a framework for reflecting on position and power in a way that... physical and virtual realms are intertwined in an interactive, immersive large environment" (Morse, 1997). In discussing related issues of the work, Druckery (1995) states that "technologies of new media map a geography of cognition, of reception, and of communication emerging in territories whose hold on matter is ephemeral, whose position in space is tenuous, and whose presence is measured in acts of participation rather than coincidences of location."

In 1995, I addressed the concepts of power and control in interaction: "Control strategies assume either dominant or submissive roles. Power and strength depends on where we position ourselves within our environment. As the viewer's awareness of the control mechanisms grow, so does the viewer's power. Each viewer will create a new and different work depending on their involvement, understanding, and transformation into a position of power. Many will leave without claiming their power." (Rogala, 1995).

Lovers Leap *(1995) was introduced as an example of an expanded interactive environment. This artwork is designed to exist in multiple forms and is a ground-breaking, unprecedented approach for creating an artwork produced in simultaneously contradictory formats. The artwork exists as an innovative immersive panoramic perspectival environment which includes an interface suitable for interactive and non-interactive experience for individuals and crowds. The work has been documented as a subject for theoretical research and analysis by Kluszczynski (1998), Morse (1997), Shanken (1996), White (1996), Druckery (1995), and Cubitt (1995).*

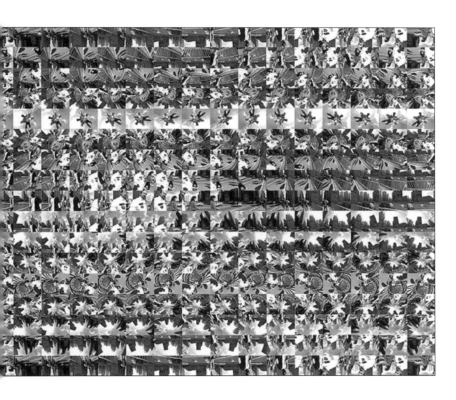

In the 3rd Lyon Biennale exhibition, the CD-ROM version of *Lovers Leap* (extracted from Artintact 2, 1995) was structured differently with a positioning 3-D interface. The CD-ROM was designed for a small screen personal computer experience, yet was placed in a public environment with a large projection screen and sound. This curatorial decision of transforming a private domain into public experience was indicative of the uncertainty of positioning the new artform. The CD-ROM was suitable for personal experience, contradictory to the form for which it was designed in the interactive installation; this same principle can be applied to displaying websites on a large screen. When Nam June Paik (along with Paul Garrin) walked into this installation, he declined to use the interactive devices, insisting that the work be "shown" to him. My reply was, "It can't be 'shown' – I would like you to experience it personally". The project required his understanding of the interface through direct participation, navigation and involvement for a certain amount of time.

Miroslaw Rogala Lovers Leap, **CD-ROM 1995**

Interactive Public Art:
Electronic Garden/NatuRealization:
Disappearance of Interface

Electronic Garden/ NatuRealization **(Rogala, 1996), a site-specific, outdoor, large-scale, public interactive, free speech installation
was undertaken as part of** *Re-Inventing the Garden City***, sponsored by Sculpture Chicago. An on-line World Wide Web counterpart
of the project was constructed (http://www.mcs.net/~rogala/eGarden) and includes QuickTime VR visualization and simulation.
Imagine a garden in which you feel the presence of the surrounding community, where you run into shadows of the past and
hear whispers of your neighbors, past and present – an "Electronic Garden" in which your presence and movement define your
experience. Driving in a car through Chicago streets, I re-visited a neighborhood where I spent my early immigrant years. I saw
a woman on an empty street, walking with a child held in one hand and talking on a cellular phone with the other hand. I had a
feeling she was both connected and disconnected simultaneously – physically being in one location, engaged in conversation in
another. Let us imagine there is a burning car in the background. Let us expand the meaning of the phone: wireless in its connection,
but also a tool for liberation – safety, feel freedom to walk or go anywhere. This interactive situation inspired me to reach for
associative dimensions and inspirations. As a tool for community participation, I use the expression "imagine" as a way for
inexperienced people to relate to my ideas of interactive, participatory art.**

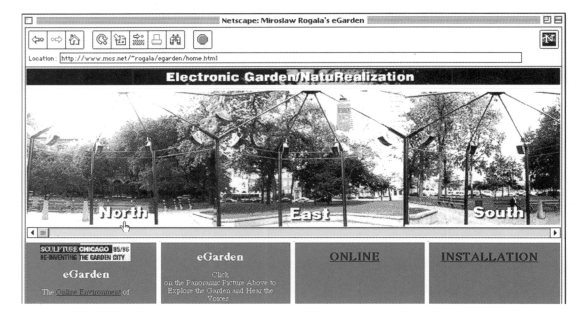

Miroslaw Rogala eGarden, **Website 1996**

Ability, energy, and identity depend upon where we position ourselves in the environment. Relationships are contrasted, and changed. The juxtaposition of the woman's actions using this remote device in the street simultaneously and the dialogue that she was carrying on suggests a new context for the displacement/roots of people and their surroundings. People express themselves by actions in the surrounding environment; the response depends on the acculturation and assimilation of cultural backgrounds and values. In an age of global instant telecommunications, identity merges the 'old' and the 'new' roots.

Miroslaw Rogala *Electronic Garden/NatuRealization,* **Interactive Public Installation 1996**

How did interactions occur? People walked, strolled, came on roller skates, rode bicycles, rolled in on wheelchairs, wore different clothing styles. Participants ranged from single persons or large group of (v)users. During my interview with National Public Radio, a large group of 60 foreign visitors from China walked inside the installation. School buses would bring school children, who would jump, listen, behave or misbehave. The installation was not obtrusive, and harmonized with the existing environment. The installation served as a center of park activity. By having a modular design, an open-ended capacity existed to accommodate new variables: park users adapted the space to hold dramatic readings, play chess and checkers, reconstruct "bug house" debates, and hold art classes, art exhibits and a book sale.

The background of this project involved an expanded role for communities working with me in all stages, including pre-planning, researching the site, making video and voice recordings, seeking neighborhood involvement, arranging for concurrent activities, and evaluating the project.

The artist's statement points to the installation "recreating the sense of placement experienced in culturally diverse environments. Characteristic of the site as a free speech environment, "the reinvention occurs through technological intervention, image processing... and multimedia activity". (Rogala, 1996).

The placement of the art work affects the site, transforming it from a landscape into an interactive environment. Writings on the project [Alben (1997), Kluszczynski (1998)] have stressed the relevance of "humanizing" through technology. Alben (1997) refers to "human experience – not technology – as the essence of interactive design" and provides a vignette of the project "that portray(s) the elements of vision, a sense of discovery, common sense, truth, passion, and heart".

Divided We Speak:
Multi-(V)User Media Laboratory:
3-D Interface for Multi-Users and Multi-Locations

Divided We Speak/ Divided We Stand **is an artist's statement emphasizing the ways of uniting people through new, interactive technologies in physical and virtual spaces.** Divided We Speak**, (Rogala, 1997b) is a Media Laboratory Workshop for** Divided We Stand**, An Audience Interactive Media Symphony in Six Movements.**

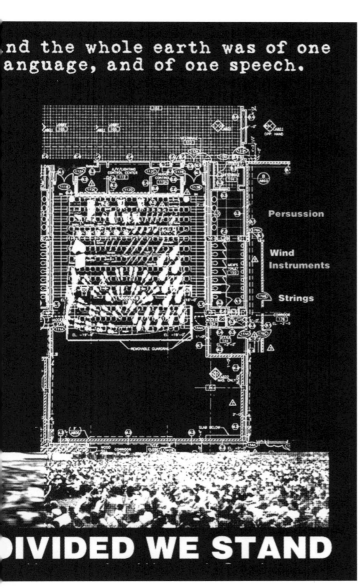

nd the whole earth was of one anguage, and of one speech.

Persussion

Wind Instruments

Strings

IVIDED WE STAND

Shanken (1997) perceives the project as "a virtual, artistic enactment of the contingent relationship between freedom and limitation":

"In this light, Rogala's interactive aesthetic – in which viewers become active participators in regulating the qualities of the work – can be seen as an artistic embodiment of First Amendment rights and elected, democratic government in action. The viewer-participator in *"Divided We Stand"* can metaphorically cast a vote which influences the state of the piece at any given moment. But this freedom is always complicated by the contingencies of behavior, the inextricable inter-relatedness of the individual and the community, the need for limits that demarcate acceptable ways of being in the world, and the random elements of unpredictability that inhere in any real environment. Such issues are especially of concern with regard to art and technology at the turn of the millennium, in the wake of the conservative controversies over artistic decency that plagued the art world in the 1980s, and the threat of the Clipper Chip that ominously looms over the Internet like Orwell's Big Brother. Can we agree to disagree? Or are the terms of our disagreement such that we can find no room to allow each other to coexist without unduly compromising our freedom?" (Shanken, 1997)

Audiences tend traditionally to be spectators. Bronson (1996) gives a historical perspective on new audience roles: "The 'real' audience found themselves in the difficult position of having their role taken away, a role they had never before considered as even being a role. Highly disconcerted... they hit upon a more creative solution to defining their own roles". With the added dimension(s) and role(s) of participation, audience members become active (v)users, requiring new roles and methods of interaction in public space.

Miroslaw Rogala Divided We Speak**, Virtual Sketch: Stonehenge 1997**
3D modeling by Alan Cruz

A significant contribution to my line of artistic inquiry was the use and adaptation of wands, devices that enable the triggering of sounds, in addition to mapping the 3-dimensional space for multiple users. Testing required physical programming and necessitated immediate feedback in decision-making. To my knowledge, such models do not exist. As participants exclaimed, "it is really amazing that you can actually touch the sound" and another stated: "I wanted to keep touching the words".

Because of the problems that have arisen in the interpretation of the movements and gestures of multiple participants in the same shared space, the spatial grammar of experience and behaviour need to be redefined. The mapping of horizontal movement in the space becomes mode of interpretation. Thus, both hand and body movements dynamically create new art forms.

Conceptualizing was done in a virtual digital domain to further develop the ideas of behavioral space. The necessity for feedback became apparent during the twelve months of programming, testing, interacting, and implementing. The methodologies of reality check, feedback, and computer memory are in reality inseparable (Shneiderman, 1998).

As a project-in-progress, *Divided We Stand* is conceived as a large-scale audience interactive media symphony. It is inspired by the idea of audiences playing the role of virtual orchestra, interacting with string, wind, and percussive instruments/sounds. I am continuing to develop and create various elements and parts of this project involving musical composition for piano and synthesizer and large screen interactive sequences. Audience-interactive musical and visual composition will emphasize a variable level of interaction occurring simultaneously with live performance and dance. In development of the web version of this project for larger participation and input, I am continuing to explore the effects of density of mapped spaces to singular and group interaction dynamics among linear and non-linear musical and behavioral components and continue to question the need for interfaces.

Miroslaw Rogala Divided We Speak**, Website 1997**

Conclusion

Interactive art relies upon collaborative engagement requiring new kinds of venues, different kinds of reception, unusual technologies. As a consequence, the artist engaged in this practice must concentrate on issues of content, interface, location, and community involvement.

In the three projects described, I explored diverse subject matter (free speech, issues of power, relationships of language to space, private versus public domain), contradictory spaces/places, challenging interfaces, adaptation of new technologies, modes of engagement and interactions, placement and use of public physical and virtual space – providing important solutions to the processes involved in framing an analytical system for dynamic behavioral space.

A spatial grammar of experience and behavior has to be defined in new contexts as there are problems involved with interpreting movement and gesture of multiple participants in a single shared physical space. Life tends to be based on horizontal movement: how this is mapped in the space became the mode of interpretation. Current usage of interactive spaces ties the body to a stationary position; in this case study, both body and hand movements and gestures became dynamic, thus creating new art forms.

Interaction in new spaces requires new behaviors. The complexity of human interaction and behavior defines constraints in undefined territories. It is not only the hand that can move in multi-dimensions: the human body can jump, walk, accelerate motion within the space and cause effects. Dimensional relationship within spaces, accepting or altering constraints of behavior, and interactive environments are key elements in the dynamic use of public spaces and multi-locations.

The ambition of the works has grown from the individual (v)users responsibility for their experience to the social construction of the work by multiple (v)users – a more complex model of democratic art experience – and finally towards the practical construction of a utopian network in which the possibilities for and demands of global media democracy can be explored.

References

Alben, L. 1997. At The Heart of Interaction Design. Design Management Journal: Summer 1997

Bronson, A.A. 1996. quoted by Robert Nickas in "A Brief History of the Audience: 1960-1981", Performance Anxiety, Chicago: Museum of Contemporary Art

Cubitt, S. 1995. Sound: The Distances. Modernist Utopias Conference. Montreal: Musee d'Art Contemporain Montreal

Druckrey, T. 1995. Lovers Leap: Taking The Plunge: Points Of Entry...Points of Departure. In Artintact 2, CD-ROM Artist Interactive Magazine. Karlsruhe, Germany: Zentrum Fur Kunst und Medientechnologie The Center For Art and Media and Frankfurt, Germany: Canz Verlag

Ihde, D. 1990. Technology and the Lifeworld: From Garden to Earth. Bloomington: Indiana University Press.

Kluszczynski, R. 1998. Dynamiczne przestrzenie doswiadczen. O tworczosci Miroslawa Rogali. In Obrazy na Wolnosci (Images in Freedom): Studia z historii sztuk medialnych w Polsce. Warszawa: Instytut Kultury

Lovejoy, M. 1997. Postmodern Currents: Art and Artists in the Age of Electronic Media. Second Edition. Upper Saddle River, New Jersey: Prentice Hall

Morse, M. 1997. Miroslaw Rogala: Lovers Leap. In Hardware Software Artware Confluence of Art and Technology. Art Practice at the ZKM Institute for Visual Media 1992-1997. Frankfurt, Germany: Canz Verlag

Rogala, M. 1997a. Dynamic Spaces: Interactive Art in Large-Scale Public Environments. In Abstracts of the Proceedings of the First International CAiiA Research Conference. Newport: University of Wales College

Rogala, M. 1997b. Divided We Speak, An Interactive multimedia laboratory of Miroslaw Rogala's Divided We Stand, An audience interactive media symphony in six movements. Program brochure. Chicago, Illinois: Museum of Contemporary Art

Rogala, M. 1996. Artist's Statement, Electronic Garden NatuRealization. Unpublished.

Rogala, M. 1995. Artist's Statement, Lovers Leap. Unpublished.

Rogala, M., Boyer, S. W. 1997c. Building a Vocabulary for Multi-User Interaction in a 3-D Environment. Workshop proposal for ISEA '97 Conference

Shneiderman, B. 1998. Designing The User Interface: Strategies for Effective Human-Computer Interaction. 3rd edition. Reading, Massachusetts: Addison Wesley

Shanken, E. A. 1997. Divided We Stand: Interactive Art and the Limits of Freedom. Website essay: www.mcachicago.org

Shanken, E. A. 1996. Virtual Perspective and the Artistic Vision: A Genealogy of Technology, Perception, and Power. Lecture presentation. Rotterdam: The International Society for Electronic Art (ISEA) Conference

Warren, L. 1997. Divided We Speak. Exhibition program booklet. Chicago, Illinois: Museum of Contemporary Art

White, C. 1996. When Two Worlds Collide: Rogala's Lovers Leap. Digital Video Online. (available on the artist's website).

The artist wishes to acknowledge the contributions of Roy Ascott, ART(n), Will Bauer, Joel Botfeld, Steve Boyer, Sean Cubitt, John Cullinan, Alan Cruz, Rob Fisher, True Fisher, John Friedman, Barbara Iverson, George Lellis, Margot Lovejoy, Darrell Moore, Timothy Murray and Mac Rutan. Portions of this writing were adapted in varying forms from the artist's writings, lectures and presentations. Special thanks to the many contributing collaborators and artists who participated in the three works; the complete list is available on the artist's website.

Artist Miroslaw Rogala 1996
Photography by Bob Kusel

It was a very quiet day **Suky Best**

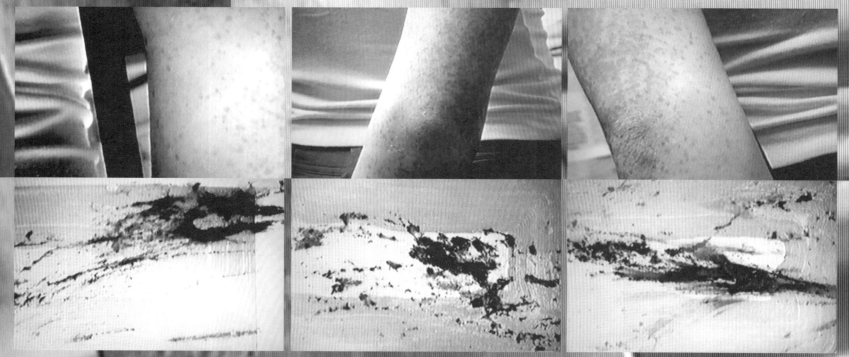

~ [mutant flesh] ~
clinical identity

Adrien Sina

ritualised iconography

Since the first steps of European medicine, from Greek Antiquity to the Renaissance and the Baroque period, with the practice of dissection, anatomical arts and sciences including engravings and waxworks, a concept of the "opened body" has mediated our knowledge of the principles of life and the human body has been depicted through its "clinical identity". Centuries before, in ancient Egypt, the ritualised process of mummification had focused the same questions within the terms of "opened, then carefully sealed bodies" preparing the clinical passage from mortal flesh to the eternity of history.

The use of photography for the study of physiological responses and psycho-pathological expressions in the second half of the nineteenth century offered a more external and bloodless approach to the body: a "clinical identity" especially attentive to the "closed body": the skin, hysterical postures psychic disturbances or the effect of disease. A similar approach had been developed a thousand years before with the Chinese and Buddhist psychosomatic mapping of the body analogically linking points on the skin to internal organs: acupuncture, the structure of human body represented as a Mandala.

This transition from the necessity of "opening the body" to reveal its mysteries towards an iconographic, almost iconic and theatrical interest in external expressions may be paralleled with developments in surgery, beginning with the medieval saw and more recently the scalpel to micro-surgery, laser operation and nano-technologies.

Duchenne de Boulogne (around 1860) and Jean-Martin Charcot were among the first to undertake comprehensive and systematic research via the iconography of the clinic, using photography to constitute a system of signs. This makes them precursor figures, comparable Paul Virilio's Bunker Archaeology in the 1960s within the field of architecture.

~ [mutant flesh] ~
an archaeology of clinical wastes

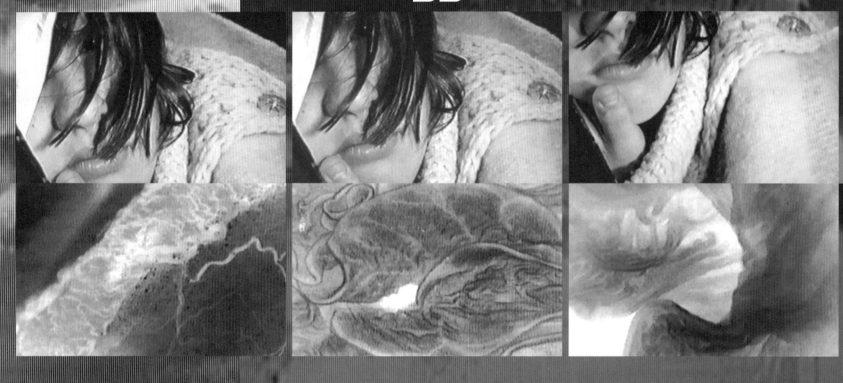

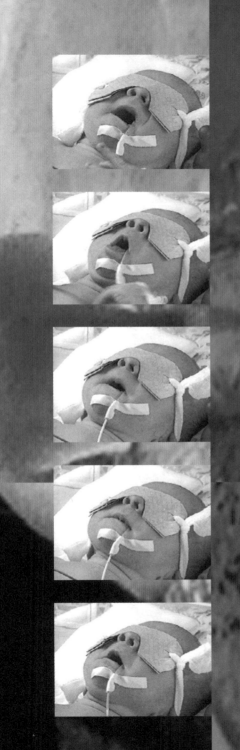

X1- Psychic and bodily wastes____ All objects that enter into contact with our body, clinical instruments, daily or intimate objects of hygiene, carry the trace of our genetic identity (hair, blood, secretions, epidermal cells) but also of our psychic identity (obsessions, fears, fetishisms)... These wastes of our technologised hygienism can return against us, betray our most intimate secrets, innocent or pervert, transform each of our traces into witness-pieces of a crime story, a permanent guiltiness of having an identifiable identity.

X2- Video and digital wastes____ Parallel to the bodily wastes we leave everywhere we are, through the use of any kind of our nomadic technology — credit cards, while surfing the Internet or using a cellular phone and soon with technologies of telesurgery — we leave billions of electronic traces, video or digital wastes that can divulge information about our precise location, our habits, our health or sickness state, our private acts. This global tracking or violation of privacy and intimacy, followed by the personal webcams, surveillance cameras in public spaces, shops, streets, underground stations or airports, even medical endoscopic cameras for the interior of our bodies, will exacerbate a new era of hygienism related to this electronic pollution, an obsession of a digital-hygiene related to the wastes of our virtual-DNA and electronic-gene.

X3- Eroticism and fetishism of clinical wastes____ Vaginal swabs, biopsies, menstrual wastes, placenta expelling, are linked to a fetishism of clinical acts and instruments: enema, endoscopic examinations, close-up observation or touch, on the edge of an erotic ritual of pleasure and pain not decently considered as such. This ritual replaces the more archaic and barbaric one of torture with its own eroticism of mutilation, humiliation or genital manipulation, its own indoor or outdoor, private or group voyeurism.

X4- We, future genetic wastes____ The more the body becomes clinically transparent the more the social corpus, culturally ritualised, is threatened, dislocated, atomised, and the more the play between identity and alterity is disturbed. The issues of wastes are crucial in this sense that our own body will be a waste of the "normality" which derives from our eugenic and technologised hygienism already in question in the selection of embryos according to their genetic provisional identity. With the cloning of human cells or organs, large parts of our genetic patrimony will be considered as pathogenic or as useless wastes. The histological exæresis will be relayed by the exæresis of the DNA, by the manipulation of the genome, if we are not assimilated into an embryonic or foetal waste before we are born.

Many of our organs will be considered as obsolete waste, because of a lack of resistance to toxic or genetic aggressions. Unforeseen functional or sensorial organs will be genetically engineered to increase our adaptive abilities to deal with polluted or interstellar and abyssal extreme environments. The limits between the self and waste will be one of the most indeterminate ethical confusions.

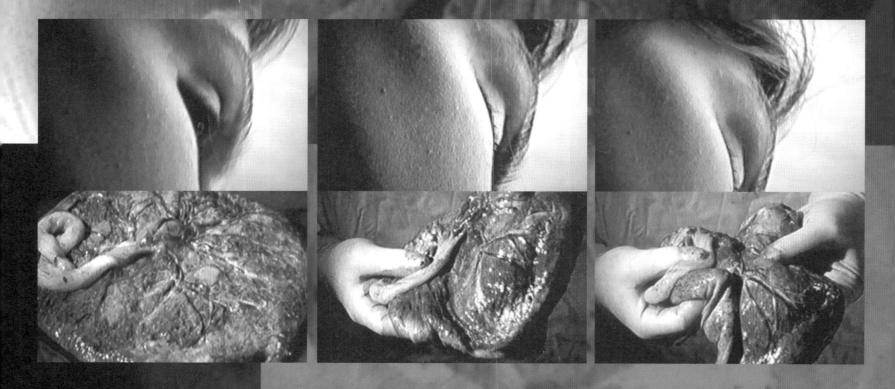

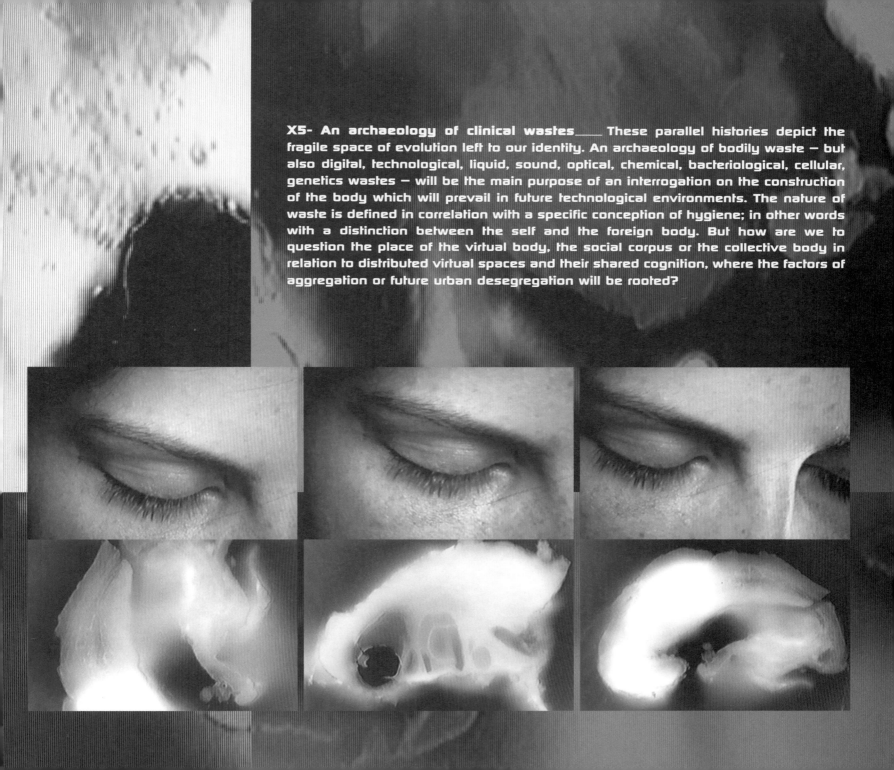

X5- An archaeology of clinical wastes____ These parallel histories depict the fragile space of evolution left to our identity. An archaeology of bodily waste — but also digital, technological, liquid, sound, optical, chemical, bacteriological, cellular, genetics wastes — will be the main purpose of an interrogation on the construction of the body which will prevail in future technological environments. The nature of waste is defined in correlation with a specific conception of hygiene; in other words with a distinction between the self and the foreign body. But how are we to question the place of the virtual body, the social corpus or the collective body in relation to distributed virtual spaces and their shared cognition, where the factors of aggregation or future urban desegregation will be rooted?

~ [d(t)oxic landscapes] ~ I
social corpus, togetherness, a silent
hyper-perception of urbanity

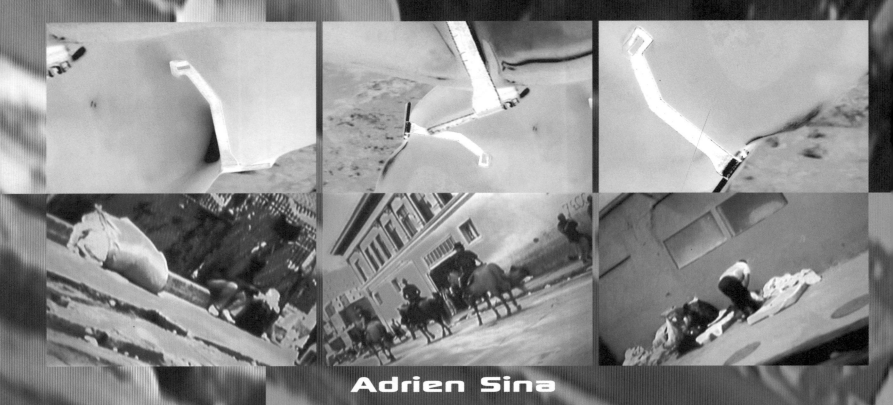

Adrien Sina

[E1]. Cybercities, Megacities, Homelesscities, Slumcities: Missing links, missing urbanity and togetherness

The urbanity considered within the terms of a human dwelling and togetherness has been a missing issue throughout the 20th Century. This was partly a result of the breakdown of utopia, the disillusion of the social body and the failure of the collective body experienced in between and beyond the wars. Whereas factors of disintegration of the real cities and urban territories are slowly shifting into factors of aggregation in virtual spaces for social and economical activities, links are still missing between Cybercities, Megacities, Homelesscities and Slumcities as parts of the multifold layers of our planetary habitat. The factors of aggregation and desegregation allow us to perceive the relative positions between the self and others, to have an awareness of alterity, in our technological environment where all positional references are more and more blurred in favour of a sightless timeless and somehow rootless flux of information.

These questions of social corpus, of un-centralised quasi-perception of the position of the other members of the community, are among the most determinant phenomena in the embryogenesis and most enigmatic steps in the development of a cell society. Through these processes each cell, each individual has a certain perception of the exact position and role of the others. While the destiny of one cell, a priori identical to the others, is to become a bone cell, the destiny of others is to become nerve cells through processes of differentiation using genetic architectures of position, aggregation and migration. Today, how can we think of any meaningful concept of exchange or transmission if we have no idea of the architecture of otherness, the position of the high-technologised or the under-technologised since the reality hardly ever corresponds to the spilled assumptions? The flux of knowledge is not necessarily from the north to the south, or from the pharmaceutical companies to the Amazonian Indians and to the treasures of their ancestral pharmacopoeia.

Among the large variety of cell societies such as our immune system, some bacteria communities or colonies accomplish extremely complex social and urban tasks without any central command, just by using a diffuse sense of togetherness carried by a fluctuating environment of information, like our

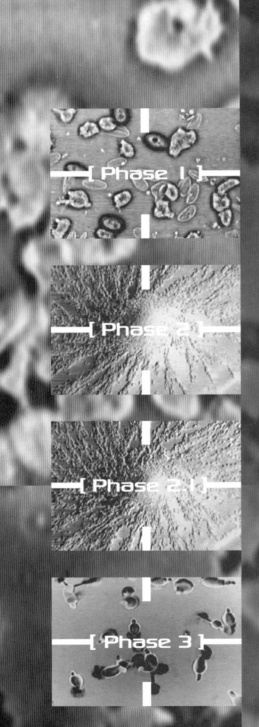

[Phase 1]

[Phase 2]

[Phase 2.1]

[Phase 3]

infosphere. There the language is structure, doxa or communication but is also a toxic weapon at higher dosage. This leads us to think about organic societies similar or different to our own, within the terms of [~ d(t)oxic landscapes] — a pun involving the Greek doxa, between doxic and toxic. Human civilisation has only surrounded itself with an infosphere since the 1950s, but other societies of living organisms, which are also based on an information environment have, in some cases, million years of evolutionary experience of mastering this medium which is still new to us. Taking the case of the society of myxomycetes we could briefly focus on some aspects of these infra-ordinary societies as a key to the topology of otherness which is paradoxically more and more missing in our human technological societies.

[E2]. A non-neuronal hyper-perception of urbanity
survival, social, architectural and urban structures by myxobacteria

Myxomycetes are single-celled individuals — amoebas — which normally live separately. However, whenever there is a situation of crisis, such as a lack of food or difficult living conditions, they emit tiny alarm signals. It is as if a group of homeless people sent out an alarm signal and the entire human community grouped around them: in the case of these amoebas, the entire community of single-celled organisms, who don't even have a brain, converge around them. This is one way of looking at how information-based societies can operate without any central control, comparable to our cyberspace and the virtual urbanity in project inside. This leads us to think how societies which are created and destroyed by the vagaries of aggregation and desegregation factors manage to structure themselves, and go even further; in the case of these single-celled creatures, they join to form multi-celled social bodies.

In this type of social organisation of the cells, which comes close to embryogenesis, some processes of differentiation occur that result in each individual specialising in order to perform individual and collective tasks. Indeed, the entire community is capable of some degree of movement, comparable to Archigram's Walking Cities, albeit with liquid and oscillating movements, until it finds a more suitable environment. Then the quasi-animal phase is replaced by a quasi-vegetable phase: part of the society commits mass suicide in order to create small rigid offshoots on which, rather like television broadcasting pylons, another part of the cells mutate into packets of spores, genetic messengers which can cross time and space, resisting long periods of drought and extreme temperatures.

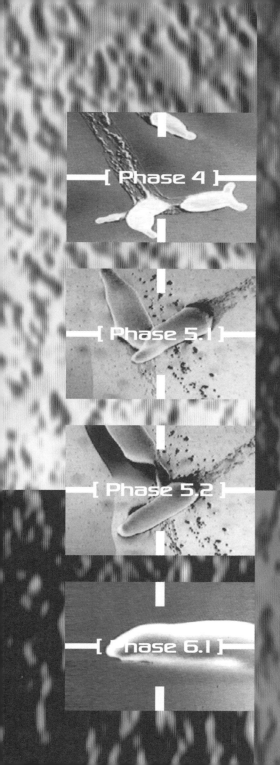

[Phase 4]

[Phase 5.1]

[Phase 5.2]

[Phase 6.1]

~ [d(t)oxic landscapes] ~ 2 mutagenic aggressions, genetic collisions between communities of social living organisms

These community organisms also use biochemical information as a language, allowing them to structure a social body, to coordinate the collective movements which make migration possible. At the same time, though, this reiterative high dosage of information becomes an info-chemical weapon or bomb, which can be used to kill or neutralise other competing organisms also living in an information-based social environment. The fact that each individual in the colony has a certain memory or a perception of the position of the others makes it possible to perform coordinated social tasks, such as oscillation, migration or germination. The issues of forgetting the position of the others in our societies are comparable to what Paul Virilio calls the path-being which marks the simultaneous loss of the subject-being and the object-being, the topographical amnesia and the geographical collapse.

[E3]. Infra-social landscapes:
Disseminated genetics and d(t)oxic societies.

Society exists since there is interdependence between individuals, exchange, specialisation of these individuals according to reciprocity and distribution of tasks. Society exists since social tissues inscribe themselves into the architectural tissues or tissues of spatial extension: colonies of bacteria meet these criteria just as much as human cities. Society exists since there are individuals and recognitions, perceptions of the position of otherness, of identity. Society exists since the factors of aggregation and desegregation with shared or competing aims define the rules of community life.

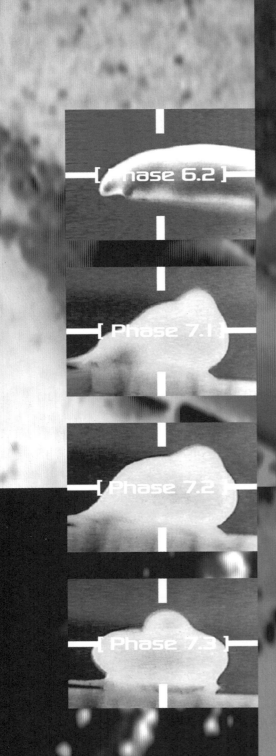

[Phase 6.2]

[Phase 7.1]

[Phase 7.2]

[Phase 7.3]

If, as Paul Virilio says, it is dangerous to compare human societies with other societies of living organisms, confusing the sociological and the biological, then by decoding the specificity of social acts that are inherent to the different communities of living organisms we can unfold new paradigm shifts, invert acquired points of view, destabilise preconceived ideas. Our brain is a cell society. So is our immune system – the most evolved and most complex of all – and a cancerous tumour is one too. The human community lives in a state of permanent collision with communities of viruses or retroviruses, genetic or toxic messengers. We also live in symbiosis with communities of bacteria that colonise the micro-landscapes of our digestive system or of our skin, protecting us from the aggressions of other competing micro-organisms or helping our metabolism.

Our blood is salty, because we are just drops of sea water enveloped in a membrane. At the dawn of our first cellular quivers, a few billion years ago, we were made of the same substance as the liquid landscape surrounding us. We think, we breathe because our cellular ancestors incorporated into their body many other social or independent living organisms which applied themselves to the tasks of data transmission, detoxification, and transport of oxygen, minerals and nutrients. The most common and visible forms of these interdependencies between cell societies and evolved organisms can be seen in the photoluminescent organs of abyssal oceanic creatures: anglerfish, jellyfish or squid, colonised from birth by symbiotic photobacteria ready to react to the slightest nervous inpulse of their host and to produce the light-based communication signals in the dark underwater depths.

Social signals, togetherness, the perception of otherness, are not specific to human societies. Other societies of living organisms are also based on complex codes of exchange, of reciprocal development, of identity recognition, of strategies of deceit or lying, of relationships of force, of relationships with the dead and with ancestors, of hierarchy, of exclusion, of sexual taboo, of clan warfare, but also of dialogue and aggressive or symbiotic exchange. Without reducing human societies to the level of other societies of living organisms, it would also be relevant to look at the phenomena of solidarity, altruism or mass suicide among other living organisms in order to question the relativity of our place in the extensive landscape of the whole earthly life set.

texts, design, videos and photographic works : Adrien Sina, 2000

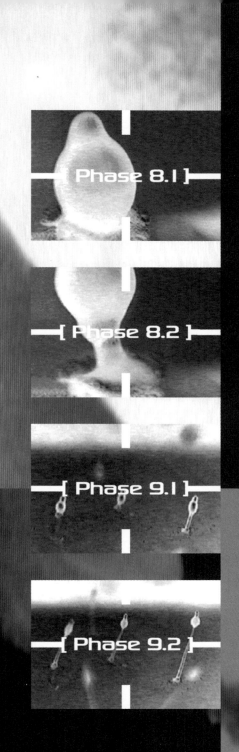

[Phase 8.1]

[Phase 8.2]

[Phase 9.1]

[Phase 9.2]

[E4]. D(t)oxic wars, mutagenic factors:
Genetic aggressions, collision between communities of social organisms.

In each genetic encounter between communities of social organisms and mutagenic factors — organelles, small pieces of genetic program, viruses, retroviruses, biotoxins, neurotoxins, carcinogenic materials, radiations — all the processes of recognition, of identification of oneself with regard to the other, all the processes of cell division and renovation, all the programmed processes of cellular life and death are affected. In each collision between communities of living organisms, all the genetic and evolutionary heritage of the species involved is altered, even mutated.

The question of the transformation of the human genetic patrimony by all the biological aggressions to which we have been exposed over thousands of years through natural evolutionary immunisation or large-scale epidemics, increases as the disturbance of our environments is speeded up, displacing pathogenic species from their confined medium and inciting them to virulence and migratory expansion. Each biological aggression leaves its genetic prints, not only on the immune system, but also on the evolutionary memory of whole species, conditioning them to a blind adaptive genetic self-defence aggressiveness.

Info-biological warfare reaches a higher magnitude with transgenically programmed aggression and belligerence. Transgenic organisms are programmed to respond to biological aggressions. They have integrated in their genes self-defence, belligerence and aggressiveness to other living organisms that their programmers consider harmful. Societies of transgenic organisms, no longer comparable to small groups of isolated individuals, are armies of bellicose individuals, injected in the midst of large-scale natural balances, fitted with decoys and info-biological weapons that are unknown to other living organisms.

Beyond binary logics, artificial intelligence, the intelligence in question in the high-scale phenomena which affect the whole planetary balance requires a reflection on the d(t)oxic landscapes inherent to the future technological environments based on rather genetic and generic architectures than informational, rather cognitive processes than algorithmic. A paradigm shift is then necessary in order to assimilate into our approach to the planet the massive phenomena related to infra-perceptible fringes of the whole life set, with still unveiled limits, temporalities, scales and magnitudes.

After Amnesia

Nikos Papastergiadis

Since the 1980s Australian artists, with the help of various funding bodies, have attempted to gain a presence in the international art world. One of the few artists to achieve a strong and persistent presence in major international exhibitions is Juan Davila. In contrast to painters like Jeffrey Smart, who live in Europe but only appeal to an Australian elite, Davila's significance is not confined to either provincial prejudices or fashionable themes. Collectors seem to prefer Australian scenes when they are painted from a distance, ideally from the hills of Tuscany. Charm of the local accrues when it is linked with the romantic perspective that pervades the culture of the new global elites. For Davila nothing could be more abhorrent than a new romanticism that conjures signs of the local in way that only further lubricates the ruthless machinations of globalization. While his paintings engage with the turbulent incorporation of transcontinental symbols there is a consistent refusal to cast this traffic in nostalgic and palliative frames. Rather than consoling us for our alienated existence or reassuring

us about the superiority
of our contemporaneity, his paintings make us return to the
question of how to make meaning out of the cultural differences
that collide and cross over each other in our bodies. The complex
narrative forms of his paintings, the use of the canvas as material
for installation, the irregular shape of frames, the incorporation
of photography, computer generated imagery and time based
media all combine to question the limits of art and politics.

Davila's own journeys between Chile and Australia, from
living in Melbourne and showing in exhibitions in the Americas
and Europe, are significant. The relationships between first
and third worlds, modernity and tradition are never posed in
absolutist or impersonal terms. The borderline between the
self and other in his portraits is always ambivalent, cutting in
multiple directions, revealing histories and positionalities that
would be suppressed from popular consciousness. The contours
of identity, even when depicting the famous and the powerful,
never hold firm. Their edges often bleeding. Their weeping eyes
and exposed orifices depicting a vulnerability that is usually
hidden from the public gaze. Davila presents an identity that is
invariably crossed by cultural and sexual differences, but this
subject cannot be known by simply decoding and aggregating
the constituent parts. The transvesting of subjectivity that
emerges in his paintings is one which leads us away from the
familiar icons of split or multiple personalities, and moves
towards a more uncertain self image. His paintings suggest
an identity that comes from the criss-crossing of the symbolic
boundaries that would separate the master and the slave.
Such ambiguous identities often defy recognition within the
conventional categories of classification. Hence the critical
discourse that has followed Davila's work is pinned between
the twin poles of either aggressive resistance or sympathetic
oversimplification. Apart from those who wish to attack his
critical gestures as if they were merely perverse habits, there
are also critics who while claiming to feel an identification with

Juan Davila, The Dealer of Indigenous Art, 1999 (oil & collage on canvas)

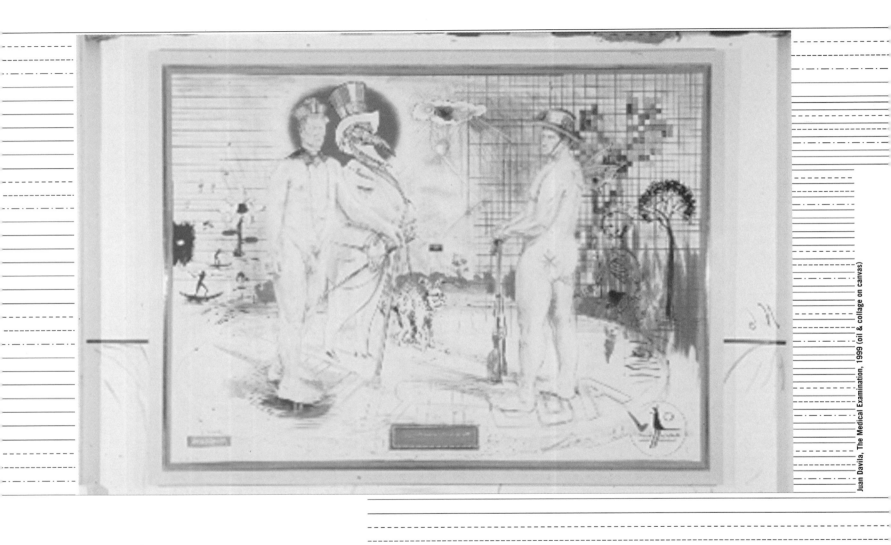

his position seek to explain the whole field of his paintings by reference to a singular thematic. The significance of his work, while often categorized as merely 'gay', 'ethnic' and 'postmodern' art has never the less exceeded the parameters and duration of these labels.

The content of Davila's images is not the primary source for determining the meaning of his work. Nor can his practice be resolved within the formal boundaries of painting. His incorporation of diverse media and narrative forms can be situated between the contesting eulogies for the end of painting and the celebration of the moving image. It demands a new framework for understanding visual narratives, one which can accommodate a heightened form of reflexive and subjective experience. The disruption of the conventional perspective for viewing a painting, and the use of a frieze with a 3D effect in his installation at the Ikon Gallery 1996, had a perplexing effect. It forced me to move around the space to experience the work that always seemed to elude my grasp and lay beyond any point where a close observation was possible. It was like being in an ornate basila but in reverse and on the move. In a letter about his monumental installation of *Yawar Fiesta (Fiesta Sangrienta)* in the 1998 Sao Paulo Biennale,

Davila defines his relationship to new media and the incommensurabilities of cross cultural symbols.

"My concern is to argue about the history of decoration against the current conservatism of the genre 'installation'. Decoration of rooms has always been an exercise in power, display of wealth, scenarios for power negotiations (uncertain rules of behavior in such space), and the display of conquests (chinoiseries, a-la-grecque, etc.) through the medium of visual representation of the concerns of the State or Capital. My room can be displayed upside-down, sideways, contains grand paintings and craft, frieze in Spanish and Indian languages (mixed as in the novels of the Peruvian writer Jose Maria Arguedas). I have made painting operate as the medium to represent debris and minor figures on the laser imaging on vinyl of the computer. It does create several tensions, between the notion of painting as the frame, image and signature of high art and the commercialism of laser billboard. Between the handmade and the electronic imaging. Between young art as the computer has been promoted and old art as oil painting has been labeled by Duchamp. ... As the work proposes a narrative – one of another power – it brings a layered effect: scenes of bullfight in the 19th century Spain rendered in popular prints layered by the Peruvian bullfight rendered by oil paints (there the bull has a condor attached to its back, there is gold thrown into the arena, the doors open and the bull/condor charges because dynamite is thrown to it, the workers jump in the ring to bullfight and get the gold, 20 or more killed per bullfight, wild music, drunkenness...) Layered on that Tommy McCree images of the emu hunt. Imagine the three scenes in Madrid, Lima and the Australian outback at the same cultural time. Imagine the protestant ethic of say, Lichtenstein in America with the clean Ben-day dot technique and his idea of the popular: clean rooms. Since in my proposition, techniques and narrative and time / space compete and are not coincidental one can speak in Spanglish of a space resilient to World wide capitalism."

Along with the artist Constanze Zikos, Juan Davila and I have began a collaborative project in which we have sought to problematize the relationship between art and politics in the context of globalization. While noting that the 'other' has become increasingly visible in the institutions

of art over the past decade, we take as
a starting point the collective amnesia
over the histories of otherness and the
resistance to discuss the conditions of
visibility. This has prompted us to frame our
investigation not only in an oppositional
manner to the selective incorporation
of individual artists within the given
structures of success, but also to pose
questions about the frameworks for
constructing narratives and representing
symbols which have been excluded from
the mainstream histories. While not
concerned with our individual positions
within the dominant discourse we were
interested in the possibility of collapsing
many of the conventional distinctions
between author and artist, critic and
creator, as well as returning to the
broader and unresolved issues on the
representation of the readymade as an
index of the everyday, and questioning
the place of folkloric and national icons
in the context of the international art world.

   Support towards such a collaborative
project was, perhaps not surprisingly,
rejected by the Australia Council. We felt
that this rejection was symptomatic of
a deeper level of cultural change. Like
most state institutions across the western
world, the Australia Council has been
torched by economic rationalism. Under
the guise of promoting greater levels of
accountability and delivering higher

quality service to the public, radical transformations have been introduced into the structures of numerous institutions which are effectively rendering a scorched earth policy on the cultural landscape. The new pressures have displaced the original aims of serving the producers of culture and promoted the function of satisfying the consumers. The constituency of these institutions has also been redefined in the discourse of market rules and client needs. The broader ideals of promoting cultural development and enlightening the citizenry have been effectively jettisoned in the pursuit of the most effective forms of cultural populism that tourists will find entertaining. The simplification of cultural and political ideals into economisitic commodity units, whose circulation can be measured and regulated, reveals the fundamental shift in government's priorities. Most Western governments are more anxious to demonstrate that they are good economic managers over the more complex role of a sophisticated civic leader.

Davila's visual response to the perceived gap between the criteria and the conditions of support by the Australia Council was decisively stated in the The Medical Examination (1999). In the corner of this painting Davila displayed the Australia Council's logo of the leaping kangaroo and added the motto, "Australia Council for the art dealers". The theme of this painting also addresses the subordination of the national symbols under the tyranny of the increasingly commercialised and puritanical priorities of the 'new world order'. It depicts in caricature form an image of Pax Americana leading the Australian Prime Minister John Howard like a mongrel on a leash. Accompanying them is the befrocked Archbishop George Pell, who is revealed in full morning glory with a cross hanging low over his naked body and pointing to the proud gold cock ring. Before them awaits the angel winged digger ready and willing for his fitness examination. The background scene presents a blazing red earth with the failed grid of modernism on one side and indigenous realism on the other. Clearly, this is not the work that the Australia Council would wish to promote. However, the reluctance to discuss the conditions of visibility and the violence between the local and the global does not end with the formal institutions of the state. For instance, the art magazine Art & Text, with which Davila had a close relationship in its founding stages when they pioneered the theoretical reconfigurations of art criticism, now seems reluctant to engage with practices which take a more critical position towards local politics. Despite the re-location of its editor from Sydney to Los Angeles, the magazine continues to depend on grants from the Australia Council. Judging by their response to my review of Davila's most recent exhibition which they had commissioned it appears that their interest in this work was restricted to a formalist account, one which might appeal to their global readers and not offend their sponsors. After all political references to the local context had been censored from the text, Davila refused copyright permissions for any reproductions of his work and I withdrew my essay.

There are important reasons why Davila's practice should not be ignored both in the local and global context of art. His very practice has in effect been an interrogation of how they can or cannot relate to each other. The dynamics of translation and incommensurability in the contemporary cultural fields that Davila constructs can be addressed on three levels. First, Davila's paintings begin with the desire for transgression that drives the traffic of globalization. As different symbols and political priorities compete for attention in the global arena, Davila stands witness to the violent clash and the jagged translations of difference. Within a single frame of the painting *Woman in*

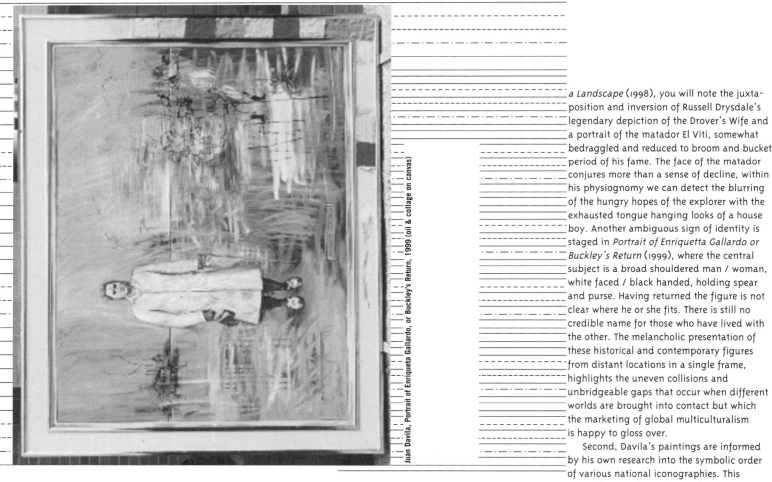

Juan Davila, Portrait of Enriquetta Gallardo, or Buckley's Return, 1999 (oil & collage on canvas)

a Landscape (1998), you will note the juxtaposition and inversion of Russell Drysdale's legendary depiction of the Drover's Wife and a portrait of the matador El Viti, somewhat bedraggled and reduced to broom and bucket period of his fame. The face of the matador conjures more than a sense of decline, within his physiognomy we can detect the blurring of the hungry hopes of the explorer with the exhausted tongue hanging looks of a house boy. Another ambiguous sign of identity is staged in *Portrait of Enriquetta Gallardo or Buckley's Return* (1999), where the central subject is a broad shouldered man / woman, white faced / black handed, holding spear and purse. Having returned the figure is not clear where he or she fits. There is still no credible name for those who have lived with the other. The melancholic presentation of these historical and contemporary figures from distant locations in a single frame, highlights the uneven collisions and unbridgeable gaps that occur when different worlds are brought into contact but which the marketing of global multiculturalism is happy to gloss over.

Second, Davila's paintings are informed by his own research into the symbolic order of various national iconographies. This research is not directed at archival material but draws from a peculiar mixture of academic and popular sources. For instance, Davila excavates the work of Tommy McCree, a late nineteenth century Aboriginal artist whose silhouette paintings of native scenes satisfied the empirical and colonialist taste of his masters. From his various trips to Latin America Davila retrieves examples of 'folk art' which he regards to be worthy of inclusion within any museum of contemporary art. Realizing that he can do no better than quote them in his own paintings, he dutifully stitches them into the canvas

as is evidenced by the presence of a flower in *The Medical Examination*. The effect of introducing found objects into the frame of the painting is twofold; it disrupts the linear narratives and questions the conditions of remembering and forgetting in the dominant institutions of art.

Third, Davila has honed both his understanding and critique of the discourses of art history, the trajectories of contemporary art practice and the machinations of the institutions of art. While the language of his critique is mostly understood in terms of deconstructive and psychoanalytic theories it also draws heavily from the oppositional practices of the early avant garde. Davila attacks the Eurocentric boundaries between folkloric and fine art, the valourization of second order modernism and the collusion between the marketeers and the curators of art. These strategies are powerfully deployed in, *The Dealer of Indigenous Art* (1999/2000), which depicts a ghoulish driver in a retro sports car dashing through the desert with a crate full of empty bottles and swarms of locusts attached to the aerial and crate. This painting is cast as one-liner, stripped of all other references other than the indictment against the most recent phase of neo-colonization; the infamous exchange between art and alcohol. This visual one liner, while being as long and as bloody as the nearly eight meter long horizon of this tryptich, also carries within its depiction of the car a hidden debt to the contemporary Spanish painter Eduardo Arroyo. Since his famous attack on the commodification of surrealism Arroyo has pioneered a strategy that tackles art historical references in order to make visible a history that is otherwise suppressed.

The emergence of a new vocabulary for defining the status of cultural institutions, evident in terms like 'flagship institutions' and 'centers of national excellence', point to the growing convergence, or rather the imposition of commercial criteria to measure the value of cultural production. The commodification of art is not a new phenomenon. Despite a longstanding Marxist critique of the context art, and the utopian spirit that underpinned early modernist experiments with form, the intellectual priorities which domi-

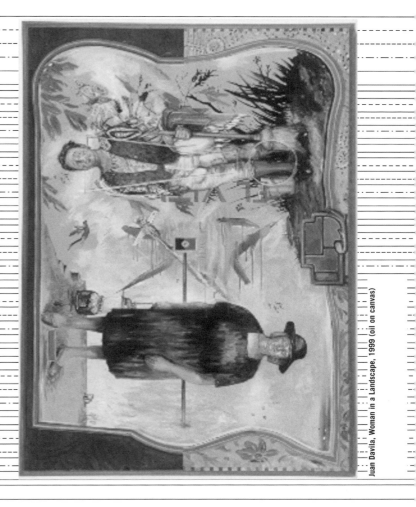

Juan Davila, Woman in a Landscape, 1999 (oil on canvas)

Juan Davila, Yawar Fiesta (fiesta sangrienta), 1999 (oil & jetspray on vinyl)

nate in the institutions of art are now fundamentally alienated from the critical discourses which shaped debates in the previous decades. The populism that is being stressed within the policies of the dominant cultural

institutions increasingly mimic the structures and values of commercialism and puritanism in the new world order. Narratives, like those presented by Davila which display the brutal domination of the local by the global, the emptiness of the current styles in contemporary art and the hypocrisy of the dealers would clearly clash with the rhetoric of our political leaders. Figure heads like Howard who prefer to uphold the illusion of independence while clinging to a corner of the Union Jack and swinging in whichever direction the Americans blow.

Responsibility for the transformation in the social and cultural landscape across the world cannot be accounted for in the traditional left / right political camps. Economic rationalism is the discourse of governance across both sides of the political divide. In Australia, during the regime of the Keating Labor government, this contradiction was manifested in the torsion between the steps towards promoting a new republic, finding reconciliation with indigenous people and the ruthless restructuring of the city and country interests to match the priorities of global capital. Symbolic and economic imperatives were on a head on collision course. Keating has a semantic difficulty over groveling before the monarchy but showed no modesty when it came to bending over for globalization.

While the current conservative government of Howard finds itself stuttering and gagging at the mere approach towards any apology for the "sins of their colonial fathers", they too are delighted to sell every public asset to any foreign bidder. Howard's own choking silence is graphically portrayed in Davila's painting *Buckley's Return* (1999), furious at the sight of a cross-dressing, trans-racial Buckley, the little door-stop of a leader is busy erasing the word 'sorry' from his thought bubble. Howard still yearns for the 1950s suburban white middle class fantasy of Australia as the lucky country with a big backyard. His successful attempt at out maneouvring the republican movement has left the majority of the Australian people in a symbolic void. Knowing that an overwhelming majority were opposed to the monarchy but uncertain about the implications of a republic, he engineered the terms of the debate in such a manner that the ensuing dissent and confusion amongst the pro-republicans would be sufficient to allow the status quo to remain. This was Howard's historic moment of triumph and he didn't even take the stage of victory. Hiding in fear of negative public backlash he gloated in private. Like all the other 'quiet' leaders of our era, John Major, Helmut Kohl and George Bush there is no sign of vision in his leadership. The contradictions between the local and

the global blister and spread as their stature shrinks. There is behind the rhetoric of governance, the deep wish that the 'problems' of identity, the 'questions' of history, and the 'rules' of the market would just look after themselves. They are our leaders who enjoy authority but bawk at responsibility. There are few better places to confront our void then when before Davila's painting, *The Australian Republic* (1999), it consists of a decoratively painted frame and an empty center.

Bill Viola interviewed by Stuart Morgan, June 4 1996

This interview took place in 1996, when Bill Viola was planning the showing of a work for Durham Cathedral, *The Messenger*, amongst other projects. Stuart Morgan included Bill Viola's work *Tiny Deaths* in the exhibition he co-curated at the Tate Gallery in his landmark exhibition of 1995, *Rites of Passage*. An earlier interview with Viola was published in frieze magazine (reprinted in Morgan's selected writings, *What the Butler Saw*, 1996), and an essay on Bill Viola's work by Stuart Morgan featured in COIL 2. The interview has been edited for publication by Ian Hunt, who is currently preparing a second volume of Stuart Morgan's selected writings, *Inclinations*, forthcoming from Durian Publications, London.

Do your current projects relate to earlier work?

This year I'm making a series of works that in some ways connect with the piece at Documenta a few years ago. I'm working on three large-scale pieces to do with a single action by an isolated figure – two of the works will be shown in Savanna for the summer Olympics. They are about the same scale as the Durham project and involve a double-sided screen in the middle of the room. They are 14 feet in height, with projectors on opposite sides. What you see, as with the piece for Durham, is an action with a beginning and an end – not an eternal loop as in some of my other installations. You're looking at an obscure space, grainy and mysterious, and there's something moving although you can't quite see what it is. Then you realise it is figures, but very small, but they are getting larger and travelling towards you and coming in and out of shadow so nothing is distinct. Eventually you realise it's a man and not a woman. There is a little more light and you see more of this person, the clothes he is wearing. Finally he arrives, never fully illuminated, and they stop.

Are there two figures or one?

It's happening simultaneously on both sides of the screen, but the action is the same: moving out from a grainy black-and-white environment. One comes close, stops, and at this moment a fire breaks out in his feet. It spreads up his leg and consumes his entire body and burns until there is nothing left. You're left with an empty floor and a few smouldering flames which go out, leaving you with the grainy, black-and-white nothingness. At that point the loop is complete and the figure emerges

The Messenger
Bill Viola (1996)
video/sound installation as installed
in Durham Cathedral, England

Collection
Edition 1, Chaplaincy to the Arts and Recreation
in North East England.
Edition 2, Collection of Solomon R. Guggenheim Museum,
New York, gift of The Bohen Foundation.
Edition 3, Albright-Knox Art Gallery, Buffalo, New York.
Photo Edward Woodman

again. And in parallel on the other side is the same thing. Except this time the figure comes close and stops, looking straight ahead, and a thin stream of water starts pouring on his head, spatters out, then turns quickly into a deluge which gushes over him. He is washed away and nothing is left. These two are playing simultaneously, so that when the fire starts at the feet, the water washes over the head, the light and sound roar up – and then it's over quickly.

The Durham piece also has to do with an approach to the figure.

It comes out of an idea which has been in my work from the very beginning: an approach to clarity, this process not only of perception but also of cognitive clarity, a resolution of something. I have made a number of works, even in the early 70s, with a person approaching from a distance. And also I've been working with breath a lot more. This year I've been doing a series of exercises for my back, which have involved holding my breath for periods of time: something I've been able to do since I was a kid. I used to scare everybody because I could go underwater and hold on to the bottom rail of the steps at the swimming pool, and stay under while everybody started to panic. Or I would flop face down on the surface. This year I made some portrait pieces for Anthony D'Offay, which involve holding the breath and keeping the muscles tense; so that the moment of releasing the breath is violent. I've been thinking a lot about that and connected it with water in the *Messenger* piece. One of the D'Offay pieces – which are called *Nine Attempts to Achieve Immortality* – served as a study for the *Messenger* in Durham. Or at least it was a precursor in that it involves a violent release.

Nine Attempts to Achieve Immortality
Bill Viola (1996)
video/sound installation

Collection
Edition 1, Cartier foundation of Contemporary Art.
Edition 2, Celebrity Cruises. Edition 3,
Detroit Institute of the Arts.
Photo Kira Perov.

Breath plays a large part in Indian culture.

In Pravanadra's writings, breath is connected with wisdom, whereas we don't consider breath to be connected to knowledge at all.

How is it connected?

Well, prana is also translated as 'life force', the force that animates. The connection became most clear to me when reading this after my mother passed away. That was also the first time I had witnessed someone dying. It was not a violent death: just a release. I was extremely aware of a few last breaths which were not just an ending of life in a clinical sense but an ending in a spiritual sense: the idea that the last breath was the end of any kind of animate life force. My brother was with me in the room and we both commented on something leaving the body. To witness an exhalation followed by an inhalation was one of the most profound things I've ever experienced. It was shocking and humbling to see someone exhale and never inhale. Many months later I remembered about prana, and the meaning of an experience which many more people would have had in the past. To witness it would mean seeing a connection between breath and knowledge.

Is it important to show *The Messenger* in a church?

Well, it will definitely add something that affects the work.

Do you believe in an after-life?

Yes, I do, but I will need to explain.

What form would it take?

There are many interpretations. Just now we live in a period when one of the strongest statements about 'after-life' comes from biological science: that our genes outlive our selves, that in a sense they are not part of us. They are not going to die with our bodies but have been linked, genetically and biologically, to reproductive cycles. That's one idea. Another is creativity. If you think of the creative act – whatever that is – as something that transcends your own self, your own life, that lives on.

And which continues and renews itself by being communicated?
Art has a special place in that way. That's part of the magic of looking at Dutch paintings, at Vermeer for example. A bridge is made between times and it is connected by experiences held in common. Also when you have children you feel this link in the circle. All of a sudden you are in the position that your parents were with you. You find you're not sitting at the little children's table at holdidays, but at the big grown-ups' table and your offspring are at the kids' table. I'm not a strong believer in the literal idea of an after-life – literally having another body with the same configuration. It's more profound than that. But I don't believe in death as an absolute finality.

Do you believe that people are unitary: solid blocks?
No, people have a consciousness that is unique, as the Buddhists have found. And it permits us to extend this table to Holland in the 17th century, to Indian villages, to go far beyond this time and place. And our doing so permeates these objects on the table in this physical environment with another plane of existence. Perception always goes two ways – it's an extension, penetration, permeation of being, an intermingling of being. You feel this most strongly with animals; that's why the Buddhists talk about 'sentient beings'. This is what makes us distinctive, the ability to move beyond our bodies as simple physical containers.

Are bodies unimportant?
They are and they aren't. The external world is real, on the one hand; but the world can be seen as illusion, objects as illusion, the physical world as illusion. Pure materialism holds the spiritual world to be an illusion. I don't believe any of these things; I believe in both because both are true.

You went through a period recently in which the air that surrounded the shapes in your work seemed to be pullulating, as though everything took place in a very dense atmosphere.
I've always been fascinated by grain, the fabric of the image. It comes up again and again. Some of that might be my formalist background in the 70s – some avant-garde film-makers were trying to persuade us always to move to higher and higher image quality, overlooking grain which can be just as interesting as this kind of transparent view through to the representation. That density of fabric has always been interesting; and to me it makes the image not more visual but more conceptual.

It's perhaps like thick paint... Within it there's no up or down, left or right. And events simply occurred. The definition of events was difficult to work out; it could have gone on forever. Was *Pneuma* your first piece concerned with breath?

There was no real breath in there, though *Pneuma* also refers to breath. It was a white noise generator that made that hissing sound. When I made *The Passing* in 1991, that had breathing on it. But the videotape work in general is much more concerned with point-of-view. That's one of the most important things in the history of cinema; from what point of view is the camera looking at these people in this situation? Physically, how high is it, how wide is the view, how narrow. Once you take away the presumed third person position of most cinema, and step outside the cinematic version of the literary third person into the first person, you're into either this kind of situation – Stuart and Bill talking, the vérité view, the documentary view. Or outside of a social context, a solitary view. Cinema has a lot to do with the social view; my work is more the view of one person. When that person is presumed to be the camera, then what is in the frame apart from that person? Very early on I started working from that position within my videos. It's from a solitary view even when it might appear to be documenting people doing something. That's part of my interest in landscape, a visual form strongly connected with art history. I was primarily interested in the idea of the solitary encounter – hiking in the woods alone, not with ten people. If you're very quiet in that situation, as in the desert, then all of a sudden the only sound for you is breathing – no river, no breeze to rustle through the trees. I remember waking myself up one night while camping and shooting *The Passing*. The sound of my own breathing woke me up. At three in the morning there's that twilight zone you're in, neither awake nor asleep, and when I came out of that, I realised that I had been listening to myself breathing without knowing it was myself. That was in the late 80s and I started working on what became *The Passing* and most of the Whitechapel Show in 1991 or so.

Is there a crisis or a transformation now in our whole idea of point of view?

Absolutely.

As when a woman is having a baby right in front of you? The issue with the woman was one of privacy, of voyeurism, which is very difficult. ... That TV show a few years ago, *Max Headroom*, addressed it in quite an interesting way: any time the camera was 'on' everything was OK, then when the camera was supposed to be 'off' people started behaving quite differently. But now there's a more general sense that we're in an age of self-consciousness embodied by the camera as archetypal instrument, like the axe or the blade was. And what does the camera represent? It is the deliberate awareness of taking an image, of

Pneuma
Bill Viola (1994)
video/sound installation

Collection of the Artist
Photo Kira Perov

looking, so it's like formal conscious seeing. And therefore a formal conscious, response: how you look, how you behave, at what point you decide which moments are private. For a lot of people this kind of evil, in-your-face interview with a guy who is dying on the street was very much there in *The Nantes Triptych*. I knew it would be and in a way it had to be because that's what this piece was about. Those images of the woman giving birth weren't treated in any way, they weren't personally expressed... the treatment was no treatment, but it was THE embodiment of those experiences in my life. Those two experiences were the unvarnished camera. I felt as if I was seeing for the first time. So when I saw my son's head come out between my wife's legs and this old shrivelled man was there with a wrinkled brown face, and he wasn't saying anything and was completely immobile with just the head, that image had nothing to do with photography, film, video, anything I'd ever witness: it was an image beyond an image.

There seems to be something we still have to get over, something about privacy perhaps, or just good manners. (*Max Headroom* was bad manners.) What's the relationship between Freud and his patients? What's the relationship between Proust and himself? The first works I ever saw by you were about distant places: things I had never seen. When you forget you know nothing about what you see, you enter into it and let events take over. At the end of *I Do Not Know What It Is That I Am* suddenly something is over and I had missed it. It was of such importance I've blocked it out.

The connection you make with the relationship between the analyst and the analysed is interesting... I don't think we completely recognize the import of quantum physics in the 20s and 30s.

How has that affected your work?

You can't pick up a camera at the end of the 20th

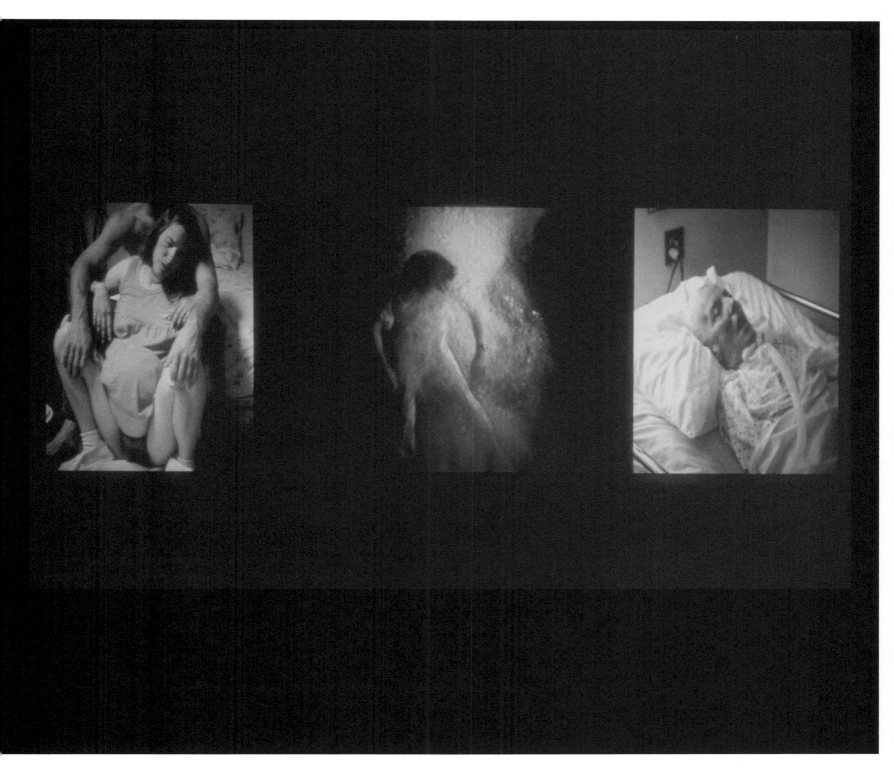

century... You can't write an anthropological text or do a number of things you could once do without an awareness of what's on the other side of the pen or the camera. It just doesn't work that way any more. We're beyond the scientific- materialist notion of the independent observer, culturally and scientifically – and it was a powerful idea. Science has been concerned with it from Roger Bacon on. That has been overturned in the 20th century and people like Freud did it in a different way; it has happened on a lot of fronts.

So we're not so much talking about the big problems that have to be solved; we're talking about an entire other way of looking at what a problem is. You seem to be talking about personal things but in fact you're talking about larger, more complex relation-ships. I didn't choose video; it chose me. One of the things it gave me was the necessity of dealing with the real world directly. You could say that the image is not direct and that's true. You could say that its potency derives from its being removed from the world. It's not actual seeing and breathing and tasting but it is close to other things we've experienced and it captures movement, unlike photography. But then photography and cinema are other examples. Look how much photography has changed art and postmodern notions of art criticism. There's something about capturing an impression of the world outside with a mechanical device – which in a way is what your eye is – that's very potent for our time. Once I picked up a camera and started going around with it I realised I couldn't hide behind theory. And that since it was not hand-rendering I didn't have to make a decision about whether it was going to be impressionist or Abstract Expressionist or whatever. Those decisions are made in the design of the machine. So you're not consciously dealing with style; you accept a certain image quality and assumptions about what image is that the machine gives you, and it's an optical one, modelled on the human eye. But beyond that, you are taping your street; you go home and play it and there's your street. Your street, not some idealised street that you've painted from your imagination, an amalgam of fifty streets you've seen and now draw by hand. All of a sudden it's your street, a literal, unique, individual one, and your friend sticks his nose in front of the camera and is on that screen right now. There's a direct encounter with the real world and the theory and concepts come later. We perceive, then conceive. So you're brought back to the primacy of perception and you're dealing with this direct experience of the world, which brings matters down to a real, concrete domain of being, and not knowledge, as the central act. It's really more about being than about presence. When I started out, I would tape inanimate objects like a tea cup. I would play it back for two minutes and compare it with the same image simply paused on screen. I remember thinking, yes, there is a difference. It fascinated me.

Things and pictures of things and our perception of them... We seem to need to go back over this time and again until we understand it. I think perception is the doorway to liberation. One of the great dangers of the media, which Gene Youngblood has examined, is 'perceptual imperialism'. It's not so much the content of the work, it's the way that perception is organised. One of the things yogis do in India is to change their perception, render it malleable, by changing their bodies. And what John Berger has written about is another example of changing the ways we see.

You mentioned Gene Youngblood's *Expanded Cinema*, and that's not a

new book but it's still about problems that have not been solved. Look at these enormous photographs people are showing in museums all over the world. What is it all about? Not hyper-realism. It's about the way we order our mind to appreciate something that is difficult for us. Why *is* it difficult? Something is being thrust at us time and time again, but we still don't understand it, so the process continues.

We also have to watch out for that. Mystics have always regarded the senses as a trap! Perceptual stimulation should not be confused with true intellectual (in the broadest sense) awareness. Used properly, these are powerful perceptual tools. If misused, or even used mindlessly, they end up being ways of passing time in a pleasurably stimulating way. It's fun. I tickle my children. But I don't want them to grow up with tickling as the primary importance in their lives.

Interventions:
an Interview with Isaac Julien
Devin Anthony Orgeron &
Marsha Gabrielle Orgeron

Isaac Julien, *The Conservator's Dream* **from** *Three,* **1999**
Installation View, Victoria Miro Gallery

Museums are very important spaces for filmmaker Isaac Julien. He is a former art student and museum lurker; his films frequently explore the thematic, architectural space of the museum (*The Attendant, Vagabondia*) or call upon its specific and perhaps occasionally stagnating iconography (*Looking for Langston*). His latest work, which is, in fact, more "work" and less "cinema" in the popular sense, is designed to be displayed in a museum context and creates of the moving image a different sort of architectural space within the museum. He utilizes DVD technology, multiple screen formats, rear screen projections; his images themselves often escape the confines of the museum and are projected outward, onto the surrounding streets. Julien's work continues to push the envelope of art and film and their various points of convergence. *Three, Long Road to Mazatlan* (made in collaboration with Javier de Frutos), and *Vagabondia* are visually enticing, formally challenging, theoretically sophisticated, and humorous in ways that avant-garde film rarely is.

The following interview took place in Julien's home, which is located next to The British Museum. His home has itself become a sort of gallery of personal eclecticism. A small, British made and very early 8mm projector is stationed on his fireplace mantle between two Chinese figures, between which also hangs an Andre Serrano photograph. To the right of the fireplace hangs a painting by Glen Ligon with Zora Neale Hurston's words from *How it Feels to be Colored Me*, repeated in virtual perpetuity: "I remember the very day that I became colored." Julien, we would soon learn, is not *just* a cinephile.

Devin Orgeron   The goal of this interview is to establish some ideas about your cinematic aesthetics.

Marsha Orgeron Largely because we feel it's something that has been neglected. In the criticism about your work and even in many interviews with you people tend to focus upon the theoretical aspects of your work. Obviously your cinematic and theoretical ideas coalesce, however we feel that the aesthetic and cinematic issues are often pushed to the side.

D   Which worries us particularly because your recent films, *Three* and *Long Road to Mazatlan*, are so clearly aesthetically grounded, they're so indebted to the idea of the image. *Three* was originally intended as a museum installation, right?

Isaac Julien   Yes. As is, *Vagabondia*. It's another installation film. It was shot at the John Soane Museum; it is an interpretation of that architectural space. It tries to explore something on the outside of modernity that is not really visible to the eye. There are many of references to Soane's architecture; in a way it's very much about empire.

D   Clearly the idea of galleries and museum spaces are important to your work. *Long Road to Mazatlan*, in fact, is presented sculpturally.

M   What compelled you to making something that could be projected in this fashion?

I   It was through doing work on *Three* for the Victoria Miro Gallery show last September (1999) and thinking about how you could, in a small space, architecturally explore that space. I wanted to shape the cinematic realization of that space around that concept, and this is what challenged me to present these two pieces in this fashion. The whole idea of the Victoria Miro show was to have *The Conservator's Dream* as the three screen piece, but this screen outside of the gallery space on the street was like a visual sonata; the idea is that you'd have these images that were rear projected outside and would utilize DVD technology and then in the back was this antiquated projector in the dark where people would sit on the floor if they wanted (there were no chairs). The idea was to have a physicalized commentary on new technology versus old technology. But since 1990 I've been making works which always somehow stem from making films, that try to engage you to some degree in the process of the filmmaking itself.

M   When will *Vagabondia* be first screened?

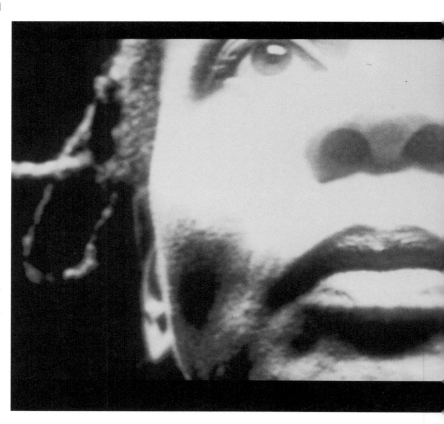

I   It will be at a show in Manchester's Cornerhouse Gallery for an exhibit on cinema; we're also going to be showing *Long Road To Mazatlan* and also a set of photogravures called *After Mazatlan*. Since *Looking for Langston* I've been involved in making work which derives from a film context but usually in another arena or mode of presentation.

D   Can you comment on that transition from film to this new context that you're currently working in? For example from *Looking for Langston*, which is avant-garde cinema but presented in a fairly traditional format. What made you want to do the kind of work you're doing now?

I   I could go back to my initial involvement in making work which is grounded in an art school context: studying painting first, and then thinking about making work that would be image work – taking photographs – and in a way being frustrated and excited by the prospect of making films – that seemed like the future. My work has always been in dialogue with visual arts: which is obvious in *Looking for Langston*. After I made *Looking for Langston* in 1989 I staged a live performance and the whole idea was to make the spectator experience what it's like to be on a film set. The audience would go from one location to the next location, almost in the same

vicinity where I shot the film, and there would be these staged happenings. The first one was an encounter at the bench, and then we'd move to another space where there would be a cruising scene with these angels. Meanwhile, outtakes from *Looking for Langston* were projected on a church façade; the actual performance began with the spectator entering this space where an exchange between my lawyers and the Langston Hughes estate lawyers over the copyright problems that occurred when trying to get the film shown in the United States could be heard in the background.

I was trying to call attention to some of the dilemmas that I had faced when trying to get that film shown. Rather than make a documentary about it I decided to make a performance. The whole idea was that it would be live; whatever happened would become part of the performance. And there would be snippets of the *Looking for Langston* music, but the whole idea was that it would be this sort of public space and then you move into more subterranean areas where you go into more of the fantasy/private space, where eventually you have this torch-bearing figure. These performances took place in London, Newcastle, and in the States. Since 1990 I've been interested in making interventions, which are not always primarily moving images.

M   I think the word interventions that you use to describe your work is an interesting one.

I   It may be a bit of an eighties word. (laughter)

M   But it does seem that on every level – visual, critical – that you are performing interventions on your various subjects.

I   The word interventions is a good one, I think.

D   You mentioned earlier your art school perspective, but we are also curious about your cinematic influences. I think the artistic ideas, or the static arts in your films – the poetics, paintings, and sculpture – are pretty prominent themes, but we're curious also about the filmmakers you look to.

I   In the immediate vicinity – not that I'm very interested in the idea of national cinema – but I think probably in the context of what has been tied to British cinema, I've been very much influenced or felt aligned with several independent filmmakers. I'm talking about filmmakers like the late Derek Jarman, Terrence Davis. I've always been *pleasured* by seeing films by Powell and Pressburger – *The Red Shoes* in particular – and then I've always been a quiet fan of some of the avant-garde film-makers – Maya Deren's work, for example.

The course I attended at St Martin's School of Art was actually quite a strange film course because they encouraged you to make anti-narrative films; to make narrative

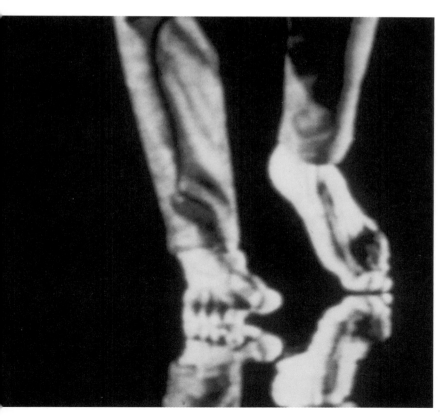

Isaac Julien, *Three*, 1999
Micro Piezo Prints

films was really frowned upon. And so it was there that I actually saw the films of Maya Deren and was first exposed to Pasolini, but also to the rigorous structuralist films, as well, so the films of the filmmaker Rose Lauder and also some of Sally Potter's early works, such as *Thriller*. I was aesthetically indebted to the films of Laura Mulvey and Peter Wollen and was very much interested in the theoretical exploration they were undertaking. I was watching Godard films and some of Jaques Tati's films and also filmmakers like Chris Marker; I was impressed by *Sans Soleil*. Then there were a number of films that I was interested in that constituted the Third Cinema; I'm thinking of *Last Supper*, some of the early films of Charles Burnett or Julie Dash's work. In a sense those films are very interesting to me because they had some relationship to content that I could indentify with. I'm not quite sure I thought those films were aesthetically the kind of films I wanted to make, however.

M   Since you bring up Mulvey and Wollen, it raises the issue of the relationship between politics and art and how they can come together. It does strike me that your films, like *Looking for Langston*, are almost diametrically opposed to, say, *Riddle of the Sphinx* in terms of your investment in aesthetics; obviously the term "visual pleasure" would be the one to use here. Can you talk a bit about the way that you conceive of the role of art and criticism in your own cinematic practice?

I   In a way I've always been interested in language and translation. I was interested in utilizing some of the aesthetic strategies of those films; also, however, when the Sankofa video collective was making films – this is early 1980s – the debate around film culture, generally the left in Britain, was an extremely important one. In the structuralist filmmaking circles there was a debate between the notion of aesthetics and pleasure, and obviously I think the dimension of the anti-aesthetic – the notion of not giving audiences normative narrative readings that were readily available in normative, patriarchal films – was crucial. But we became quickly stagnated by the debate around theory and notions of spectatorship versus pleasure.

On one level the debate between Sankofa, Peter Gidal and the Black Audio Film Collective in the conference of 1982 called "Cultural Identities" crystallized the positions (Peter Gidal's work I think actually would fit perfectly in a gallery context). But I also think perhaps that the avant-garde at the time were rather ambitious about what they thought that their films aesthetically could do. Obviously, the debate around audiences was never the question; it was the idea that the film actually had some presence and didn't adhere to audience demand. The fact that it was shown – even if it was a film which was essentially no sound, black leader, sprocket holes – but still in a sense beautiful in its own right, that was enough.

For us, as young Black people making films about questions of representaion, it became overberaring. In a way, the questions of audience address were never as important to the films that we were making as they were to our critics, so I think

there was a way in which we wanted to explore aesthetically something else, and I think that maybe that something else was the question of desire and the visceral relationship to those questions. We wanted to utilize different histories, which we saw as being quite repressed in the current context. So I think in that sense the Greenbergian notion of an aesthetic formalist exploration was never really enough. I think in retrospect some of our works were far more influenced by that aesthetic, and I think we were interested in the hybridization of those aesthetic strategies, which would also take on the question of critical address and the politics of representation. In that sense our work does follow a line from Mulvey and Wollen, but there's an inversion to that because that inversion occurs not just on the level of language but also on the level of audience identification and notions of pleasure. It wasn't so much about unlearning those categories but really trying to take some of those that were taken for granted and imbedding them with hybridized aesthetic approaches.

We were also very aware of the background of postmodernism; we were very aware of the idea that there could be several aesthetic strategies in one piece of work, and in that sense we weren't the neo-formalists of structuralist filmmaking. At the same time I think we were much more interested in questions of form and representation than was ever really debated.

M   You raise a very important term: your audience. When you're making your films, who constitutes audience in your mind's eye? Who do you think ultimately sees your films and in what context?

I   The problem with that sort of question, for me, is that I have always felt that the notion of audience wasn't the central idea – as I said long ago, one wasn't in the business of doing social work. The notion of pedagogy was always interesting, but it wasn't interesting to us on the level of address. It was interesting on the level of enunciation, but the way in which you formally constructed something and what was being articulated in its form.

I really think it is an important question, because for me the notion of authorship always seems to be questioned once it was in black hands – John Akomfrah of the Black Audio Film Collective said this ages ago. That question began really around authorial intentions and the intentions get linked to the question of audience address, as well. In a way, you had to say to yourself, would the same questions be beholden to someone who is non-black? No-one would say it to Godard, for example.

D   It's a question I've wanted to ask him. For people who love the cinema,

Isaac Julien, *Three*, 1999
Micro Piezo Prints

it seems such an obvious question to ask: who are you addressing? And particularly I'm interested in this in relationship to the *Looking for Langston* performance you discussed earlier, which is so linked to the idea of the spectator, albeit in a different context. With *Mazatlan*, which seems to position the spectator in all of these different ways, it seems as though if your ideas of audience haven't shifted that at least there is a real critical thinking about that role.

I   In *Mazatlan* the spectator is subjected to a multi-perspectival approach. The film has a lyrical structure – the three screens enhance this – which results in a spectator who is always shifting. *Long Road to Mazatlan* is specifically about the "white gay experience." But it differs from other films I've made, whose characters are typically gay *and* black. Here that's not the case.

The thing about audience address is that one wants one's work to be seen by as many audiences as possible. *Vagabondia*, *Mazatlan* and *Trussed*, in that sense, and to a certain extent *Three* all get shown in a gallery context. *Long Road to Mazatlan* and *Three* also get shown in a film context, at film festivals in single screen versions.

Before, when I was making films that had funding from television broadcasting companies, they would be shown on television as well as in the cinema and at film festivals, so there was a multi-address that was built into the work. When those questions were asked about audience address before, you realized that surely the experimentation in your work would be alienating for some audiences and specifically, perhaps, black audiences themselves if they weren't familiar with art or art criticism.

I personally grew up on television and was quite alienated by it, even disliked it, so it's ironic that I actually made films that had funding from television. I never felt terribly indebted to these mediums, but I saw them as spaces which were precisely *sites of intervention*. You could make something that was really formally different but could exist in that context. Eventually, of course, television became indifferent to the things that I was making as well; *Darker Side of Black*, for example, which was a BBC arts documentary for the *Arena* series on the questions of nihilism in black culture. That was very much a political intervention and it was made for a television context. So sometimes I've made work where I feel the aesthetic considerations are somewhat compromised in order to make a direct intervention. At the moment I'm working on a television series called *SWEN* where artists take over the news for about a half an hour; so we're actually *reconstructing* news archives, transforming them into video art. My piece is called *Blairspin* (as in Tony).

D   Did you study dance in art school? Especially in the more recent films it seems like such an important part.

I   I actually studied dance prior to art school. But it was a long time ago. It was the mid to late 1970s at the London Contemporary Youth Dance Theatre and I studied the Martha Graham technique and my dancing partner was a dancer called Gaby Agis, and it was actually her work that I first saw in a gallery context where she did a dance that was a sort of meditation, an interpretation of a painting, and I just thought this was very strange and I didn't really understand it at all. But it was interesting to me. My current interest in dance stems from a collaboration with Bebe Miller and Ralph Lemon to make *Three*.

D   You don't necessarily see any special relationship between dance and cinema?

I   In some ways I do because of Powell and Pressburger and things like *The Red Shoes*, and so there is for me something about dance and the possibility of a language that is expressed via choreography rather than through text.

M   And dance is an even more ambiguous language.

I   Yes, it is. It's more ambiguous and interpretive I think in a refreshing way. You can't have a theoretical rap about it in the same sort of way, which I like. I'm quite interested in people coming up with their own reading, not being too burdened by what was written before – by me or others – and looking at something from a fresh perspective.

D   This is interesting in a way and brings us back to someone we discussed earlier, Godard, who is very interested in textuality – in words and language. Your interest seems to be more musically oriented; there is such an indebtedness and consciousness in all of your films to sound and to dance and choreographed movement – poetics, in a more general sense.

I   To me, sound is as important as the visualization or the mise-en-scène. The reason for this prioritization of sound has got to do with the notion of black vernacular signifying practices, which is a creolized notion of certain black expressive idioms. So, for example, in films like *Frantz Fanon* the composers were both black and both saw themselves as being between two classical traditions: Western, on the one hand, and on the other side, African. One of the instruments, the chora, which is an Ethiopian sixteenth-century instrument, was an instrument that I was very interested in using in that particular film. It's a whole other aspect of the work which is not really written about, but also it's quite hard to write about music aesthetically.

D   You work in music video, as well.

I   Interestingly enough, I've found when I've worked in music video that it is far too restrictive because the record companies want to control so much of what you're making. Actually, I think music videos have become rather derivative.

M   Actually, we wanted to ask you something that has to do with you being both a filmmaker and a spectator. With the time you spend in the States teaching and the time you spend here in London, what do you think of what's happening with contemporary cinema? What are you seeing out there, particularly in relation to black British independent cinema?

I   I think black British independent cinema is dead, and that's been the case for some time. I've never been particularly interested in the notion of *just* a black British cinema because I've never been really interested in the notion of cinema as a form of nationalism. My work has always tried to position itself somewhere in the middle of those ideas; *Looking for Langston*, *Frantz Fanon* and *Vagabondia* are all about Diaspora.

In the British context, at least, there's a contestation that's taking place, but it's not fully acknowledged, which is that in terms of cinema as an institution and cinema as a space for certain theoretical reflection, there has been a shift away with the academicization of something like the British film journal *Screen* at least 12 years ago.

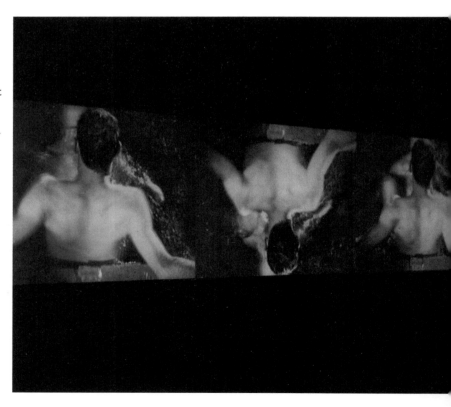

When it moved from London and moved out of its metropolitan context to Glasgow it changed its relationship to practice. At the same time, there was a very short-lived romance with independent film; Black British film was stopped dead in its tracks in the same way that other cultural endeavors were – it is over, gone, and dead. In relation to British contexts, that notion of *independent* is no longer with us.

Black British film in a way was stopped in its tracks in the same way everything else was. In a sense, the move into a museum space is also about the looking for a space and the recognition that perhaps the notion of independent film somehow competing with global models (like Hollywood) couldn't work. At the same time with the museum contexts there has been a certain body of work, a certain language, a certain way of exploring the culture of the moving image that has flourished which might be antithetical to independent or experimental cinema. Some call it necrophilia , others see it as testament to the death of cinema and through those ashes we can see the likes of Douglas Gordon, The Wilson Twins, Steve McQueen.

It seems to me that someone like Matthew Barney and his *Cremaster* series, which is interested in the exploration of performance and its relationship to cinema in the art world, wouldn't stand a hope in hell in the cinema world. In the cinema world you

Isaac Julien, *Long Road to Mazatlan,* **1999**
Installation View, Victoria Miro Gallery

would recognize it for what it is – a sort of permutation of some of the things that Derek Jarman might have done in the 1970s. But in the art world it's fantastic, he's the cause célèbre. That's the transformation that seems to be taking place. I can think of other filmmakers and video artists whose concerns are cinematic, like Doug Aitken and Douglas Gordon. One might consider what that exploration, in that context, might be like; and so there's a certain development. It seems to Mark Nash (film curator and producer) and I that there is a huge gap in criticism of films that exist in the cinema context and the art world; the development between those films and video works and critical reflection is extremely limited. I think there are interesting developments taking place but they're lost without any context. This seems to be the fate of cinema studies.

D   One thing that seems to be really underplayed in a lot of the writing about your work is the sense of humor. Can you talk about humor as another artistic device – I don't want to call it a weapon, because that sounds really trite – at your disposal as an artist.

I   I think that there were some things about popular culture that we found interesting and we wanted those things to be in the work. We wanted the work to be tarnished, sort of corrupted in that sense. The other corrupting influence is irony, which is very traditional in black vernacular cultures. Carnival is only one example.

In my work there is a question of irony and ironic address that is part of the undermining strategies but also the return of the repressed, and so in *The Attendant* it's used to underscore what would become a very moralistic question in terms of ethics and the notion of master/slave relations in a gay context, and what that means across racial lines. At the same time *Long Road to Mazatlan* is very much looking at the ways in which stereotypes are perhaps the things that we cannot live without... maybe... instead of the constant repudiation of the stereotypes. In *Long Road to Mazatlan* this idea is explored – this idea of thinking about the stereotype, or laughing at the stereotype and viewing it from an ironic position, is to try to place certain ambivalent questions in a controllable context. In a way it's sort of mastering, or calling into question, or exorcizing things which are deemed undesirable or hegemonic. I think that it is very important to remember that aesthetic ideas can get lost or get imprisoned by theoretical constructs.

M   Well, it paralyzes you as a filmmaker because you have think within these small boxes instead of being able to open up to larger ideas, aesthetic or political. Which brings us back to the idea of audience in a way because it's an issue of who gets the jokes, whether it's the reference to Scorsese's *Taxi Driver* in *Mazatlan* or the appearance of Stuart Hall in *The Attendant*; it's a question of who is able to recognize the references.

I   Well, one is popular culture, the other is cultural studies. [laughs]

D   Speaking of the popular, have you thought about putting images up on the internet? Perhaps in coordination with the museum space, is this an arena that you have any interest in?

I   Well *Three*, for example, at the London Film Festival was put onto the internet so you could download the film if you wanted to. That's interesting to me and I can look at is as similar to television; I can conceive of it as another sort of space. But whether or not you'd experience the film aesthetically is up for grabs.

In terms of making an internet piece I have been approached by an organization to make an one, but I have to admit I'm not really convinced by internet pieces in the same way because I find the movement of them not desirable. The way you get from one place to the other and the mechanics and operation, the mise-en-scène is all start-stop. The technology has to be developed more before it really works. If they could be of the quality of DVD then I'd be convinced. It hasn't been an area I've completely concentrated on but it is something I could develop in the future.

D   You teach at Harvard and hold research positions at various universities. What is the importance – since we're talking about spaces – of the academic space for you?

I   It's a space that's been very supportive and centrally important. At one time I saw myself very much as making interventions into those spaces, but doing that from the position of an artist and filmmaker. Ostensibly that's still the case and there's been some kind of dialogue and development. Teaching the course at Harvard influenced the making *Long Road to Mazatlan*, so maybe there is quite a direct relationship. That course was about black representation. The film, on the other hand, is about whiteness. Richard Dyer's book *White* was quite influential. He writes about the cinematic Western and *Mazatlan* thinks similarly about the genre and about race. When the Mexican mariachi band starts singing, they are ignored. There are all those sort of things that one recognizes as social commentary about race, so questions of whiteness and representing whiteness are very much a part of its construction.

I guess in a way I'm talking about the role of the unconscious; and the question of emotionality in relation to teaching cinema is that there is something fairly irrational in the cinema about the ways in which it consistently constructs representations of blackness in a specific, narrow repertoire of images, or stereotypical figures.

White cinema is there as an invisible rod to measure everything against and I think it's interesting to explore those questions in the academic context. Teaching a blaxploitation course, at least at Harvard, becomes rather like the Bete Noir of film studies because it's not just a formal exploration of film as you would undertake if you were doing silent film or European art cinema class. I think the idea of being in one camp is just completely boring and retrograde.

M   What about teaching film production?

I   I've never taught production actually, but I have taught studio practice. The idea of actually doing a film course could be interesting. I don't like the idea of being so schematic about one's work, because one's work really comes out of the practice of coincidence, about making a film that doesn't derive from a script in that institutional sense. Obviously there was a script for *Looking for Langston* and *The Attendant*, but for my recent work there are no scripts; *Vagabondia* or *Mazatlan* or *Trussed* are all unscripted

M   Do you consider choreography a script?

I   Well we had some ideas and that is a kind of script but it's very loose. In a way it's about the making of work that's not bound to all of those conventions. Improvisation is key.

D   So what's your relationship like with the cinematographer in a situation where those traditional rules aren't being adhered to? When you go to a shoot what is being communicated to a cinematographer?

I   Basically we talk about scenes and the thing that is always important are locations because they also speak in important ways.

D   So again we return to the expressiveness of space and how characters or bodies and objects occupy space.

I   Right. In a way I'm very interested in the cinematographer having a lot of freedom when they're shooting something; I want them to work with what is visually interesting for them as well as for myself. It was a different sort of approach for something like *Young Soul Rebels* and *Looking for Langston*, which were actually quite planned. In *Vagabondia*, conversely, the script comes out of the actual architectural space and what that space represents for the cinematographer and I.

Devin and Marsha Orgeron wish to thank the University of Maryland's Committee on Africa and the Americas for making this interview possible.
There are several exhibits currently featuring the works of Isaac Julien as well as some forthcoming in the United States and Europe, including: Cinerama at Cornerhouse, Manchester (August 17-September 17), then at the South London Gallery (September 22-October22); The Film Art of Isaac Julien at Bard College (September 24-December 15); Museum of Contemporary Art, Chicago (October 22); and Vienna; Julien's works are also featured at a group show at the Studio Museum, Harlem (October 15-January 17).

Isaac Julien, *The Conservator's Dream* from *Three*, 1999
Installation View, Victoria Miro Gallery

dot●jp:
/a curator's tour
Barbara London

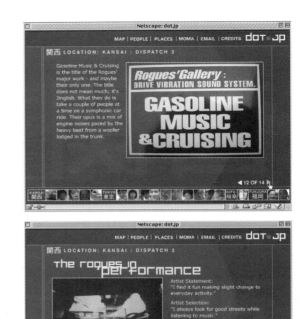

Hitoshi Nomura

A new blip recently appeared on the screen that monitors risks to human survival. Plagues, nuclear war, and catastrophic weather changes now have to compete for attention with meteors. Astronomers monitor the sky for neos (near Earth objects), meteors whose orbit puts them on a collision course with Earth. A big one wiped out the dinosaurs, and we too had better watch out.

Nomura has a benign view of meteors and notes that they predate humanity. Stones that fell from the sky have been venerated since ancient times.

Nomura has his hunk of metal fly on a magic carpet wing powered by solar panels. He theorizes that meteors are the foundation of life -- the life blood. Iron is an essential constituent of hemoglobin, the molecule that transports life-giving oxygen in the blood stream.

Soft Landing Meteor, 1996
(Detail , bottom)

2 OF 9

KANSAI 関西   TOKYO 東京   GIFU 岐阜   FUKUOKA 福岡

The façade of The Museum of Modern Art where I work has gone through many facelifts. I favor the version inaugurated in 1938 because of the motto carved above the entrance: "Art of Our Time." Alfred Barr, the Founding director, envisioned that the mission of the Museum was to foster, assemble, promote, and show up-to-date art.

My experience with contemporary art in Japan began in 1978 while researching an exhibition for The Museum of Modern Art, *Video from Tokyo to Fukui and Kyoto*. At the time, I met many artists who were presenting videotapes in small galleries and were carrying out "parcel post" video exchanges with colleagues all over the world. Back then "alternative" experimentation was the underground norm. Artists wore the hats of revolutionaries, evolutionaries, feminists, conceptualists, and modernists. Ever since I have foraged in foreign countries for emerging artists. I visit studios, gather documentation, and slot the information in file folders, where the materials remain accessible only to me. As the artists mature, gradually I include their works in shows.

A chance encounter with Shu Lea Cheang at the American Film Institute's 1989 Video Festival seeded a new kind of digital project. Cheang showed me several videos by artists from China, whose work was as innovative as her spiky hairdo. I wondered about the future of these Chinese artists as they emerged from isolation and digested contemporary art trends.

Finally in September of 1997 I had the opportunity to indulge my curiosity. I headed off to China accompanied by a colleague toting a backpack stuffed with a computer, camera, tape recorder, and cables. I hoped to document my curatorial visits by posting them on the web. At the time the Internet in China was unmapped territory, and contacts in Beijing doubted I'd be able to transmit data to New York.

The China I discovered had plenty of computers, though tracking down a decent connection to the Internet was arduous. In most cities, I managed nearly every night to email data to New York, where a design crew assembled and posted what in effect was a diary of my research. On this excursion, I wanted to make public my research. Instead of squirrelling away the information in file folders as before, my findings would be available on the Internet for curators and anyone else interested in the contemporary art of China.

Moreover, I thought demystifying the curatorial process would be refreshing. A casual visitor to www.moma.org/stirfry gets a chance to travel with a curator on a research quest. I think it's salutary to let people look in on the gestation phase of a museum exhibition.

For www.moma.org/internyet, the project in 1998 that took me to Russia and Ukraine, I was better prepared. I had a top-of-the-line computer capable of video capture, a digital DV camcorder, a DAT tape recorder, and a digital still camera. *InterNyet* includes many videos and movie clips, all the taping and editing handled by my associate and me, now dubbed "Studio London."

The Internet presents museums with novel dilemmas. Artist Olia Ljalima's *Web Gallery* is wonderfully archaic; she has hung art pieces (links) on a web page as if the works were for sale on the wall of a gallery. Ljalima claims that her site is the first traditional art gallery on the Internet.

Kazuhiko Hachiya

Hachiya   Some tools of Hachiya's trade

Hachiya created the commercially successful software, PostPet, which Sony markets through a subsidiary.

1 OF 5 ▶

KANSAI 関西   TOKYO 東京   GIFU 岐阜   FUKUOKA 福岡

The Japanese version of PostPet is a commercial product, but an English and a German version can be downloaded free from a site in Singapore. Hachiya is offended when I inquire about his financial connection to Sony. He works with Sony only because he wants wide distribution for his creation.

PostPets is exceptional art. Most interactive art is just that - art that allows for participation. Whether an interactive work is brilliant or banal, it is rarely animated by an artist's longing to connect to another person.

▶ Hachiya raps about his PostPets as he plays with them.
(Japanese dotted with English)
RealAudio 4:20

▶ Summary (English and Japanese)
RealAudio 2:00

3 OF 5 ◀ ▶

PostPets are little creatures that live in an email universe where they enliven communication between correspondents. They are not passive pets; if they're abused, they leave; and sometimes they write emails on their own initiative.

Some PostPet nests

2 OF 5 ◀ ▶

The interactivity in Hachiya's projects issue from a passion to communicate. His works exhibit a curious pattern: Viewers are presented with an obstruction that obliges them to communicate with other participants. One installation, for example, entails a totally dark room outfitted with a few infrared glasses that enable some viewers to see. In another work, each viewer wears goggles that blocks their own eyesight, but can see via a camera installed on another person's goggles. Two people joined in this fashion must help each other move about, guiding each other around obstacles.

4 OF 5 ◀ ▶

Seems simple, you pay your money and you get a Web Gallery work. When I returned to New York and considered buying one of the pieces, I discovered a purchase would not be straightforward. What exactly would the Museum receive by purchasing a work in *Web Gallery*? Right now the Museum has use of the works without paying a fee. InterNyet provides a link to *Web Gallery* (www.webgallery.com), and the art there can be browsed. (I can legally quote the URL, but presenting a photo of the site in a magazine requires Olia Ljalina's permission.)

At the serving end of the URL, Olia Ljalina frets over permitting the Museum to exhibit a work, under whatever terms a purchase may be consummated. Internet artists repudiate the common practice of art dealings whereby artists forego all rights to the work they sell. Clearly, the boilerplate for Internet acquisitions is still in rough draft shape.

To date there have been few sales of net art. Rather then buy, museums commission work, and on occasion they acquire entire curated sites. When AOL dissolved ada'web, the site was deposited on the server of the Walker Museum. Similarly, Dia Center received the site developed by Stadium when the Stadium crew disbanded. These are "transfers" in the interest of preservation. Individual artists retain all rights to their works, and reputedly can withdraw them from the site whenever they wish. (I wonder who will pay a programmer for excising the work.)

Netscape: dot.jp
MAP | PEOPLE | PLACES | MOMA | EMAIL | CREDITS dot.jp
東京 LOCATION: TOKYO : DISPATCH 9

a cloth that melts

In recent months, the ever-experimental Sudo has developed fabric from bandage material, employed rusty nails in creating a design, and produced a cloth that melts.

Sudo points to holes in a boiled swatch where the interim binder has dissolved

2 OF 7

Netscape: dot.jp
MAP | PEOPLE | PLACES | MOMA | EMAIL | CREDITS dot.jp
東京 LOCATION: TOKYO : DISPATCH 9

impressive engineering

Chikamori's installation 0 [en] is an impressive feat of engineering. Visitors to the work manipulate glass balls cut in half, combining two of them to form a sphere. Depending on the color of the balls and where they are placed, various iconic figures rise on a dome screen above the visitors.

Chikamori aims for simplicity in his work. The game-like 0 [en] is easy for children to use and understand.

Chikamori demonstrates what's under the hood of his piece.
RealVideo 1:57

5 OF 7

Netscape: dot.jp
MAP | PEOPLE | PLACES | MOMA | EMAIL | CREDITS dot.jp
東京 LOCATION: TOKYO : DISPATCH 9

Sudo believes the achievements of Japanese design derive from its craftsmen---men like papermakers and kimono fabricators. Issey Miyake's pleats may be world renowned, but they're old hat to these artisans. Centuries ago, samurai had their outfits pressed under heavy rocks to create pleats. Japan is high tech, but 30,000 skilled artisans still ply a traditional trade.

I try on a blouse. I decide it's a "media art work" that I'd like for my personal collection. I buy it.

samurai pleats

3 OF 7

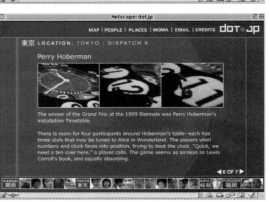

Netscape: dot.jp
MAP | PEOPLE | PLACES | MOMA | EMAIL | CREDITS dot.jp
東京 LOCATION: TOKYO : DISPATCH 9

Perry Hoberman

The winner of the Grand Prix at the 1999 Biennale was Perry Hoberman's installation Timetable.

There is room for four participants around Hoberman's table--each has three dials that may be tuned to Alice in Wonderland. The players whirl numbers and clock faces into position, trying to beat the clock. "Quick, we need a ten over here," a player calls. The game seems as aimless as Lewis Carroll's book, and equally absorbing.

6 OF 7

Netscape: dot.jp
MAP | PEOPLE | PLACES | MOMA | EMAIL | CREDITS dot.jp
東京 LOCATION: TOKYO : DISPATCH 9

INTERACTION

Motoshi Chikamori

Motoshi Chikamori

The hub of technology art in Tokyo is NTT's high tech museum, ICC (Intercommunication Center.) Currently showing is the 1999 ICC Biennale, a juried exhibition of works on the theme "interaction."

4 OF 7

MoMA too is involved in a confusing cat's cradle of web ownership. The Museum collaborated with ada'web in creating the series *Technology in the 90's* and *Stir-fry*. MoMA owns the copyrights and hosts the works, though they also reside on the Walker Museum server as part of ada'web's oeuvre.

Fortunately issues of ownership have not interfered with browsing art sites. Links connect when you click on them, on whatever hard drive the data sits, and resolutely the web spins wider and wider – at last count one web page for every ten people alive.

Information on the web is remarkably resistant to obsolescence. The first experimental web page I posted in 1995 still gets hits. This homepage of the exhibition *Video Spaces* resides in the Museum's Online Projects (www.moma.org/onlineprojects,), along with several golden oldies.

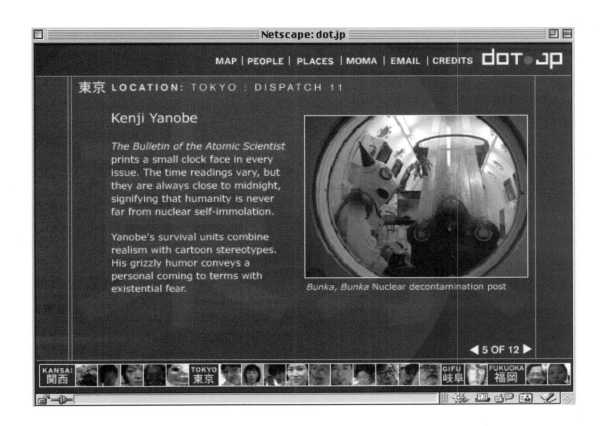

MAP | PEOPLE | PLACES | MOMA | EMAIL | CREDITS   dot.jp

東京 LOCATION: TOKYO : DISPATCH 11

Kenji Yanobe

The Bulletin of the Atomic Scientist prints a small clock face in every issue. The time readings vary, but they are always close to midnight, signifying that humanity is never far from nuclear self-immolation.

Yanobe's survival units combine realism with cartoon stereotypes. His grizzly humor conveys a personal coming to terms with existential fear.

Bunka, Bunka Nuclear decontamination post

◀ 5 OF 12 ▶

KANSAI 関西   TOKYO 東京   GIFU 岐阜   FUKUOKA 福岡

In some respects, web sites function like books in a reference library; and the dead. A year ago last September, after a long dormant phase, General Idea's screensaver sprouted and blossomed. For reasons that remain a mystery, during September and October it received more hits than any page on the MoMA site. (www.moma.org/onlineprojects).

I have continued my art and technology research in Japan. In November 1999, I spent a month in Japan, which resulted in my third curatorial diary project for the web, www.moma.org/dotjp. I discovered that media art in Japan is still at a formative stage, yet I see the field poised for rapid progress. The elder statesmen of media art have assumed influential teaching posts, and innovative art forms are being integrated into art schools.

Most of all, I'm heartened to see young rebel artists initiating their own spaces and networks. They are forging connections to the international community in a way that never happened before. Historically, contacts between Japan and the external world occurred formally, through institutions, and consequently changes happened slowly. That won't do in today's accelerated world. Through the web and by personal globe-trotting, young artists are in touch with international trends as they unfold, and have the chance to make their work known and appreciated.

Hisao Sotoda

Sotoda

Personal Channel

Personal Channel (1995) is Sotoda's representation of modern living. After visiting a friend, Sotoda learned the following day via TV news that someone had been murdered next door. "Often we know more about New York than what's going on next door," Sotoda laments.

Personal Channel has a rotting bull's head walled in by cinder blocks and surrounded by a metal fence. Reality is hemmed in by many barriers; the rotting head can only be viewed on a TV monitor.

◄ 3 OF 5 ►

Keiichi Miyagawa

Metastank, 1995-99

Metastank is postal-service art--Miyagawa's version of an art exchange. He set up garbage cans in five cities as places for people to deposit art. Then the garbage cans were shuffled between the cities and people could take art from the cans. Or something like that. I think the reliability of this delivery service gave rise to the expression "it's in the mail."

Miyagawa Gallery director Miyagawa is an activist. He likes to organize and rabble-rouse.

◄ 4 OF 5 ►

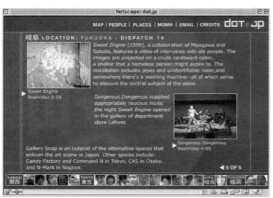

Sweet Engine (1999), a collaboration of Miyagawa and Sotoda, features a video of interviews with old people. The images are projected on a crude cardboard cabin, a shelter that a homeless person might aspire to. The installation includes pipes and unidentifiable noise, and somewhere there's a washing machine--all of which serve to obscure the central subject of the piece.

▶ Sweet Engine
RealVideo 0:58

Gorgeous Dangerous supplied appropriately raucous music the night *Sweet Engine* opened in the gallery of department store Laforet.

Gorgeous Dangerous
RealVideo 4:05

Gallery Soap is an outpost of the alternative spaces that enliven the art scene in Japan. Other spaces include: Candy Factory and Command N in Tokyo, CAS in Osaka, and N-Mark in Nagoya.

◄ 5 OF 5 ►

FUJIHATA'S FUJI

Masaki Fujihata

Fujihata recently returned to Tokyo from a sojourn at ZKM Institute for Visual Media in Karlsruhe, Germany. He came home to establish a media art department at Japan's foremost art school, Gedai (Tokyo National University of Fine Arts and Music).

My favorite piece of Fujihata's prolific output, *Personal Fuji* (1994), weaves together art, technology, and personal expression. The work is based on Fujihata's trek up Mount Fuji carrying a GPS (Global Positioning System) unit that recorded his position once every second. The data, when organized, created a digital representation of the mountain.

In addition, Fujihata fashioned a system that enables anyone to do the same with their GPS data. Using Fujihata's recipe, any hike up the mountain can be a fashioned into a portrayal of Fuji--a personal Fuji.

1 OF 4 ►

An example of the revolution just beginning can be seen in the career of Ben Benjamin. He currently has a job in Science City, Kansai, designing the interface for the city of Kyoto's web site. Ben never applied for the position. Until recently, he was a freelance designer in California, where he evolved a web site that people liked and accessed regularly. Now in Kansai, Benjamin is on display as well as his work. Art students are bused in to meet him, and learn directly from the artist in his 'atelier' (at the computer.) Another worldwide trend is evident

An anime figure. Devotees collect elaborately sculpted dolls

Fujihata with Ultraman, Japan's version of Superman

Akihabara is the place to go for everything electronic. Fujihata first came to this area of the city with his dad to buy components for a radio. Later as an artist, he prowled the stalls for unusual devices to incorporate into his work. The character of Akihabara is changing. Fujihata regrets that many engineering-oriented businesses closed shop, replaced by vendors who flog manga comics and anime models.

Masaya & Kiri Matsuura

Child-oriented e-game business provides a trough where multi-media artists feed. The artists furnish the audio-visual fizz that compels kids to push buttons manufactured by Sony, Sega, and Nintendo. This arrangement works well, and often delivers imaginative results.

Masaya Matsuura is a composer/musician who produced more than a dozen records for Sony in the 1980s. He still works with the company, but now he's creating games in alliance with graphic artist Kiri Matsuura. Their big hit was PaRappa the Rapper (1996), a collaboration with artist Rodney Greenblatt that sold three million copies worldwide.

Masaya Matsuura

Kiri Matsuura

MAP | PEOPLE | PLACES | MOMA | EMAIL | CREDITS
岐阜 LOCATION: TOKYO : DISPATCH 17

Just about now, Sony is releasing Matsurras's Vib-Ribbon for Playstation. The game is based on a music analyzer that converts any music CD into a graphic line with oddly shaped obstacles. To play the game, a button-pusher has to flip and skip the stick figure, called Vibri, through the musical obstacle course. Every time the player fails, poor Vibri gets a bit fried.

Vibri - Animated stick figure that dances a music tightrope

▶ Vib-Ribbon, the game (demo clip)
RealVideo 1:59

in Japan: Artists generate their own funds in pursuit of an independent vision. The technical abilities of media artists are in demand. Not since portraiture went out of style have artists had a skill as marketable as web design and computer programming. I often run across artists doing key work for major corporations. Consider this as a turnabout! No corporate headhunter recruited Jackson Pollock to dribble paint for a Fortune Five Hundred company.

The weakness in media art, if any, lies not with artists, but with the supporting art community. Only one commercial gallery, the Watarium, devotes its space to media art. Other museums, such as the NTT InterCommunication Center in Tokyo, do an admirable job of introducing media art to the public. However, by technology at the expense of personal expression, exhibitions take on the character of a science museum.

These are minor issues that I expect will soon be addressed. Media art is simply too dynamic to be slowed by institutional inertia. Everything I have seen in Japan suggests that art schools, as in the United States, will be inundated by students interested in media art. I plan to follow closely these revolutionary developments in contemporary Japanese art.

IN PLACE OF FIRE; [1]
insects and the death of Pan

Nicky Coutts

A Consilience by Jan Fabre

Natural History Museum London 13 Jan – 29 Feb 2000
An installation of two video screens showing curators and research scientists from
the Natural History Museum, in 'bug' costumes, behaving as the insects they study.

The Cast

....

A Butterfly
Dick Vane-Wright
Head of the Department of Entomology at the Natural History Museum.
Area: The classification and evolutionary biology of tropical butterflies, notably their colour patterns and scent systems.

A Fly
Dr Rory Post
Deputy Head of Entomology.
Area: Medical Entomology, the study of insects which cause human disease, e.g. the blood-sucking blackflies which transmit 'river blindness'.

Another Fly
Dr Martin Hall
Head of the Veterinary Entomology programme.
Area: The taxonomy, biology and behaviour of blood-sucking horse flies, parasitic flies and the infestation of live animals with fly maggots.

A Dung Beetle
Martin Brendell
Curator of 10 million beetles of the 30 million insects housed within the Department of Entomology.

Another Beetle
Jan Fabre
Artist and playwright.

A Parasitic Wasp
Ian Gauld
Flora and fauna division.

A Book
No Go the Bogeyman (2)
Marina Warner

A Murderer
Grimsrud
A man who kills in the snow, *Fargo*, Coen Brothers (1996)

A God
Pan
God of shepherds, goats, nature and the human soul.

The line-up of participants in **A Consilience**, is impressive both from the point of view of science and art. Rarely do scientists from such differing specialist areas work together on an even footing to evolve a project. And how, from an artworld perspective, did Jan Fabre convince them to do it? Clearly having a famous grandfather, such as H.J. Fabre, the eminent entomologist, lends the artist credibility in the scientific community where others would flail. But nevertheless, by establishing a meeting place between art and science, an area recently much beleaguered by language difficulties on both sides, Jan Fabre managed to ask what for most of us is, in practical terms, are inaccessible questions. Leading scientists were encouraged to consider with him the very basis of their engagement with the Natural World. **A Consilience** asks, what is the nature of 'explanation'?

Rory Post and Jan Fabre *A Consilience* courtesy of the Natural History Museum

"*A Consilience*", for Fabre, literally means "a jumping together of knowledge and facts across disciplines to create a common groundwork of explanation". Interaction and communication are, therefore, clearly subordinated to the activity of jumping – to the analogy of insects buzzing from plant to plant, settling briefly, behaving indecipherably, moving on. 'Explanation', for Fabre, is, therefore, conceivable within the act of causing entities to jostle. The relentless humming of neighbouring particles replaces the outsider's myth of the measured scientist at work ponderously reaching conclusions. It is the artists' premise that disciplines crackle and fizz when they meet. They are noisy visually and aurally, and the discharge of their encounters, the 'explanations' reached, should not be hardened, unnaturally and prematurely, into the annals of fact and knowledge. His work alludes more to an investment in fragmentary languages, it is here, within a landscape of bit part buzzings and crawlings that 'explanation' must take its place. Fabre enacts the dethroning of the solitary man of whitecoat science, dead specimen limp before him, and his subsequent replacement with a buzzing crowd of imposters.

Marina Warner quotes Aristotle, "INBORN IN ALL OF US IS THE INSTINCT TO ENJOY WORKS OF IMITATION. WHAT HAPPENS IN ACTUAL EXPERIENCE IS EVIDENCE OF THIS; FOR WE ENJOY LOOKING AT THE MOST ACCURATE REPRESENTATIONS OF THINGS WHICH IN THEMSELVES WE FIND PAINFUL TO SEE, SUCH AS THE FORMS OF THE LOWER ANIMALS AND OF CORPSES." [3]
For Warner, these ancient thoughts, on our endemic attraction to mimicry, are described within the context of an analysis of fear. "Corpses" and "lower animals" are taken as examples of knights, the nights of our deepest imagination, terrible yet desirable reproductions of dread. Warner does not, however, venture an opinion on the differences between Aristotle's given examples although there seems to be an important disjuncture here. The corpse's causal relationship with living bodies is, in itself, straightforward in terms of mimicry, evoking, as it does, the inevitable interpretation of before and after imagery, for example, the mocking, moralistic, Medieval tale of 'the Quick' addressing 'the Dead'. [4] However, our perceptions of the 'lower animals', insects, for example, do not lend themselves so neatly to dualistic inter-pretation. In the case of insects, death does not function as an intervention to distinguish the mimicker from the mimicked. As Warner later indicates, [5] "accurate representations" have been evolved and developed to extreme conclusion on the part of the insect predominantly for survival purposes. Mimicry, for the insect, is, therefore, both a tool and a condition, it refers to process, ongoing life and the living, as opposed to death and the still image, the mirror, relic, result, endplace, associated with the human

corpse and its representations. Imitation, for the insect, therefore not only deflects any perception of the afterimage but is further deployed to distance the crawling world from familiar languages of representation. Insects become endemic liars, the disguised deftly blended and melded with their disguises simultaneously enabling the dead to masquerade as the living while the living imitate the dead.

As creatures most fervently associated with the concept of metamorphosis, insects collapse a range of other forbidden dualisms. They embody every shifting shape, their past and their future – what they are and what they will become. When Fabre's entomologists agreed to mimic the insects that they studied, and were denied the possibility of appearing solely as themselves, Fabre accomplished his first 'explanation'. As demonstrated by his co-operative scientists, the insect alludes to the observer and the observed married, encapsulated in camouflaged form. As an extension of 'Science', *A Consilience* proposes that the 'lower animal', requires a considerable adjustment of language, an investment in the mythic lexicons of shapeshifting, if it is to be 'explained' with reference to observations on perceptions and the senses, from Aristotle to Warner.

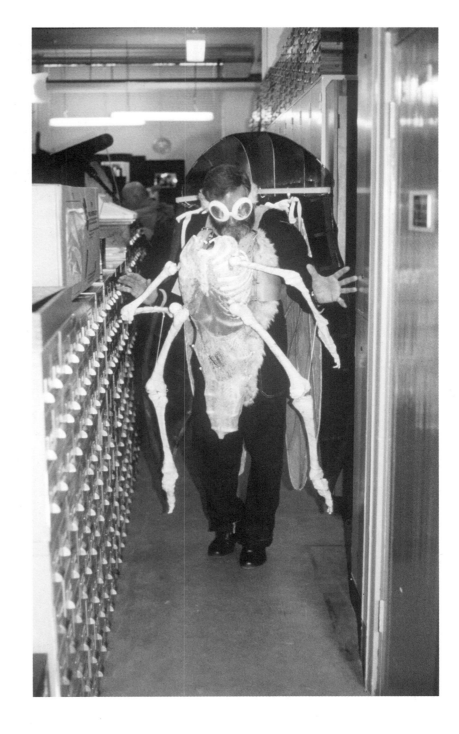

Fabre's images of the scientists' fluttering, desiring souls, enacting the habits of their treasured species, are further investigated through video editing. Images are forced to hum, insect/ human/ insect /human, the sudden and secretive moves of the participants are shortened and fractured, oscillate and spin, in seemingly random repetition. The artist flaunts his shapeshifting swarm before the viewer, who easily become involuntarily involved in their perplexing rituals. However, the puzzle of who is who and what they are becoming also has the affect of potentially alienating viewers. The participants seem oddly unconcerned about how they appear and whether anyone is watching. Perhaps, this is because, despite Fabre's emphasis on the sensory, his subjects are being encouraged to do the opposite of wear their hearts on their sleeves. The insect wears its bones on the outside. The heart, if there were one, would be entombed deep inside the miniature crusty carapace of its exterior form. Insects, for this reason, allude to the dancing skeleton, the figure of Death in the *danse macabre*, the little boys' scary toy rattling its bones. The scientists' fancy dress could therefore be likened to body armour, an exoskeleton of deceit, masking feelings, thoughts and intentions. With the basement bowels of the Museum as backdrop and with the corridors lined with specimens waiting in murky jars, this transformation of humans into insects bypasses any perceived moment of mammalian friendliness or familiarity. Although dark moments in the video piece are easily matched by episodes of farce and the ironic melancholy of drag, the work alludes defiantly to the non-human, the invertebrate, the cold-blooded at home and at one within its equally alien habitat.

Little could be perceived as colder, than the environment, the acts committed, or the significance of the activities of insects, than in the film *Fargo* written and directed by the Coen brothers. The film describes the pulling together of place, character and hidden agenda in a way that parallels the sentiment of Fabre's video work. It indicates a further form of mimicry, exemplifying its extended vocabulary and its capacity to operate not only between animate or previously animate forms but also between the animate and the eternally inanimate, lifeless mineral – the environment itself.

Set in the frozen winter of a small town in Minnesota, *Fargo* is the farcical story of Grimsrud, a man who murders for apparently no reason amid the bumbling inadequacies of the towns' inhabitants. The hollow and empty character of the killer functions as an almost anthropomorphic manifestation of his icy, exposed, improbably white, surroundings. It is the depiction of snow in *Fargo* that collapses geographies, evoking deserts of lightness, without beginning or end. Anything or anyone who might have been indicative of a precise place or time is muffled by the snow and by the obscuring clothes necessary to survive it. With orientation and distinction impossible, the snow alludes to a heartless democracy. Everything is rendered the same here, blended and smothered. A world is described which is loosing any sense of visual order or definition. The portrayal of this landscape, where it seems to be forever snowing, therefore evokes our deep seated fear of the obscuring of forms, the sedimentary affects and effects of sustained melding, masking and mimicry.

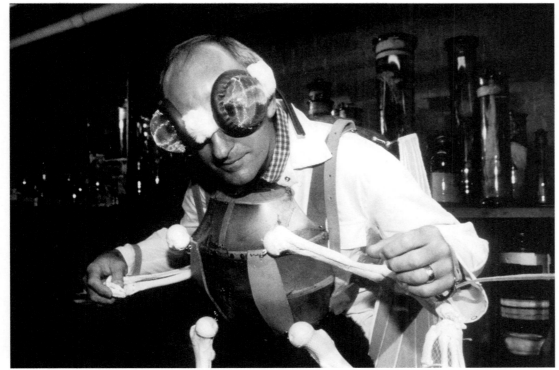

Both images *A Consilience* courtesy of the Natural History Museum

A scene in *Fargo* features, Carl, the murderer's accomplice, attempting to get the television working. With Grimsrud oblivious in the foreground, Carl, who will be his next victim, can only achieve television snow, seething, buzzing particles, imparting a lack of information, light nothingness. In the shot that follows we witness a working set tuned into a Natural History programme on insects.

TV VOICE-OVER
THE BARK BEETLE CARRIES THE WORM TO THE NEST WHERE IT WILL FEED ITS YOUNG FOR UP TO SIX WEEKS... **(6)**

The viewer only realises that the television snow has not transformed into insects when the camera pulls back from the screen revealing that we are in Marge's house (the hapless pregnant detective, who eventually captures Grimsrud). Marge and her husband Norm are seen vacantly watching the insects on television from their bed. We hear the sound of these 'lower animals' chirring on TV.

The insects, in *Fargo*, and their proximity to snow appear to indicate living death, when all else has gone or been denied. The couple watch the insects on TV, portrayed 'live' in their own natural environment. Insects and humans display seemingly mutual disinterest, a lack of connection, similar to the scientists in *A Consilience* in relation to their audience. Despite, as with Fabre's work, a tendency for farce, the Coen brothers' choice of making the TV programme a documentary on insects, appears to reflect the abject qualities of the film. The characters seem disturbingly interchangeable in their automated lives – similar, in their hollowness, stupidity, cruelty and yet, above all, will to survive.

This description of the characters in *Fargo* could be directly applied to common perceptions of the insect world (with stupidity an exception, as insects are usually credited with their own, seemingly alien, intelligence). The living and the dead, housed inseparably within the form of the insect, however, indicate a propensity for survival, which extends towards the divine territory of eternal life. Representations of the insect in *A Consilience* and *Fargo*, have precedent in the living death of Arachne, the artisan so proud of her skills that she was condemned by a jealous Goddess to weave for all eternity, cursed into the shape of a spider. Death, for Arachne, was thereby frozen into life, time was compressed into the single kill of a fly, repeated for all eternity. Weaving and repairing her hidden death trap, waiting in the centre of her web, Arachne was left as perpetrator and victim to the clutches of an environment imbued with death.

The insects' persisting pervasiveness as an agent of both life as death combined with its further associations with swarms and viruses, makes its infringement on the human domain all the more uncomfortable. The myth of Arachne bleeds into everyday citing of a spider in the home, upsetting the distinction between perceptions of the mythic, domestic and Natural worlds. As, perhaps, a final remnant and reminder of the forces of an uncontrollable and ferocious Nature, the insects' appearance in Fabre's work, as in life, literature and art in general has a tendency to induce feelings of panic.

THE ENDWORD
PAN, THE GREEK GOD OF THE FOREST, WAS A SAVAGE TRICKSTER WHO DELIGHTED IN TRIGGERING FITS OF TERROR IN HUMANS. HIS LEGACY SURVIVES IN THE WORD WE NOW USE TO DESCRIBE ANY UNCONTROLLABLE FEAR, BUT 'PANIC' REFERRED FIRST TO OUR FEAR OF THE FOREST, OF THE DENSE, PROLIFIC FEROCITY OF NATURE. **(7)**

Stills from *Fargo*, Coen Brothers, 1989

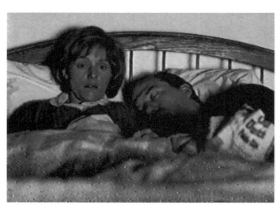

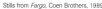

More precisely, the word stemmed from the rustic phenomenon of the sudden madness which can descend on a peaceful flock, goats and sheep sent racing, swarming, over the land which echoes with their screams. They have been struck by Pan – quite literally, 'panic -stricken' as were the Persians by his cry at the great battle at Marathon. Pan's cry was exclaimed in defence of wildness, in protection of the Natural environment. As God of Nature, Pan was oversexed, mischievous and sometimes dark and troubled by un-requited love as a result of his ugliness. He was the only God who died. According to Plutarch, Pan died around the same time as Christ which accounts for the added controversy over the significance of his death. In Pan's wake, some rejoiced over the coming of the supposed true God, others mourned embracing a fading image of a sorrowing nature. With his inner conflicts and conflicting associations Pan was variously equated with images of Christ, (the Lord our shepherd) and the Devil who began, in the Medieval period, to be depicted with Pan's goat's legs and horns. Pan was half goat and half God, partly of the Natural World and partly of myth. In Apuleius' *The Golden Ass*, the myth of Psyche, Pan is portrayed as aware of his own mythic status. (**8**) He is of the world but acknowledges that a part of him is both already dead yet timeless, alive for all eternity. The accident of Pan's perceived character due to early misinterpretations of his name have nonetheless attributed to him a powerful and persuasive identity. Etymological confusion over the word 'Pan', which during the Roman period was taken to mean 'all', and the Greek word 'paon', meaning 'pasture', extended Pan's form to include the heavens, the seas, earth, and fire.

Statue of Pan

He became the 'Supreme Governor or 'soul' of the World' and with his supposed death, as echoed in Milton's *Paradise Lost*, came the alleged loss of this soul. If insects are perceived as the last animate indicators of Nature's powers of survival and pervasion, then perhaps it could be argued that they are the legacy of Pan, inducing, as they do, [pan]ic, his namesake.

In the period of the horror novel 1890-1930, terrifying images of the God Pan witnessed a revival. Arthur Machen, in an attempt to describe an environment that scared him, conjured Pan as a manifestation of terrors that lurk beyond the veil of material things. In a scene that recalls the melding of characters and scenery in Fargo and the oscillating and visually confusing forms of *A Consilience*, Machen's heroine reaches beyond this veil of the material world in a renactment of the Edenic fall of Eve.

"WHEN AS INFINITE SILENCE FELL ON THE WOOD, SHE SAW A PRESENCE, THAT WAS NEITHER MAN NOR BEAST, NEITHER THE LIVING NOR THE DEAD, BUT ALL THINGS MINGLED, THE FORM OF ALL THINGS BUT DEVOID OF ALL FORM." [9]

With reference to Fabre's various representations of insects, Kathy Acker evokes the artists' capacity for inducing the extreme form of panic that Machen describes, in stating that,

"FABRE IS ONE OF THE FEW ARTISTS TODAY WHO BRINGS US BACK TO THE PRESENCE OF TERROR." [10]

NOTES

(1) It was Aristotle that first separated the sanguineous from the exsanguineous, those with blood from the bloodless. Pliny the Elder, following Aristotle, then attempted to further divide the animal kingdom into categories in correspondence with the four elements of earth, air, water and fire. Finding that little could live in fire, this category was jettisoned. However, insects continued to defy comfortable categorisation as they could correspond variously to all of the three remaining classifications. Because of their ability to change shape, with the process of metamorphosis little understood, insects were associated with the magic and impossibility of the missing fiery element. Entomology only began in earnest as late as 1667. Ross, H. *A Textbook of Entomology*, New York: John Wiley & Sons inc.

(2) M. Warner, *No Go the Bogeyman,* London: Chatto & Windus, 1998, p.6

(3) ibid. p. 173

(4) The story of 'The Quick and the Dead' originated in Northern France in the 1200s

(5) Warner pp. 172 – 183

(6) Full script: http://www.godamongdirectors.com

(7) K Dunn, 'Alive in Guyana', *Guyana,* (on the painting of Alexis Rockman), New Mexico: Twin Palms Publishers, 1996

(8) Apuleius, *The Golden Ass,* alternatively named 'Metamorphoses' written c. AD 150

(9) P. Merivale, *Pan the Goat God, his myth in Modern Times,* Massachusetts: Harvard Studies in Comparative Literature, 1969

(10) K. Acker, 'Fabre's Art', *The Power of Theatrical Madness*, London: ICA, 1986

MOVING

Leaving 25 Bedefield Cromer St. Kings Cross London WC1 1988 - 2000

I've been crying c 1989

Many waters cannot quench love
neither can floods drown it.
Song of Solomon

Crying
Roy Orbison/Joe Melsen Acuff Rose 1961

I made my wife pregnant to stop her crying.
When she cried it was as if a great gap happened in the earth and I stood staring into it.
I couldn't see anything and **I didn't know what my relationship to it was**.
Do I just turn away? If I look in I might fall.
It was a long time since my wife began to cry.
Unlike a lot of crying people she didn't wail or blubber, the tears just came down without any individual expression. Floods of tears, how ridiculous everything would get wet. Her hands. Her hair scraped back behind her ears, her hair the colour of cork. I could see her as *Alice in Wonderland* floating alongside the upper windows of office blocks adrift in the tears of her own making.
I made a joke once that she should be in the *Guinness Book of Records*.
At this the film of water slid off the edges of her eyes and I embraced her again as she told me the only record she knew by heart was the the record beard of bees. Seventy thousand, she wept.
Once she said she was doing her lifetime of crying. I thought she may have had dysfunctional tear ducts.
Some nights we'd sit close together at the table and talk about why people cried. She believed it was to do with impossibility.
She said she never felt she belonged because we live in time she said and tears are something you make yourself in time.
They are emotion made visible, a valorisation of pain.

Selection of b/w stills by my father John Miles: *Love's Secret* 1994, *Golden Syrup* 1990, *Damsel Jam* 1992.

Why are they different to a blush?

Blushing is for brides, she said.

Brides cry too, I said. I thought crying was acceptance: when you cry acceptance is made easier, you are exhausted and resistance is low. Marry me I said taking hold of her wet hands.

The first time I remember my wife crying like this, this sort of self perpetuating baptism she told me a story.

She had eavesdropped someone elses private grief.

Two sisters dressed in black. There was a peculiar aura of pain, the kind of pain my wife was sensitised towards. One of the sisters was expressing a deep sadness, 'I just wanted to see my baby,' she said. 'But the woman said it will be stiff as a brick, stiff as a brick. She shouldn't have said it like that. When I get angry now I hit anyone near me and if there isn't anyone I headbutt the wall. I've packed away the baby things now.' She didn't cry. Then it was a young woman friend who died of cancer, another jumped under a tube train. And her impossible relationship with her father. She never cried when these things happened but later with a different event, grief when it reached her was late.

Refusing to give any significance to the first time this crying began she had **flown at me with her stained face almost gulping for air**.

Love's Secret 1994 still by John Miles; *Kings Cross* 1999 Utopia means no place there's no place like home.

My parents' wedding photograph 1959; *Damsel Jam* 1992 still by John Miles; *Kings Cross* 1999; *Damsel Jam* 1992 still by John Miles.

When did you start? When did it all start? Weary to the point of a last sob with beginnings and more compelled by a sense of an ending.

She did smile and laugh but the tears were always there. **Tears at the beauty** of it all, the sadness of it all. She said she would see things like all the aborted foetuses from St. Mary's hospital in a heap covering all the cars in the car park. I worried about her I felt so dry.
She wept of animals, sensitivity was being privatised.
This reminded me of the Australian prime minister who became famous for crying on TV If she saw people crying on TV she stopped.
It wasn't self piteous, you know that wet pillow those shining staring eyes in the middle of the night when there's no-one to see, so alone. **The community of women** is a community of dolphins she said. I didn't understand but it sounded good. Something extrasensory plunging and rising effortlessly through **deep and calming waters**.

Kings Cross 1999.
Out of the sweetness came forth strength – *Golden Syrup* 1989 still by John Miles.
Still from *The Wizard of Oz* (MGM 1939); My mother and me 1959; Clare, friend and neighbour – *A Bunny Girl's Tale* 1998 original colour still by Ed Miles; Joan Bryant, my maternal grandmother 1921-1972; *Amaeru Fallout 1972* 1987 original colour still by Ed Miles.

The Kindness of Strangers, John Boswell: mothers tossing unwanted children into a river – *Abandonment is frequently associated with rivers or water in ancient and medieval texts, but the children were usually rescued and mythically founded the empire. John Boswell discusses the recurrence of the ancient association of abandonment and incest and the Roman influence on establishing patterns of european abandonment. These themes can be seen to be endemic in Kings Cross site of hidden rivers sacred wells Boadicea's burial.* Hopital du Saint-Esprit Manuscrit sur la fondation miniature 3; *Damsel Jam* 1992 still by John Miles; *Modern Times* – Homelessness and Independence 1999 original colour stills by John Miles.

My Mother phoned me up last night.

She said that you change irrevocably when you have a child. It was this that sowed the seed in my mind. **My father** said that people never change, there it is again my mother trying to understand my father and my father refusing to be understood. Who's the wiser? My mother dancing on the spring board at the deep end and my father paddling in the shallow end. I'd spoken to Janey about this and a fabulous tear rolled down her cheek hanging on the brink of her chin, it dropped into her cup…

Janey was dissolving becoming universal. One.

One time when I got angry, confounded, I tried leaving but her passivity held me, as she held out a wet hand and looked away. I was giving her the silent treatment, humming like a swarm of drones around the Queen, Janey's beard of bees. I told her she was a freak and I should put her on a game show where she could be a cry register. The public would air their grievances and sadnesses, their tales of woe and we'd see how wet Janey would get.

For a brief moment I thought she'd cry at my trivialisation and appeal for a chair of tears, a study of the molecular chemistry of crying. But she laid off, she said I was disgusting and that one day I'd drown in my own sexual innuendo. Then she walked straight into the kitchen banging cake trays and buzzing, whirring the cake mixer.

Janey the baker. Hours later I would follow her into this haven where the gas oven burned and the delights of her work were displayed simply. I couldn't resist, you could be a new Mary, a Neo Mary crying for the world. All that crying the world hasn't got time for. Crying for the men in the city, expressing all the grief in the domestic domain.

She slammed the oven door shut, stinging angry tears and exhausted trailed into the bedroom.

In the beginning was emotion. When I first encountered Janey I walked in on her in the bathroom at a party she was in tears. I said, 'Excuse me,' noticing her burgundy tights on her crossed legs and closed the door. Then in a moment of complete inspiration I walked back in and turned on all the taps, if a first meeting is significant in determining the nature of a relationship then this start of our slalom was my invasion of Janey's privacy, a plunge into her personal pool. Janey had a honey cap she loved it. She always had it in when we had sex and emotionally I felt this to be a barrier, physically I couldn't feel a thing.

Our first time we'd been to the funfair and excited by the big rides we reached each other variously, it was luscious. I teased her so much about not being able to feel her cap and that it might not have protected us that she took the morning after pill. A bit like being back on the carrousel she said, mechanical horseriding, an imitation of life.

Love's Secret 1994 still by John Miles; *2001 A Family Odyssey* 2000 still by John Miles; *Max and Siggi @ Bedefield* 2000 colour original; *Love's Secret* 1994 polaroid. *Golden Syrup* 1989 colour original.

I stared out of the window while she cried and vomited with the cap securely back in the honey jar, a perfect sphere of cream rubber, a holy ghostly asteroid floating in it's milky (honey) way. When I put on my suit to go to work, leaving Janey that is exactly how it felt, unhooking, disconnecting. Leaving while throwing a nervous glance at the honey jar to see if it was embodied.

A multitude of things were bothering me.
Dogs barking in the night, the damp patch on my shoulder after I left Janey.
I work as an artist, well that is I put on my suit and I teach the origins of things in an institution. I use one room of our flat to make paintings. The first time Janey came into this room I showed her one of my paintings. It was a plane field of colour interrupted by an undifferentiated spillage as if the painting wept. Janey's eyes went straight past my work and hit upon a black and white photograph of Jeanne Moreau the french screen femme fatale who starred in *The Bride wore Black*. In this picture she had a tear in her eye and a cigarette in her mouth, looking sombre and erotic.

Coming home one afternoon I surprised Janey pregnant in the kitchen. I immediately suspected she might have hidden a lover and looked anxiously for the honey jar. On seeing me she bent over and putting her head between her legs smiled ferociously. She was as beautiful as an antelope without being scared of hunted. Her eyes glistened and anticipating a flood I stepped across the room to close the window. Her tears were a slipping away of eroticism, I stepped carefully towards her and kissed her affectionately on the mouth.
As I did this I remembered our first drive together. Janey was questioning me about my affairs was I a good guy or a bad guy? I felt put upon, it was a golden autumnal day and I'd borrowed a car to drive this girl about for chrissakes, it was exciting the way she looked the way the sun bathed her the way she smelt the way we freed ourselves through the landscape. She started crying and in a flash of Kubrick horror I felt the car fill up with water. Janey was floating around the red plastic interior a close up of her watery death, after this near fatal foetal illusion I was even more convinced that a child would seal up these outpourings.

As Janey's pregnancy progressed I looked to see if her masochism would ebb or flow through nights of wakefulness we became friends again, our affections punctuated by moments of tears and sometimes sperm.

Detail from *Bacchus and Ariadne* by Titian courtesy National Gallery; *Love's Secret* 1994
I Love You 1990; *Aerial Trespass* photograph by John Miles 1983; *Kings Cross* – Utopia means no place there's no place like home 1999; still from *The Lovers* by Louis Malle 1959 Zenith Pictures.

We were in the supermarket looking at a new washing powder when Janey's waters broke. As provider and protector I panicked at the prospect of the baby suddenly left alone in a void, gleaming honey under wings of bees, oceanic continental plates moving apart. I must have looked glum as Janey's face superimposed tears onto joy, **a suffering lined with joy**. Stepping towards her I slipped and banging my head lay face down in the amniotic pool of her fluid, drowning in sorrows, a well of living waters.

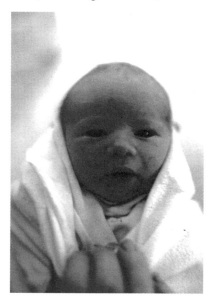

Golden Syrup 1989.
Lucas Rey – We accept you we accept you one of us one of us, colour original by Emma Miles 1999.
Me and my son, stills from *A Bunny Girl's Tale* 1999.

12 Years filmography
Golden Syrup
I Love You
Damsel Jam
Loves Secret
Amaeru Fallout 1972
A Bunny Girl's Tale
Modern Times
In development
2001 A Family Odyssey
The Black Marble Castle.

Leaving Kings Cross 2000, colour original still by Ed Miles.

David Wojnarowicz/Sylvere Lotringer

Hammer On The Head:
The Last Interview of David Wojnarowicz

Stills by Marion Scemama from *The Last Trip*, David Wojnarowicz/Marion Scemama (1991)

Still by Marion Scemama from *The Last Trip*, David Wojnarowicz/Marion Scemama (1991)

David Wojnarowicz I guess I feel a little intimidated, mostly because I've always felt intimidated with intellectuals and my experience with intellectuals has always been that they use language like a hammer.

Sylvere Lotringer Sometimes you need hammers, too.

DW True, but not when you're the one who's getting the hammer on the head.

I've always been attracted to people with information and to the idea of language. Most of my life has been without words. This is something that confused me about using language in very intellectual ways. I feel like everything I respond to is on either an intuitive or primitive level, and that I pull together language and try to form art or form these things that I don't feel I can tell artists. I just feel very alien to things being done in the art world or the intent of things. It's a luxury people play with in terms of images

Something else I'm discovering is that it shocks me that people think similar things to me. I'd get so obsessed when I was younger that if I looked at this table and you look at this table and we both think we're seeing the same thing, are we really? Then I would think well, the only way to know is to take a photograph of it and say does this look like what the table looks like? And if you said yes, then it would confirm that I'm seeing the same thing, but then I think what's the difference between the photograph and the real thing? I can't get inside your eyes and look through them. I remember having these uneasy feelings that maybe I'm seeing something very different than what other people are seeing. It still shocks me that people would think similar things to me because I've always been so isolated on a certain level, most of my sex was with strangers most of my life.

That's one thing in growing up, what I connected to in promiscuity was a vessel into which I could pour fantasy. The less I knew about the person that I was having sex with the more amazing it was to me. Because it wasn't loaded down with the collections of owls that he has all over his house or something that would really disgust me or upset me because it just seemed so absurd in the face of what living was.

I think it's great when I see kids that are fifteen experiencing their homosexuality now. They're lucky; they didn't go through a period where everything was so open and then have to close down again. At the same time, I also hate the promiscuity. I hated the experience of it because in the end I felt it killed all my dreams, not all of them, but a lot of them. It's like what I felt like as a teenager before my twenties where I was having sex three or four times a day. I would have sex and for periods of time; I felt that somehow it killed me. I had sex for money before, but I didn't feel like it was promiscuous. I don't know if it was part of the process of growing through my twenties, that age people hit where their dreams die.

I had one very powerful relationship with Peter Hujar. He was somebody who I felt saw the world the same way I did maybe with a little bit of change here and there, and he was twenty years older. His perspective was really interesting to me. He taught me a lot of things, and he connected instantly to what I felt about the world myself. But beyond him, I've always felt like a stranger among people. I'll spend years in the company of certain people and always feel like I just don't understand them. There are certain things that are familiar, but then once I get beyond that, it's like I don't have the faintest idea of where they're coming from or how they're looking at things. It just doesn't make any sense to me.

This extremely wealthy woman came up to me in one of my shows. She and her husband had bought some work of mine years before and she was just shocked by what I'd done in the show. She pulled me aside and said, "Do you really see the world like this?" I couldn't even answer her because I remember saying something to her, "But what do you mean?" And she says, "It's so negative." I said "No, it's the opposite. It's totally positive, and it's full of hope." She just shook her head and went away.

When I thought about it later, it really made me angry because I should have said: "Look, let's trade for a moment. I'll sit in your house; I'll sit in this penthouse that has this view for hundreds and hundreds of miles that mostly nobody else on the lower floors can see. I'll have the house person in the kitchen cooking and any airplane system in the country and go to Borneo or go to China or go to Africa. You have that luxury of distance. You have access to any means of transportation to escape that somebody who lives with very little money doesn't have." They depend on their own legs to run through a city and outside the confines of the city when this person has the helicopter pick them up at the top of their building.

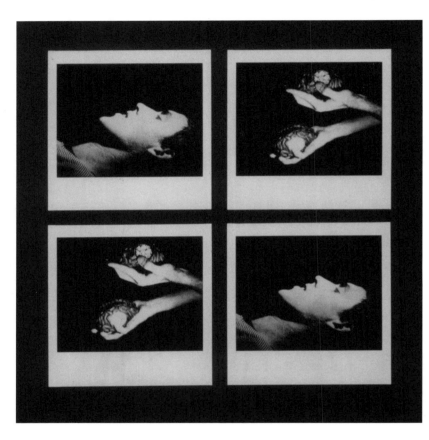

Stills from *Where I put my hands on your body*, David Wojnarowicz/Marion Scemama (1991)

I think I've always wished that I could be of value. I was not valued. I was worthless. My family just didn't value me. I was not valued in all the institutions I was in. I lived on the streets. I was not of value. All my jobs were as custodians where I guess I was of value, because I cleaned up everybody else's garbage, but I didn't feel of value to myself before I started making money from art work. I found a tape recently of a conversation in 1980 with a friend, it's a really boring tape, very pretentious and everything, but there's this one section where I'm talking about robbing a bank because I have something in my head that I want to make things, but I can't afford the materials. I was getting really enraged because it's something outside myself that determines whether I have the materials or not. Therefore, I should rob this bank and be able to do what I want to do.

If I can find value in what I do, that means something to me, or if somebody comes to me and says they've seen something I did and it meant something to them, it touches something in me. Like it's repairing something because I've made a gesture that reverberated and touched somebody else.

I see myself living my life in a capsule in a compression of time. Now, suddenly all these things are happening very quickly, and it's almost as if the length of my life is suddenly compressed to months and things that I thought were years away if at all possible are suddenly going boom, boom, boom.

It was growing up in a household with a psychotic which then became the country or the world. I did this painting recently called, *My Father was a Sailor, My Father was the Century*. It's the same thing; it was not only about his being a sailor, but also about transportation. It was about moving out where a century ago most people wouldn't know what was beyond the bend in the road outside their door. Now, you turn on the TV and you're in China, you're a thousand feet below the ocean looking up at things that exist. The painting touched on that as well as my father's psychosis. It's a world that's extremely dangerous, extremely death and destruction oriented. All of these activities about destruction or self-destruction shaped my first experience. First, if you believe that embryos pick up thoughts, if you accept that argument, which I wouldn't because of its anti-abortion implications, but just thinking of the possibilities in the world or the possibilities in forms of life, communicating without words, then that was the world I was born into. My mother, when I was fourteen, told me that she had just prayed that I would die; when I was in her belly, I would abort or that I would just be stillborn. When I arrived, because of everything she felt about my father and her two other children. I just wasn't wanted. He constantly beat and threatened her with guns. I was born with the umbilical cord wrapped around my throat. I was almost strangled. I only recently found that that happens to a lot of children whose parents want them to die. They're born with the umbilical cords around their throats.

I grew up in a society that basically wanted to kill me, and that every sign that I say as a kid growing up. Whether it was the structure of my household or the structure of schools, or the structure of the world at large. Everything was aimed at extermination in some way; especially when at the age of eight, I had my first homosexual experiences with a thirty year old guy. I knew what my family would do. I knew what people beyond my family would do, whether it was the police or hospitals, any of these things. I knew that they would try to destroy this if they found out. I've met people who experienced just the opposite, the moment they realized they were homosexual, or that they were inclined towards that experience, they were immediately open about it, immediately talking about it. Yes, they were beaten up and yes, they had rejection from their families, but they never questioned for a moment that this was who they were. For me, I remember inventing all these reasons why this was happening. Then, I remember from the age of eight on, thinking: well when I hit puberty that's when I'll start having relationships with women. I didn't have hair on my body, so I thought this was why I was making it with men. That excuse failed by the time I hit puberty. I realized I was still like that.

I know I turned a lot of death towards myself. I had attractions to death. I took myself into situations where it was possible to die. Some of them were reactions to what I understood homosexuality is. I remember going to the library trying to find out what a homosexual is and reading books that said that I had to put bottles up my ass and wear a dress and do this and do that. I was horrified; that's not what I want but then I thought I had no choice. I thought by the time I'm seventeen I'll be wearing dresses and putting bottles in my ass. It was upsetting. I thrust myself into situations that were potentially dangerous to confront this idea of becoming a "sissy." I didn't want to be this. It was also an ugly torture of somebody that society hates, somebody who's effeminate. The whole thing was informed with rage. On some level, I wanted to be accepted, but on some level it was impossible.

I don't think I ever believed that paintings could change people. The only thing I thought about paintings was that they were signs that people who felt similarly or differently could identify with in some way. They'd either look at themselves or feel that there's some sensibility that may give them more comfort.

There's the sensibility here because that was the thing I remember lacking when I was growing up. As I became more aware of my homosexuality, there were no images anywhere in the culture that gave me comfort or helped my fears. There was no role model. I could argue against role models at this point. Now, I don't like the idea of role models, but as a kid, I was looking at all these stereotypes, and I wanted to see some stereotype that reflected me, and I couldn't find it. It was completely absent and everybody else who's not homosexual or doesn't have leanings that are that far outside the norm are totally supported by every image they see in media and movies and books. They find comfort in all of these normal lives because they find direction. I had no direction and I'd just pretend I had it, but then at the same time try to figure out where I was. If I had seen it as freedom, it would have been freedom. I didn't see it as freedom. It was fear. It's the distinction of being drugged or put in the hospital, all the things done to people who are not normal. It was fear.

As I confront fears physically, either by speaking or moving, there is an incredible landscape which appears. Suddenly, I'm loosening laws that I constructed for myself – all the rules, all the laws – there's this sense that I'm not through with them or I haven't passed yet. That's what happens when you confront death; all of the things that you construct for safety become useless so you start bouncing against them. What gets revealed is something I wish I had years ago, or sensed that I had years ago because it would have really freed something in the expression of what my life became. I try very hard to be normal and accepted and try very hard to get loving, touching gestures. It is a terrific waste of time.

There was one thing Peter in his Buddhist leanings once told me. He always encouraged me to meditate and do things like that. I tried it for a period of time and it made everything I did worthless. I no longer wanted to paint these images, and I no longer wanted to deal with violence. It scared me so; I was always on this health diet. I'd given up smoking, sugar, salt, meat, all these things. I did it for four months and it scared the shit out of me. I just said the one hold I have in the world is dealing with my expression. I was at a total loss as to what to do, what to paint, what to make. None of it made any sense because I didn't want to paint beauty. I can't think of an interesting way to present beauty unless it's inside of death or violence. That's where I make violent things beautiful. There have been times that I've painted flowers or landscapes, and it's actually been nice to give myself that freedom, but in the end it's not something I'm really interested in showing other people. They can go out and look at the same. Somehow it's just not potent to me; it doesn't express something. So I gave up meditation and went back to eating sugar and pancakes, and I became violent again. It made me feel much better.

Actually, I remember having an image of bathing my brain, holding it under running water or woods or whether it was in nature or out in the woods or forest, it just became a beautiful image, the idea of being able to wash your brain like you wash your pants and squeeze it out and start fresh.

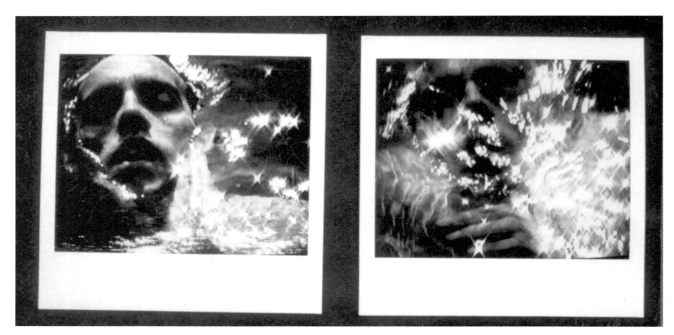

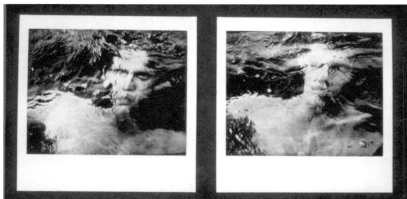

Stills by Marion Scemama from *Rushes From Death*, David Wojnarowicz (1989)

I've always had a reaction to the sound of TV. It makes me sick. I mean it does. If I watch TV for five minutes sometimes during the morning or afternoon hours, it colors the rest of the day, and it's more about frequencies in that it hits something in the head that makes me numb. For the rest of the day, I feel uncomfortable. So, I've gone through periods of watching TV just trying to drown things out, but really in the end, I feel like I want to throw up. It's just that it's so ugly and the sound waves and everything else are so distorting... plus all the information. All the information puts me in a rage and I can't do anything about it. That's why I scream at the TV. I yell "Fuck you!" Sometimes I draw things on the front of the screen like a big dick or something so that every announcer has this dick going into his mouth or into his face just something to shift it because it's so full of shit, and it's so predictable, emotionally or otherwise. It's like fucking with the images, putting them through some sort of change so that they mean something else, or pushing them in directions so that they can mean a variety of things.

I'm sitting there always in a dialogue with this box. I imagine murdering these people on TV. I confront them at every turn. If I'm watching the news it's so insulting, but the people to whom I'm attracted have the ability to control language that's beyond what I've learned or what I understand. That's where I become overwhelmed or frightened.

I had a therapist confront me not too long ago, saying that I found it easier to develop relationships with my objects than with people, that I invest so much emotional energy that I'm afraid to invest in people. It's fairly true. It doesn't speak back. I love animals. I've loved animals all my life because of my early experiences with my family. I would spend all of my time in the forest and watch animals catch animals, read about animals. I've always loved them more than people or always trusted them more than people. I bought a bunch of crickets to feed a scorpion that I'd bought to use in a film, and the crickets started eating each other. Within twenty four hours, two crickets killed the other twelve. I couldn't under-stand what was going on. I didn't realize they were cannibals. What the hell is this? Maybe it's a virus that's attacking the crickets, and they're dropping dead. Then one day I looked in there, and I saw this cricket bite the leg off of another cricket. There were two left, and I fed them to the scorpion. I didn't feel so bad. The scorpion eats them like popcorn.

I think about mass murderers and how they seem to really love death and murder. They keep doing it over and over and over. They even do it with a lot of thought and care. They're in love with it, that sensation of death or what they imagine death to be. Most people you talk to would be or at least say they're horrified at the idea of death or the idea of killing.

Peter had just enormous rage, incredible rage and ugliness, the last year of his life. It became an ugly spectacle because there was nothing that you could do to touch it. Finally he hit a point where it was as if he had let go of something, and maybe it was a string leading into life or something, but he let it go and then it was just passivity.

I think I've worked at rage all my life. I used to feel very self-conscious about it because when I first began showing in galleries, all the people who worked in the gallery would say, "Can't you, you know, ... Is that all you see?" or, "Can't you paint something nicer?" or "Can't you be like Keith Haring?" or "Can't you, you know, create something that's fun?" I was extremely uncomfortable. I felt terrible. All I can do is produce misery.

All my life, I tried to fit. One of the things that happened with my diagnosis is that I don't care if I fit; there are still parts of me that want to be touched or accepted or embraced, but in the end it's absurd. It's not going to keep me from dying.

Part of what I felt in the year of Peter's illness before he died was this incredible rage about everybody I knew. I hated them. I hated them so much because not one of them would ever say anything. And if they ever said anything, they would touch on it once or twice and then never bring it up again. They would look at you with certain eyes. I would feel people looking at me because they knew that I was going through something in relation to Peter's slowly dying. They would say something here or there, but basically it's the same thing that I feel about memorials for people who die. On some level, it's great to make a private grief public because it makes people more aware and makes them witness to what's happening. But, at the same time, memorials eventually just become this preparation for death, and everybody refines their words about this person who's about to die so that when the day comes and there's a memorial, they get up and

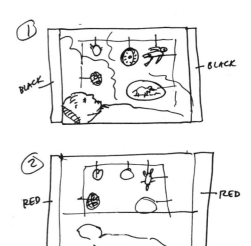

Storyboard for *Rushes From Death*, David Wojnarowicz (1989)

say, "This is who this person was. This is what this person meant to me." It's beautiful, but then they all go home and prepare for the next death.

There are moments when I have a slide machine in my head, and suddenly one slide that I carried for years and years gets knocked out and another one comes in. It could be for a minute or five minutes, when suddenly I'm looking at death, seeing the end of my life. My body grows still. I have absolutely no fear. It makes perfect sense and there's nothing loaded or attached to it. And, what am I afraid of? What am I afraid of? I know I'm afraid of loss of control mostly. Because of the rage that I've carried, I used to be afraid of that monster coming out. It was loss of control, where I was suppressing this for years, ever since I was a tiny kid, for this thing to suddenly jump out, I think I was always afraid I would kill somebody. That if provoked, I would lose control and then I would kill somebody. It's the same thing about my death or the view of my death, the loss of control or the loss of the ability to mark it or change it or shift it or construct things in order to make it not exist or exist less. But for that five minutes, it's a wonderful sensation because everything is meaningless.

My friend Keith Davis died two times of a heart attack, and the doctors came in twice and jumped up and down. Finally, they brought him back and then attached him to a machine. The family was trying to get them to remove the machine, but it was a Catholic hospital, which said, "look, you know, we don't have the decision to take away this life." They stuck him on the fucking machine, and they made a decision to bring him back from death because of their own fear of death.

I had to argue. I screamed at these doctors, "What the fuck is wrong with you? Why did you put him on the machine if now you can't make the decision to take him off the machine and why did you suddenly feel that you had the right to do that? Keith expressed that he never wanted anything like that. Anyway, as we were fighting with these doctors, the family, after five days of fighting with the doctors went out to sight-see around New York. Most of his family who visited New York to witness his death were in the Empire State Building on the observation deck around the time that his sister and I finally convinced the doctors to pull the plug, and in something like thirty seconds, he was dead. In thinking about it later and finding out that they were on the observation deck of the Empire State Building, it was wonderful.

I loved the idea that they were up in the sky so high above the ground, and that at the moment of death all that energy just gets dispersed and covers everything or mingles with everything and then dissipates. This energy is free of gravity and moving up into the atmosphere, and here are these people looking through binoculars into the sky or the city and through the depths of this height. It was wonderful. I thought it was the perfect death, or perfect moment in the relationship to this family for him to achieve death while they were sightseeing.

One of the things that I remember Kiki Smith saying to me was that when you die you become fly food. I like that. That's the clearest idea that I've ever heard from somebody; that it's nothing less. The idea that at the same time you nourish things in your death is kind of comforting. It's sweet. That's what I've been seizing on lately; that idea of death. That actually makes me fairly comfortable.

I'm attracted to the idea of existence after death in the form of objects. I have a pair of Peter's glasses, and they are the saddest things I've ever seen in my life. They're sadder to me than his death because they become totally useless, and yet they possess all of this personality. They're silent.

I'm having a lot of odd thoughts of what death is at this point. Partly because when I watched Peter and another friend, Keith Davis, die, I was in the room with both of them when they went, and it confronted all my feelings of what death is. I realized that suddenly everything, every idea I've had about death seemed so stupid. Stupid because it was so totally about living of life or that the words seemed ridiculous.

Peter wanted to believe that there's experience after death and that there's travel after death. I even did some little rituals in his house after he died that were according to some Buddhist papers that somebody gave to me to make a drawing of him and burn it at some point so that after seven days or three days or something his spirit can receive all knowledge and I totally believed in those things as I did them. It made me feel calmer about his absence in those moments, but now, facing my own death I don't want to believe that there's an afterlife because I think it's bullshit. This is what they do to enslave people. You tell them, "Oh you get your reward after you die," not when they can question it, not when they can confront it.

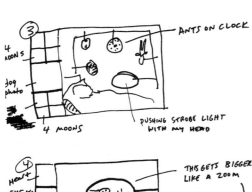

③ ANTS ON CLOCK

4 MOONS

dog photo

4 MOONS

PUSHING STROBE LIGHT WITH MY HEAD

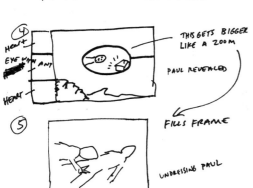

④

HEART

EYE WITH ANT

HEART

THIS GETS BIGGER LIKE A ZOOM

PAUL REVEALED

FILLS FRAME

⑤

UNDRESSING PAUL

 ⑥

1. HETERO SEX W/ ANTS
2. GLOBE (NO HAND)
3. HOMO SEX W/ ANTS

UNDRESSING ~~LICKING~~ PAUL

⑦

1. FLAG AT NIGHT
2. WOLF HEAD
3. CHRIST WITH ANTS

 ⑧

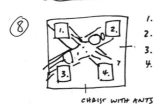

1. UNDRESSING ~~LICKING~~ PAUL
2. WOLF HEAD
3. BIGOTS
4. LICKING PAUL

CHRIST WITH ANTS

⑨

1. ATOMIC BOMB
2. ANTS ON CROSS
3. BIGOTS
4. ~~PEOPLE~~ GEARS
5. ANTS ON MONEY
6. ~~OR~~ ROLLER COASTER

CLOSE UP LICKING PAUL

⑩

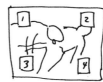

1. MAP FIGURE
2. CLOUDS/STROBE
3. TRAIN
4. 2 MEN: BRIDGE/RIVER

Storyboards for *Rushes From Death*, David Wojnarowicz (1989)

I love playing with all the contradictions in a surface. To be limited by only what you experience seems really boring, but then I realize that is one of the things about which I like to write. What I experience, what I think, or what I see in terms of whether it's my experience or someone else's experience, whatever attracts me, I pull together for my own writing.

I've done so many things that were against my religious upbringing that I've never considered that there's a reward waiting for me at my death. And at the same time it's hard to shake the religious training that I have. I was thrown out of Catholic school in the first grade for "molesting a little girl" my own age. I tore her shirt playing tag, and they made it into a big sexual case. The mother superior, this red-faced woman, who was just screaming day in and day out, told me that I was going straight to hell; I was in the wings of the devil, that I had no hope and never to come back to the school again. This was in the first grade.

I once asked God to meet me on the side of the house because my father forced me to put my hand on a bible and tell him whether or not I stole some money that I'd actually stolen. But, I knew he would have taken me to the basement and killed me if I said yes, because he was extremely violent, so I said no I didn't. And then I prayed to God. It was the last communication with God I ever had; asking him to meet me outside in five minutes and I'll explain everything. I waited out there until the sun went down, and the son of a bitch never showed up. I thought, "Well that's it, it's lost. If he didn't come now, he'll never come."

It's just something I told Marion yesterday, that I remember really clearly when I was first taught in kindergarten that God is everywhere, sees everything, knows everything and that everything comes from his hands. The next time I bumped my leg on a tree or something walking through the woods, I just started saying, "you son of a bitch," and cursing like a freak. In that moment, I wished I had more language than I really had because I wanted to think of the most incredible curses I could throw at this figure and just say you could have stopped it, you could have saved me from banging my leg instead of just watching. I see him up there like this just watching me. How cruel! How vicious! He could step down and make all this different.

I get angry at the idea of what it does to people to believe that there is this God and that God is this thing outside of themselves. The closest I could come to believing that there's something that people call God is just what sparks our bodies into movement and makes us move across the room. Or when we get cut we don't leak all the liquid out and become like plastic bags. Or why ants aren't the things that destroy the world instead of people. It's something of the construction of things about which I don't know that much and don't understand. In the times that I've flirted a little bit with spirituality, it's always been something outside. It's why we take this form, and are we really seeing what all this is, and are there things that move faster than we can see.

When Peter was diagnosed with AIDS I made this enormous construction of what this man was going through, what he was thinking and how he saw life. He gave me an indication early on the first day he got the news that he was diagnosed with AIDS. I came over ten minutes later from my house to sit with him for a few minutes. He went to meet me at the door. There was some mail that arrived, and it fell on the floor. He picked it up and turned saying, "Even something like getting a piece of mail in my home has an entirely different meaning." I felt very distant from him. I felt very sad. I felt angry. I felt fear. And yet the moment I got diagnosed, it was a shock that nothing changed, that people were still running back and forth on the street, that the mail still comes. You wake up in the morning and you have to eat. Other people have the luxury of time where they can abstract it into their nineties or when they reach fifty. Suddenly I'm doing it at thirty three.

Right after my diagnosis, the things I appreciated for a period of time about people who were dying from AIDS was their courage, and all the words that connect to courageous or courage in people's eyes for people who aren't facing death. I thought Peter was courageous even in the midst of his rage, he was courageous. Everywhere that I experience a friend's death or knew of a friend's death or illness and experienced part of it, I thought it was with great courage that they were living. Once I was diagnosed, the idea of courage enraged me. I thought this is bullshit really they're talking about politeness, that the more politely a person dies, the more courageous he is, that he should contain his experience of his death within himself

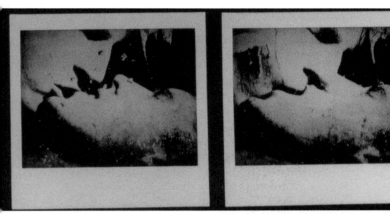

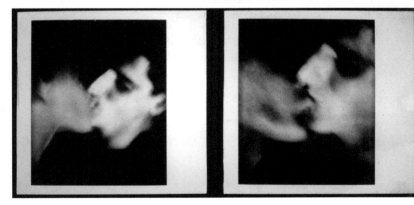

and make it very easy for everybody so that he slips through and dies.

I got this thing in Germany. They're now illegal in the United States because they look too real. (click) But I think it's a cap gun or something. I don't know.

Peter threatened to throw himself in front of a car because he was mad, but he didn't have the strength to walk to the curb and throw himself in front of the car. He talked about killing himself endlessly, brutally, "I want to go to that building across the street, climb to the top and jump off the roof." He would say, "I'm gonna do it, I'm gonna do it." And he said it every day until one day we gave him the number of a doctor who could help him find the number of somebody who would give him medicine to kill himself. Once I gave him the number, he tucked it away and never spoke about killing himself again.

I've been feeling this fear of getting trapped in language like in doing interviews, talking about AIDS, talking about death, talking about these things. I used to fear my contradictions as I grew up. I didn't understand. I wasn't in contact with enough people to understand that everybody has contradictions. I think the contradiction is containing contradictions all at the same time.

The first time I explored the promiscuous sex scene in the warehouses, I always stayed away from it and had judgements about it on some level because I wanted a relationship or I wanted to be connected to somebody and not just run around and have sex for the sake of having sex. I remember telling a friend of a friend from high school who was ostensibly straight, but then suddenly admitted to me, after all the years knowing him that he had fantasies of having sex with men. We were sitting on a river, and he was telling me about this. Then he saw these men going in and out of the warehouse. I mean dozens of men. And he said: "What's that? What's going on?" I said " Oh you know they're stupid. They go in there, and they just fuck all over the place." I used to get really frightened by contradictions in people and get really upset at contradictions. Mostly because I was upset at them in myself, and recently I've been enjoying more and more confronting my fear of contradictions because I love contradiction. It makes perfect sense to me. I mean it's becoming less and less scary, and I'm feeling more strongly about accepting them and holding them or embracing contradictions. The more I think about death, the less I want to find my feet in the cement of one form of thought.

I feel like I'm riding on a current of very nervous energy. And it's part fear and it's part exhilaration and it's about what I'm approaching, about the possibility of it and also confronting all these fears in myself. Not just about death. It's pretty abstract to think about death, but I feel like I'm trying to break down everything at once, cut through the bullshit, cut through all these constructions I made all of my life in order to feel somewhat comfortable or somewhat safe.

It's like breaking all of those down because they're going to become meaningless as death comes close. There's a tremendous amount of fear in doing it, because it's only in a really recent period of time that suddenly I'm confronting all of these things it would take me a year to confront. Suddenly it's just like plowing through everything, and I'm scared to death at moments of confronting. This confrontation of these privacies is exciting at the same time.

Talking about sexuality is something I've hardly ever done. If I did it, I would always displace it to another person or something I witnessed. Even in the first book of monologues I wrote, some of those monologues were me, but I was afraid to reveal that, so I would make them some kid in Times

Square at 4 A.M. They really are my stories. Now I write my stories, and it's exhilarating to confront that fear in myself about revealing those things.

Marion and I had a rough fight recently. In part it had to do with documenting myself. On one hand I'm attracted to it. When Peter died, I saw all the photographs he left and how little of himself he left clearly. It was all contained in the photos, but it's also hidden in the photos because it's other people, other images. I have some tape recording trying to do interviews with him. He was having such a hard time with the gallery system that I thought well maybe I could write an interview, but it ended up being too self-conscious and we never did it. But there are these pieces of tape that exist in different people's houses. Ten years ago in one of these tapes, he's talking about what he imagines death is. Things like that are valuable.

I went through a period of eight days in the last month or the beginning of this month where I couldn't function at all, and I felt everything shutting down inside me, inside my head, inside my body. It was about making gestures. Making gestures at this point suddenly became meaningless in the face of dying. It just felt stupid. It was like, "well so what." So what if I make a painting? So what if I write? What the hell, it just felt totally meaningless. It wasn't going to stop the illness. Those are scary moments because I felt if they continued there was the possibility that those would be my feelings for the rest of my life. If that's what I feel for the rest of my life, there's no reason for me to live. I've always found reasons to live by making things ever since I was a kid. It's the only thing that remained constant, or the only thing that ever made sense or gave me proof that I was here because I felt so completely alien; that's one of the reasons I began writing in my late teens. Seriously, I was just writing constantly because I couldn't speak to people.

Recently, I felt everything shutting down and it was scary to shut down. This train of thought relates to my fear of death more than fears about loss of speech, loss of movement, loss of sight, loss of the senses. Maybe I have some claustrophobia and death seems claustrophobic. I got into a fight with Marion about the loss of what's inside of me in terms of video tape or recording and being trapped in that language that's becoming my existence after I'm dead.

One of the things that happened after my diagnosis is this feeling that this may be the last work I do. Trying to focus everything and channel it into this square or into this photograph, into this thing that it's all got to go in, and it ends up not being everything.

I have the attraction to document things because through Peter I saw how little was documented of him other than filming the super eight of his body after he died. As soon as I could get everybody out of the room, I shot a Super8 of his body for maybe a minute and a half and then took a number of pictures of him, which served like a modern death mask for me.

Edited by Ron Palmer and Sylvere Lotringer from a film shot by Marion Scemama.
Marion Scemama is a photographer, videomaker and curator for Galeries Photo FNAC.
Born in 1950 in Morrocco, she currently lives in Paris after five years in New York.

Installation Lower East Side NYC, David Wojnarowicz (1985). Photo Marion Scemama

David in His Studio on Bowery, NYC. Photo Marion Scemama

Life in Music

Nelson Henricks

The song begins and without realizing it, you begin to sing along. You like to sing, even if your voice is not very good. So you sing when you are alone. You learn to sing through repetition and imitation. You don't want to be the singer. You want to know what the singer knows. You sing because it feels good.

In 1978 you could browse through any teenager's record collection in Forest Lawn and find three albums. These records were the cornerstone of a good music collection. Possessing them was a mark of the owner's coolness. There were other albums between and around them, but the following three appeared without fail: Led Zeppelin *IV*, Pink Floyd *Dark Side of the Moon*, Supertramp *Crime of the Century*.

I remember seeing boys who had Led Zep logos embroidered on the backs of their jean jackets and wondering what "Zoso" meant. I was always fond of Zeppelin, but I never got *totally into them* the way I did with Supertramp and Pink Floyd. These albums I played religiously. I even made a point of listening to them through headphones on LSD so I could study them more closely. It was on acid that I discovered the cuckoo-clock sound that ends side one of *Crime of the Century*. I am baffled by the totemic status these albums had and wonder what their equivalents are today. 1

In 1994 I was sitting in an espresso bar in Lucerne with a friend from Hungary. Her English was limited and we struggled to maintain a conversation. The cafe's sound-system played Crime of the Century on CD. The crispness of the music was almost painful. I had not heard this album for at least twelve years and was not a little surprised by how annoying it sounded. I found Roger Hodgson's warbling and the bright, melodic, piano flourishes distracting, like being attacked by a swarm of bees. It made me conscious of how much time had passed and how much had changed in the interval. I tried to explain to Sonia the role this music played in my life and describe the strange transformation that had occurred. "Theese museek," she said haltingly, with a hint of sour-faced revulsion, "eet eese wary... SWEET."

The change occurred not in the music, but in the lis-

tener. This fact amazes me, not because it means something as banal or obvious as "I can change," but because it indicates that what we hear in music is never stable; that what is heard is heard differently by different people. When this happens, I have a split second glimpse of a world outside my subjectivity. It can be as simple as the difference between whether a song sounds happy or sad, complex or trite.

Imagine making the loudest sound you can make. Bare your teeth, loosen your tongue. Force air out of the lungs. Let this feeling lift you up. The chest, head and throat vibrate together. The voice emerges from the viscera. It feels good.

1999. I am back in Calgary for a visit after living in Montréal for eight years. When my Lebanese cab driver (who spoke an unaccented working-class Western-Canadian English eerily similar to my brother's) determined that I was once a native, he asked me what high school I went to. "Forest Lawn." "Forest Lawn?" he said doubtfully, glancing at me in the rear view mirror with one eye-brow raised incredulously. He looked over my faggoty clothes, my short hair, my nerdy glasses. "That's a tough school."

It wasn't until years after I'd graduated that I learned that Forest Lawn, both the school and the suburb, had a bad reputation. Forest Lawn wasn't tough in that urban city-center/gang activity/crack-house kind of way. It was more of a rural, trailer-park trash/Jerry Springer-style, conjugal violence sort of toughness. If I now consider drug use, vandalism and other minor felonies normal parts of growing up, it was because I spent my adolescence in Forest Lawn. 2

In spite of its reputation, F.L.H.S. paled when compared with my earlier junior high school experiences at Ian Bazalgette (pronounced Bazal-JET by the teachers, and Bazal-GETTI – to rhyme with Alphagetti – by the students). The school was overcrowded: two-to-a-locker. My locker partners were always hoodlums. If I modeled my school persona after Marcia Brady, my locker partners emulated Charles Manson. My first partner, Terry Henderson, was the embodiment of pure meanness. His gang got into chain fights with other gangs on the roof of the gymnasium before later setting the same gym on fire (thus interrupting a full year of dreaded gym classes). Terry regularly locked his adversaries in our shared locker, serving the double purpose of scaring the shit out of both me and his victim. When Terry was pulled from school – presumably bumped to yet another fosterhome/detention center – he was replaced by Doug Herkel, one of the school drug dealers (and truth be told, a pretty nice guy). Our teachers had frequent and spectacular nervous breakdowns (but isn't that normal for any school?). We tortured our alcoholic music teacher, Mr. Robinson, by locking his keys in a metal cabinet week after week. The only thing I remember doing in music class that was remotely musical (there were no instruments except recorders) was talking about bands with my fellow students during the long intervals when Mr. Robinson absented himself. The logos of AC/DC (the early Bon Scott version), Alice Cooper and KISS were carved a quarter of an inch deep into 47% of the dilapidated antique wooden desks at Ian Bazalgette. I never listened to these groups much, but if I had to pick a fourth album for my mythic list, it would be *Highway to Hell*.

The Greeks believed in a beauty so perfect that to gaze upon it would cause blindness, to hear it would drive a person mad. Our image of the power of the singer is that of sound waves breaking a champagne glass. It is the destructive power of beauty that fascinates us.

I listened to *Dark Side of the Moon* so much that I wore out one copy and had to buy another. My parents were hip enough that they listened to a lot of the same music I did. But their taste drifted more towards America and Southern California: Fleetwood Mac, The Eagles and Chicago. I only listened to music if it came from England. But there was some overlap. My dad was very excited when I first played *Dark Side of the Moon* for him. And I listened to Fleetwood Mac *Rumours*. I remember playing Christine McVie's "Songbird", holding my dog on the couch in the living room and crying my eyes out, thinking how someday my dog would die. I don't think I was stoned.

This text is to some extent about embarrassment and humiliation. We all like to claim that "we-saw-that-group-when..." or "we-were-the-

first-one-on-our-block-to-buy-that-album," but how many of us really want to admit to the really icky stuff? Listen, the first long-playing album I ever bought was by The Captain and Tennille. I was smitten by the single "Love Will Keep Us Together" to the point where I felt it was time for me to make a major commitment. I remember that when you opened the gate-fold sleeve, you could see the Captain without his sunglasses! (One of the gimmicks of the group was that you NEVER saw the Captain without his sunglasses: a bit like never seeing the four lads of KISS without their make-up.) Anyway, the Captain had brown, sensitive, puppy-dog eyes that were painfully large, almost to the point of physical deformity. If anything, he resembled one of those weird, doe-eyed, children so popular in the ubiquitous kitsch paintings of the epoch. I speculate that the Captain had certain insecurities regarding his ocular endowment and hence, the shades. Incidentally, Tony Tennille sang backing vocal on Pink Floyd's *The Wall*, another life-shaping album I listened to with a pharmacopoeia of psycho-active drugs playing bumper-cars with my neurons. ③

       Patsy Cline is singing a happy song, but the sadness of her voice cuts through the music. Patsy's voice is serrated with pain. It rips through the meaning of the song like a saw-blade tearing a log in half. The content suddenly becomes doubled. It's as if we're looking through binoculars the wrong way: joy seems impossibly distant and remote. We stab at happiness from the heart of mean-spirited envy. But the knife blade always falls short of piercing the mocking target.

       At the pool, the men all look the same when they are in their bathing suits. But when we get out of the water, go to the locker room and get dressed, our relationship to one another changes. We become coded as soon as we are clothed. When I see what you wear, I can begin to imagine what kind of music you listen to.

       Music, more than anything else in our culture (with the possible exception of clothing), brings out our tribal nature. Walking to work two years ago, I noticed someone had spray painted a fresh "Led Zep" on the wall of a disused parking garage. What does it does it mean to paint "Led Zep" on a wall

now? John Bonham has been dead since 1980; the group disbanded not long after. Instead of writing their own name, someone felt it was important to make this mark: writing a band logo on a brick wall. Yet the gesture is intensely personal; a declaration of one's taste in music also expresses a social position and a philosophy towards life. 4 The degree to which we identify with bands, recording artists or certain musical genres is profound and complex. We can't imagine someone identifying with, say, films genres, in such a primal way. Saying "I like westerns," is not the same as saying, "I like country and western." There are vast webs of associations that emerge from such utterances.

The singer sits hunchbacked on a stool. She seems far away, perhaps in a trance. Her face is in front of the microphone. Eyes closed, nose crinkled up, her mouth, open. The jaw pumps up and down with a muscular tightness. Now and then, she throws her head back violently, removing her hair from her face. When she is not singing, she turns away from the mike and breathes deeply. Her left arm jerks up and down, punctuating the downbeat with each descent. Fingers splayed. Her right hand sways back and forth, marking the tempo. Periodically her fingers curl, forming or releasing a fist. She draws her hands together in front of her chest, as if she is holding someone's severed head between her palms. She lifts her chin. Her mouth forms a perfect O.

1987. I am sitting in a coffee shop in Calgary with a friend from the UK when the song "Dreams" by Fleetwood Mac starts playing on the radio. "My god," he sighed, "ten years ago I was listening to this. Then my girlfriend played *God Save the Queen* for me. The Sex Pistols changed my life." Music can do things like that. It seems impossible now that *Rumours* and *Never Mind the Bollocks* were released the same year. Ten years later, in 1987, I found it sort of pathetic that people still dressed up as punks, as if they were trying to crash a party that had been over ages ago. Now, in 2000, punks have been loitering around for over twenty years. The squeegee-toting teenagers I see jockeying street corners between red lights are young enough that they could have had punks for parents. Punk is not just a style now, but a *life style*. Punks are a tribe; a social group with a history and a belief system all their own.

****

The t-shirt reads: "Become what you are." It's the slogan for a tattoo shop I visit and I like what it implies. It's as if the tattoos are already there, under you skin, just waiting for a chance to bleed through and finally become visible to the outside world.

What is fascinating to me about squeegee punks, and any number of people who have tattooed and pierced themselves into the margins, is that they have willed otherness upon themselves. Growing up queer in the working-class (and reputedly tough) western Canadian suburb of Forest Lawn, I was very conscious of my difference from the start. I tried to will myself into normality, or at least into invisibility as a compromise. I am sure that this was also true of the South Asian immigrants who passed like shadows against the gray locker-lined halls. But here are these young white (and straight?) people who refuse to play the game. This is how I choose to understand them at least: that they have flushed much of western culture's value system down the drain. I feel like going up to them and saying, "You can't see it, but under my skin, I am tattooed from head to toe."

I never really listened to punk in the late seventies, but preferred the more prog rock stylings of Yes and Genesis, or the full-on glamorama that was Bowie and Bolan. It is weird how strongly the budding proto-gays and lesbians of the seventies, who would blossom into queers in the eighties, were all fixated with Bowie and Patti Smith. One of my friends who was in a drug and alcohol rehabilitation program in the eighties told me that in all the straight groups sang Beatles' songs, while the gays and lesbians performed Bowie medleys.

Now, I would never want to be accused of saying something as wrong-headed as "celebrities belong to the people". But on the other hand, this text is partially articulating music for those who have always been presumed to be dumb and inarticulate: that faceless mass of listeners who we refer to

more or less pejoratively as fans. I am not talking about music per se, but about how music is used. Although we love recording artists, we regularly amputate music from its maker and make it ours. This allows us the freedom to reinvest it with a whole new set of meanings. 5 How else can you explain why someone would write "Led Zep" on a wall today? How else can you explain why gays and lesbians were shattered when Bowie went from bisexual to straight at what was a pivotal and defining moment for the vilification of gays and lesbians. 6

When we hear the voice, we move to a place without words. Time denies either future or past: we move sideways into this moment. Firmly and comfortably inside our bodies. The experience is like that felt when one shits, pisses, sneezes or has an orgasm. It feels almost like singing itself.

Sex and drugs and rock 'n' roll. This text is also partially about pleasure: the pleasure of living in the moment. That sacred, drug-induced, orgasmic moment where you aren't thinking about the future or past, but are securely embedded in a series of ever unfolding now-now-now's that open up into infinity.

It seems absurd that we can talk about the pleasure of music in the same way that we talk about drugs and sex. But for those of us who need music in that special way, it doesn't seem strange at all. It's the Cult of the Hit Song: that special song that you play over and over because it makes the hair stand up on the back of your neck. For fifteen minutes, it becomes the soundtrack of your life. I did it when I was a kid and I still do it now (most recently with *Saturday* by Yo La Tengo). The rush of pure pleasure still feels the same. 7

The needles are pushed into the skin. Each one evokes a different sensation. This one is a prickle of pain, like a pin prick. This one feels cold, or hot. A throbbing ache. A carpenter's nail breaking the skin. An electric shock. A tightening muscle. Distributed across the body, the array of pins creates a feeling of neither pain nor pleasure, but of INTENSITY. They remind you that the

body is a field with which to receive information.

        A bunch of young, hippie kids are sleeping in a Volkswagen van parked on my street. What kind of music do they listen to? What are their three or four life-defining albums? These hippie kids are young enough that they could have hippie grandparents. But of course they don't. Families don't exist anymore. In a world where youth is free, you are allowed to choose the parents you want — once you have disposed of your biological ones.

        The youth revolution of the sixties was not a failure, but its meaning can be misinterpreted. It was about the liberation of the young. The young have been free ever since. It's not so much that you can't trust anyone over thirty, but that once you're over thirty, you are no longer a recipient of the benefits of youth rebellion. You are no longer free.

Life is organized by sound.

        Music is being segregated again. POP is quarantined from ALTERNATIVE. It reminded me of 1979, when confused record store clerks in Forest Lawn had ROCK and NEW WAVE and PUNK sections alongside COUNTRY and JAZZ. It's curious what twenty years can do to the record bins. Now Elvis Costello, Sting and Laurie Anderson have slid into POP whereas The Jam, The Sex Pistols and Joy Division have been recuperated by ALTERNATIVE.

        I dream of a record store where there is no segregation. Where black and white music come together. Where SOUL, HIP-HOP, TECHNO and ALTERNATIVE commingle with JAZZ, BLUES, COUNTRY and POP. Where you look for music according to its name, without having to understand genre.

****

        I was worried that my taste in music would become frozen; that I wouldn't successfully make the leap from the eighties to the nineties. I would remain a curious fossil playing the same records for decades to come. Not long ago, a reunited Supertramp came to town. Musically, the nineties were partially about reunions due to financial obligations. I am glad that I am not overly interested in the reunion of Fleetwood Mac, Supertramp, The Eagles, The Sex Pistols, Duran Duran and other musical franchises. [8]

Last week, I went and saw a Japanese pop band that blends Motown with Bollywood movie soundtracks; that combines contemporary dance music with French yé-yé. The audience was a mixture of Asians and whites, not everyone was young and I saw other queers there. The band didn't really play. They just sang along with a bunch of video projections. Over the course of the evening the lead singer changed from one spectacular costume to another. I think this is what the new millennium will be like. Musicianship will be replaced by stage antics. Songwriting will be replaced by electronic spectacle. Authenticity will be replaced by pastiche and parody, and musical genres/eras/identities will be blended and distilled into strange unpredictable cocktails.

A deaf boy once told me that he danced by feeling the beat. Sound is a vibration. If you could sing higher than the highest note, it would become light. Lower than the lowest, your voice becomes touch. When I sing, everything converges in my chest. Lines emerge from my sternum and suck the world in. When I can feel the world resting in my chest, I know I am singing well.

Nelson Henricks Spring 2000

Notes

1   In 1978 or '79 I missed my chance to see Supertramp at McMahon Stadium in Calgary during the "Breakfast in America" tour. Two of my friends, Laura and Judy, went to the concert on acid. They came home exhausted and sunburned after sitting all day on the black rubber tarp that was stretched over the stadium's infield. I think by then my infatuation with Supertramp had waned sufficiently that I didn't regret missing the show. For the occasion, Judy had a t-shirt made at the mall. It was robin's-egg blue and, in glittering individual letters, she had had the word "Supertramp" ironed onto it. Laura remarked that walking around with the word "Supertramp" stretched across your tits could be grossly misinterpreted. The t-shirt was relegated to the bottom drawer of her dresser, never to be seen again.

2   I earned my criminal record changing the price tag on a copy of The Who's *Tommy* (not the movie soundtrack, the original recording). I was charged for fraud, fingerprinted and fined as an adult, only three days after my eighteenth birthday. I lost my nerve for shoplifting after this.

3   I think that *The Wall*, circa 1979/80, would have to be the fifth great album on The List.

4   Or Exhibit B: Any number of young men who make public displays of themselves by driving around in cars with loud music blaring out the windows. Over the past several weeks, there have been repeated sightings of a middle-aged man in a convertible playing (and singing along with!) *Crime of the Century* at volume levels that exceed the limits of public decency.

5   This is simultaneously profitable and terrifying for artists. Terrifying, because, in the most extreme cases, this transaction can be deadly (Charles Manson, Mark David Chapman, etc.).

6   As evidence, I cite Todd Haynes revenge epic *Velvet Goldmine*. This indictment seems to be the only substantial content of the movie, and makes it easier to understand why Bowie didn't allow his songs to be used in the soundtrack.

7   Throughout the writing and revising of this text, this song has been updated. Here are some of the others that appeared in this paragraph: "Cut You Hair" by Pavement, "Substitute" by The Who, "Ella Guru" by Captain Beefheart, "Music Sounds Better With You" by Stardust, "Tracy" by Mogwai, "Chicken with its Head Cut Off" by Magnetic Fields, "Out of Control" by The Chemical Brothers, etc., etc., etc.

8   Pink Floyd are a sad example of "the-band-as-franchise", spurting out a series of products that don't seem to be the result of any creative endeavour. The necrophilic reunion of The Beatles was also fascinating in so far as it occurred in virtual space. The release of outtakes and butchered remixes featured in *Anthologies 1, 2* and *3* seemed to destabilize The Beatles, revealing cracks and holes in the solid polished surfaces of their musical edifice. But that is another story.

John Latham: the Incidental Person

Jürgen Harten

John Latham is fighting for a cause. Seldom has an outsider persisted so stubbornly to put his radically independent output at the disposal of the community. It may be said that his work is an expression of his life, and ultimately it is the life that matters. Yet self-realisation has wider implications for him: He feels affected by a general predicament and this is what he spells out, in the course of his work.

In his search for an alternative vision of the world and of himself he has exposed the ingrained habits of perception. As long as he remains alone in taking this view he will continue to assert that his predicament is inseparable from ours. Our failure to understand accounts for John Latham's isolation, and counter-pointing the reasons underlying this failure has become an integral part of his work. He outlines the option whereby if we are not to sacrifice life to the relentless pressures brought on by an ill-conceived approach, we may choose to adopt the alternative.

What has John Latham's endeavour to do with Art? Could we find an answer by examining the question: What means can be considered viable today for making art?

The conventional craft is still alive; it is common for artists, be they painter or sculptor, to depend on traditions and styles as if their assumption of this could somehow insulate them from unease and doubt about the meaning-fulness of their endeavour, putting the responsibility for such problems on critics and others who have made promotion their business.

Faith in the avant garde, that spearhead of art history, is now badly shaken. A certain immodesty in art has emerged as one of our options: this may involve reviewing the pretensions of art, but would this imply a deterioration in the cognitive potential of art compared to other disciplines? A 'Farewell to Art', to quote Werner Schmalenbach's recent controversial phrase? Art reduced to a mere supporting role?

Accepting the implications of his work John Latham has gone further than acknowledged art. For more than twenty years his work has been developing on a line parallel to action painting, assemblage, happenings, primary structures and conceptual art. But as he remains aware of the most diverse connotations he has gradually refined the painterly and sculptural means to a point where context can be recognised as constituting half the work. In his view Art is an Event. As his interest in art is focused on what happens through art, his interest in the event advances the conception of the work. Art leads to a preoccupation with events and their further development.

Experience has taught Latham that whenever he opens his mind to the image-generating process he is energised by a directing impulse. Thus throughout the history of art it is the agitated openly-structured paintings, demonic works, those of El Greco and Van Gogh above all, that affect him as a reflection of man's nature. Whereas religious cosmic images are usually regarded as mere parables Latham finds that the creative process is directly bound up with the cosmic processes. In extreme cases the image therefore becomes an immediate representation of the structure of such processes.

This may sound absurd — but only if one assumes a parabolic type of relationship between mind and matter. Latham argues, however, that this duality can now be seen to be inconsistent with reality. In parallel with Gregory and Kohsen who had been working on a psycho-physical cosmology Latham evolved a time-base theory of his own. If in recent years physicists have been unable to describe fundamental reality unequivocally in terms of matter, then, Latham states that there is no longer any need to proceed on the assumption of that duality. Does this imply that the human mind fails to come to terms with reality, or on the contrary, that we are only just discovering its true nature? The determination of man is not something that can be elucidated by physics. The artist, however, is concerned in a practical way with the motivation of human behaviour. Hypothetically linking the physicist's knowledge with the artist's experience Latham demonstrates that the behaviour of both matter and the human mind is motivated by events.

It would be difficult here to make a detailed critical analysis of Latham's system. His formula carries ethical connotations, and this seems to be the crucial point. It is only going to succeed if man turns out to be susceptible to his cosmic determination, and is prepared to act in accordance with it. He does, in fact, when he stops asking "What is…" and begins to ask "What can you say by going on that…" Otherwise prospects look grim. Man strikes Latham as a disease organism threatened with self-extermination, and in this age of nuclear weaponry we know that the "smallest error in concept can provoke the biggest of disasters."

It remains doubtful, though, if the message is getting through. The work constitutes a self-contained system, but as such makes allowance for only two conclusions. Failure to grasp the premise registers as a faulty function. Can it be possible for freedom to change to adhere to a predetermined pattern? For any question there would be one pair of alternatives. Is man failing in his destiny because of his reliance on obsolete concepts? Or is he falling back on obsolete concepts because he has failed his destiny? The formulation can overcome this quandary. One key term is supplied by theology: Kairos, a new era, a time of fulfilment is dawning — the religion of physics, the world as a work of art.

Latham is inclined to see all his work from 1954 when he produced the first spray painting, before the Institute for the Study of Mental Images was founded — in terms of time-base, though the verbal shape of this theory was arrived as in 1973, the outcome of constant revision of the ever-broadening context of an ongoing, non-repetitive work. Latham is an observer, detachment is his method of self-discovery. He conceives the observer's distance as a differential, events are perceived relatively to that of the observation. He is not surprised to learn from experience that, where the time span of an event exceeds the comprehension of human consciousness,

it is the observer who feels he is being observed, however if the time span falls below the minimum level the observation will be by inference. Reification of events is argued on a different level of event as a disruption of human motivations occasioned by motivation interfering with the habitual processes maintaining life. This has led him to employ destructive techniques to transform objects, and thus by implication habits. He detaches himself, the better to expose their destiny. These activities are complimented by a constructive approach alerting attention to the "traps and surprises for the unwary expectation", as well as "the equation in graphic terms", visual images as a pre-verbal state; finally his formulations can be received as conceptual information.

Time-base conceptualisation is found to trigger off a chain reaction, a reordering of values. Relationships of correspondence supercede separation, a different form of communication abolishes the lack of mutual comprehension. If fundamentally all is one, if an all-embracing range of events assures each of the parts of its place in the whole, if we were to reassess the ephemeral nature of our existence, then the various branches of science would be subject to a rational collaboration, the abuse of money based on submission to the demands of the immediate will come to an end, industrial society will no longer have to waste productive energies in suicidal competition, academics will appreciate the narrowness of their outlook, education will preserve man's natural creativity, and in all fields time-based techniques will complement materialistic approaches. This is probably the first time that an artist has ever evolved such a far-reaching and practical solution. It can come true if people are unprejudiced and independent as artists are given scope for creative work in all fields. John Latham is fighting to get social recognition for a new profession: that of the Incidental Person — an intelligent and creative counsellor and watchdog.

This essay was first published in 1975 in a catalogue accompanying the exhibition *John Latham State of Mind* at Städische Kunsthalle Düsseldorf, September-October 1975.

whatever happened...?

3 Early States from *RIO (Reflective Intuitive Organism)*, 1983

John Latham

initial condition:

According to written history there has never been a specific way in which to understand the difference between systems of belief, eg. faith and non-faith, art and language, art and science. The world looks to be a kind of free-for-all where one sort of power is sure to win in the end at the expense of anything else worth pursuing. Here, though, is what has happened.

'physical'?

The twentieth Century kickoff was the discovery that everything is quantised. Then from General Relativity it appeared that one could find that at a certain point Everything = Nothing: "Gravitational collapse", according to physicist John Wheeler, was "the greatest crisis *ever to face physics*". The crisis has   persisted into the twenty-first century, but now the news is out. The concept   of dimensionality was flawed — a difference exists between 'time' and 'space' dynamics.

verbal logic

The findings in physics made it awkward for philosophy: the problem has   been knowing where to start. Ludwig Wittgenstein came to Cambridge in   1912 with the bright idea that language could be systematised by way of   atomic propositions; but when no member of the literati could specify such   a proposition, verbal 'logic' itself fell apart. This problem is now a macro- challenge to all theorists, art critics included.

meta....

If harmony in society depends on the common integration of the 'one', of the unity bhind the multiplicity of phenomena, the language of the poets may be more important than that of the scientists.

Werner Heisenberg (1)

From the mid-twentieth Century, 1951 to be exact, the literate track and the art track each began to follow that of physics. Where in a singularity Everything = Nothing, all art came to be on a par with zero action and verbal 'logic' not logical. What proved to be the flaw was *reason according to spatial appearances...*

Wordcraft or lingua franca (together with its offspring, mathematics), is the only medium in practical affairs for understanding the world, the net effect being still visible in the drift from Plato's *art* to Aristotle's *array of academic subject matters*. An artificial division between *things in space* and *ideas* (which are not attributable to the space-based framework) became the assumed reality.

From early attempts to discover the source of *idea* — mysteries, spirit, the *informing system* — people looked to the sky for signs, their cybernetics derived from stone observatories and celestial charts. But these too were found illusory, and traditions of prophets and cults began to guide beliefs. Now, at the end of this line, reason, as the key product of language, also breaks down at the pinpoint of physics, where it is now "all to play for".(2)

meanwhile

To follow the collapse of reason and the "death of God", what then..?
Did we then find out how to put all that right?
We did indeed: **money** would be the new medium of rationality, the engine
to deliver the future. We are in the present, and how is that working out..?
Has Coherence (the centuries had been feeling their way towards it) been
showing any progress..?
Electronic age notwithstanding, only fission reactors for power and fission
actors of the mind are profitable. Lethally equipped populations have begun
to swarm. Remember *Finnegans Wake*..?
Here Comes Ebola.

the currency

Shot up, head in screen, writers fill up pages; publishers pump out texts,
galleries install more debris, stadia resound with more noise... media
bifurcate wildly to gobble up attention-meal... drawn, it often seems,
towards further disintegration of the organism.

RIO (Reflective Intuitive Organism), 1983

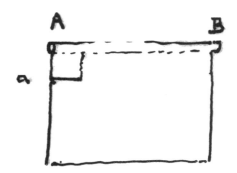

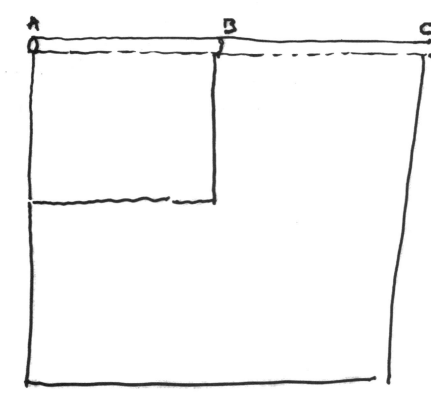

art?

Hasn't the written word been responsible for navigating the ship post 1951..?
What if all this is only a nightmare... product of a flawed, literary, common-but-disinformed sense..?

The only approach independent of the language and money autocracy manifests itself in the affronts of paradigm shifters. Behind its apparent indifference, art has been alone in being able to deride all of it. The hangup is that wealthy litterised society keeps minders and handlers in charge of its artist sniffer dogs so that you don't hear anything unpredictable. Year of the Artist: 'a thousand artists in a thousand places' is a sponsored extension of the nightmare. Off the leash though, a shift arrived at a different interpretation, a dimensionality of 'event'.

constructing the basic (T) diagram

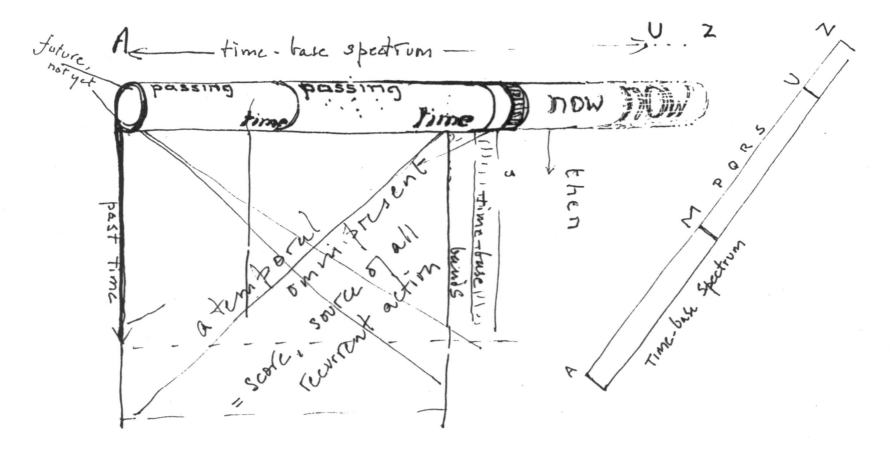

'event' structure?

After art's ascent into 'Nothing' in 1951 what came through was a logic which traces minimality in terms of 'time' which had otherwise been unthinkable.
If time is what art finds it to be, history dates back to a *proto-universe* (proto-U), chronologically anterior to 'big bang' cosmology (U). A credible proto-universe, arising from and instantly returning to a *nonextended state* of zero action puts art activity and cosmic dynamics on the same map. As for objects in space, the 'U' event has to be 'time' extended before there is distance as space, and the function of an 'atemporal score' (natural to music) is seriously event-structural. But theory in physics admits no such state.

The dynamics which work for people have little to do with the dynamics of physics. Ears hear a piece of music which has a beginning and an end; the score of the piece, which pre-exists it, is co-present with and informs the performance. However, they do not hear the score, nor does it come to an end when the performance is over. Listeners need not bother to reflect on the ordering of what they hear, they have it by direct sense. This order is a function of the score, and is moreover an ordering of time-bases (frequencies, intervals, repeats). There are here three time-related components each of which are separate and belong to a coherent point to line to plane dimensionality, having no *necessary structural spatial component whatever*. In this framework the initial units are extendedness and nonextendedness, and the dynamics, impulse and discharge of impulse.

the basic (T) diagram

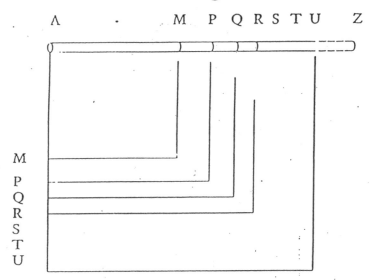

Λ   ·   M P Q R S T U   Z

M
P
Q
R
S
T
U

A turning cylinder on an axis AZ provides a point/line/plane progression where
The line AZ is a succession of points:
The point A on AU represents the time-base of a Proto-Least Event (c.10^{-23} sec.)
The point M on AU represents the time-base of a specious present (c.10^{-1} sec.)
The point P on AU represents the time-base of a body event P (c.10^{9} sec. or 30 years)
The point Q on AU represents the time-base of a boundary of reason in extended events
The points R, S, T on AU represent the time-base of 'intuition', 'conscience'
The point U on AU represents the time-base of the Universe as extended event

The line AU represents all extended events (points) on their time-base coordinate.
The square of the line AU will represent the (nonextended*) atemporal omnipresent
from which all events within AU are ordered, as from a score.

The phrase 'the people' is used of a society composed of Persons P, (body event),
        partially of Persons PQ, QP, (reflective, rational),
        intermittently of Persons PQR, RQP, RPQ (intuitive)

Such a society follows rules laid down from within the band Q, its rational institutions,
- acknowledges the influence of communications from R, S, T as art, and
- may recognise communications from the S, T, U bands as approaching
        comprehensive 'truth'.

* The plane (AU)² is 'score', a nonextended co-present with extended events. A semantic ambiguity persists in language, which can use the word atemporal but has no grammatical form to express it or functional relations between the concepts of clock time, time-base and atemporal omnipresent, – except as art.

(T) diagram

The flaw described above in 'physical' shows up when the framework of 'event' discloses itself in the visual field. The initial visual, *Early State from RIO*, 'opens the account' in its first picomoment: a 'nonextended' state as 'white' becomes definitively extended white when hit by a point mark black.

Similarly the dynamics contained within a score are 'nonextended'; the ordering (of sounds or events) from the score is informed via time-base sets of recurrent states in clock-time — time as a count of time-base units. The performance occurs in a *slice of time mediated via a body-event*, which in turn belongs within the world event U_{now}, a latterday progeny of an insistently recurrent, accretive proto-universe.

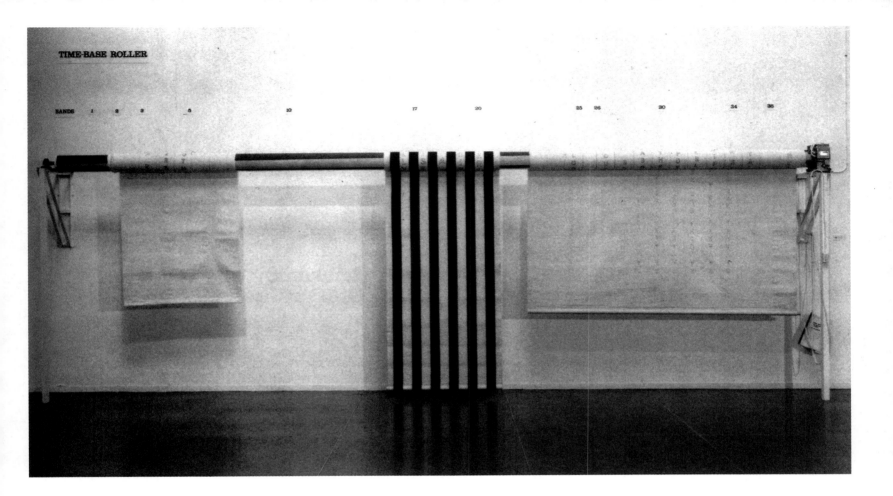

next

'The new physics' of the twentieth century still has its uses within its 3-D+ convention for *one time dimension only*. The argument has moved now to a platform where there are two alternatives: a dimensionality from "art proposing three time-related components" which constitute an envelope cosmology, and a theory emanating from Imperial College's department of theoretical physics proposing *two time-related components*.

As this comparison is just beginning to get hot, here's the verbostop.

NOTES
(1) Werner Heisenberg, *Natural Law and the Structure of Matter*, a speech given on the Hill of Pnyx, Athens, 3rd June 1964. Text published by Rebel Press, Devon, England.
(2) see Isham & Butterfield 1999, in *Physics meets Philosophy at the Planck Scale*.

All images by John Latham.

John Cage's

"Art at its most significant is a distant **EARLY WARNING SYSTEM** that can always tell the old culture what is beginning to happen to it"
Marshall McLuhan

On November 1st

On August 29th   **1952**   At the Maverick Concert Hall, in Woodstock,
Upper New York State the pianist David Tudor
gave the first performance of *4' 33"* by John Cage

The United States exploded
the first hydrogen bomb

The 10.4 megaton device,
part of OPERATION IVY
was codenamed Mike,
and weighed 82 tons. The

Tudor sat down, opened the piano lid, and played
nothing for thirty seconds, closed the lid, opened
it again, and played nothing for two minutes and
twenty three seconds. He closed the lid a second
time, opened it again and, again, played nothing,
this time for one minute and twenty seconds. This
performance constituted the **GROUND ZERO** of the post-war avant garde. the shockwaves from
Cage's so-called silent piece was experienced far
beyond the concert hall in Woodstock

of the test, Elugelab Island,
was completely destroyed

Survivors and witnesses of
atomic and nuclear explosions
often describe the experience
of the world turning

In 1950 Cage's friend Robert Rauschenberg
painted a white circle on a city map, and called it
Mother of God, a clear reference to nuclear
destruction. After this he embarked on a series of
all-black and all-   **WHITE**   paintings

at the time of explosion

The threat of nuclear attack
demanded the development
of sophisticated technological
systems for detecting potentially
hostile activities. Radar and
computer screens in such
early-warning systems were

For Cage these paintings were not empty or
nihilistic, but acted as

FIELDS OF
FOCUS

or environmental surfaces upon which dust could
settle or shadows fall. Cage felt these works gave
him 'permission' to compose his silent piece

in which critical attention
needed to be paid to the
events unfolding in front
of the operator

Crucial to the success of
such early warning systems
was the capacity to detect
the difference between
meaningless and random
signals, known as

Despite its being referred to as Cage's 'silent
piece', *4' 33"* is not about silence, but about
questioning the difference between

NOISE

and music. Deprived of a recognisably musical
experience the audience was constrained to pay
attention to the noise of the environment, which
became the work

and actual information

A number of different images
were invoked for the cloud
formations in atomic and nuclear
explosions, such as raspberries,
brains and cauliflowers.
Eventually the motif of the

Soon after writing *4′ 33″* Cage started to become
interested in

MUSHROOM

and fungi collecting and cooking. This could
be dangerous to his friends as, early on, he
occasionally served them poisonous species,
fortunately without fatalities occuring

cloud became the accepted
description of the
phenomenon

In Plato's *Phaedrus*, writing
is described as a

As a source of nourishment and a means to
mystical wisdom, as well as a source of danger
and possible fatal poisoning, fungi are ambivalent
objects, both poison or remedy or

PHARMAKON

both a remedy and a cure

Jacques Derrida describes
nuclear weapons as a
'phenomenon' whose essential
feature is that of being
fabulously textual, through and
through. Nuclear weaponry
depends, more than any other
weaponry of the past, it seems,
upon structures of information and

Cage's was a crucial influence on many artists
and movements, from Fluxus through to net.art,
who have directly concerned themselves with
questions of information and **COMMUNICATION**

The demands of nuclear
vigilance led to the
development of much of the
technology of modern
real-time

Cage's emphasis on the roles played by the
audience and the environment in making a work
of art was of great importance to later
developments such as performance art as
well as contemporary concepts of   **INTERACTIVE**   media and art, such as net.art

computing, including video
displays, networking,
graphical user interfaces,
analogue-to-digital and
digital-to-analogue conversion
techniques

The continual circulation of
messages in the high tech
systems of nuclear vigilance
is intended to deter the

Like Scheherezade we keep talking,   **APOCALYPSE**
communicating to deter the

the missives or missiles of
which are fatally marked
'return to sender'

An Endless Insurrection
Gilles Lazare

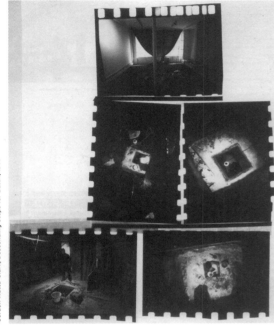

Gordon Matta-Clark, *Descending Steps for Batan*, 1977

Whither are we moving? Away from all the suns? Are we not plunging continually? Backward, sideward, forward, in all directions? Is there still any up or down?
Friedrich Nietzsche, *The Gay Science*

The summit of experience, or revelation, is not attained by singular effort, but by exertions sustained and committed in the knowledge that time and careful tending bring fruit to the vine. It is tempered by sudden sharp shifts of fate and periodic upheavals, those moments which jolt us from complacency and certainty, force us to take risks and live in a moment of radical consciousness.

In the rational West a confrontation with ritual, whether traditional or foreign, often brings the temptation to succumb to laughter – a welling up of primal energy seeking to veil a fundamental incomprehension, even intolerance, of a faith one does not have oneself. Laughter, in this case, can often be replaced by horror or indignation, as each response seeks to deny the meaning of an act which remains beyond the limits of one's own order of representation; excessive, proximate and unstable.

At the crux of a new century there is a visible dissipation of faith in the traditional religions which we have inherited yet spent the last two generations erasing as either hidebound tradition or as moderating forces in an increasingly judgemental culture. As a social glue binding the fabric of society, faith has been replaced by entertainment and consumerism. People are more often united by their desire to conform to fashion, taste and style than by a spiritual hunger, or need for something beyond our overweening preoccupation with sating the senses. An expression of this can be seen in the storefront Christian ministries of South London promising their congregations more money, a better career, or love and marriage through prayer. They are understandable delusions, the frustrations of those excluded from an economic boom, but would the God of Job and Jonah respond to such supplicants? It is as though we have adopted a course of drowning ourselves in an orgy of denying spiritual curiosity, of numbing the delicacy of speculation through a dogged pursuit of the merely rational. Sensuality has been replaced with saturation. Mystery is just a mask.

And yet, on a scale of participation possibly never witnessed before, there is an explosion of interest and desire for knowledge – for 'truth' and answers – previously guarded as the property of the elite. Popular science on television and in books fuel the public imagination for certainty, truth and fixity despite reservations as to its accuracy from within the multitude of scientific communities themselves. As perhaps our heritage dictates, the questions proposed remain the same: we are still seeking to explain our existence, but more through the investigations of science than the beliefs of religion. The babel of sects and cults associated with religion has been replaced with that of competing disciplines, each vying for pre-eminence and funding.

Gordon Matta-Clark, *Days End*, 1975. Courtesy of Electronic Arts Intermix, New York

But human nature being what it is, an enlightenment in our knowledge of the physical world has not necessarily extended to embrace our social and cultural hierarchies. A consequence of this shift from faith to rational materialism is that what cannot be answered within our new terms of reference is no longer valid, even false. These fragments of 'untruth' are swept away as though without value and the knowledge gained over generations dismissed as mere superstition. Furthermore, as folk memory and tradition suffer for their perceived naïvete, a culture of binarism has begun to exchange more speculative systems of interpretation for a cascade of hierarchical empiricism. The impartiality and rational 'truth' of science has achieved a sanctity of its own.

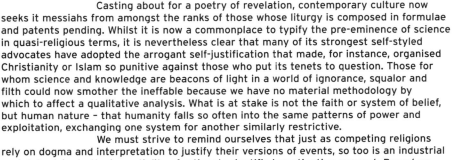

Casting about for a poetry of revelation, contemporary culture now seeks it messiahs from amongst the ranks of those whose liturgy is composed in formulae and patents pending. Whilst it is now a commonplace to typify the pre-eminence of science in quasi-religious terms, it is nevertheless clear that many of its strongest self-styled advocates have adopted the arrogant self-justification that made, for instance, organised Christianity or Islam so punitive against those who put its tenets to question. Those for whom science and knowledge are beacons of light in a world of ignorance, squalor and filth could now smother the ineffable because we have no material methodology by which to affect a qualitative analysis. What is at stake is not the faith or system of belief, but human nature – that humanity falls so often into the same patterns of power and exploitation, exchanging one system for another similarly restrictive.

We must strive to remind ourselves that just as competing religions rely on dogma and interpretation to justify their versions of events, so too is an industrial society's claim to the impartiality of rational scientific investigation suspect. Bound up in the voracious industrial exploitation of the planet, it has impoverished humanity's place within the ecosystem, attempting to manipulate our situation and extract us from its holistic chain, ridiculing and displacing those cultures attempting to live in balance with it. Science per se is no more than the quest for knowledge – but scientists and their employers within companies and governments are themselves not without motivation, greed, stupidity and ignorance – the products of our society as much as the priests of the Inquisition were of theirs. Just as the Church of the Middle Ages and the Renaissance sought to stamp out whatever it could not control, rational materialists and their apologists must be wary lest they too become the victims of hubris, without the *insight* to see beyond the limits of their own horizons. It could be a tragedy from which there is no chance of redemption – for anyone, or anything.

But nevertheless, two centuries after the Enlightenment, rational objectivity itself is still unable to satisfy that lack, that unfocussed, unfathomable primal desire at the root of the human condition; people are driven to believe, to place their trust in some notion of order, if not science and capitalism (and these two are inextricably linked, like an antagonistic pair, or two knife-fighters locked in a tango of death), then something, anything. Just as late twentieth century consumerism discovered niche marketing and personally tailored shopping, so too have faith and religion (and perhaps even aspects of science) been torn apart and reconfigured by each and every one of us in our own way – unwilling to believe in nothing at all (a step on the logical path of Darwinian evolutionary theories), yet too proud to allow ourselves to be the minutiae of something infinitely bigger than ourselves (God, or even an unthinking, unfeeling, not-conscious Darwinian Universe). Is this evidence of a growing self-confidence in the power of our own belief, or of a disturbing trend towards a sense of dislocation from community and socialisation?

Gordon Matta-Clark, *Substrait (Underground Dailies)*, 1976. Courtesy of Electronic Arts Intermix, New York

Ritual has for countless generations been part of the means by which culture, knowledge, beliefs and traditions have been passed along, for good or ill. But what does it mean to us now, we who can pick and choose our heritage from the many multi-cultural options? Could it perhaps reveal to us something of the now rather than the past? Is ritual constructed around an awakening, consciousness or awareness – or is it blind – a dumbing of our ability to penetrate the thick gloom we have called 'Progress', locking us into a ceaseless and senseless repetition of what has been before? Are we foundering upon an altar of detritus, scrabbling vainly after Walter Benjamin's Angel of History and contributing ever more (with our own feeble efforts to keep pace, make sense, try harder) to the storm blast which carries it away from us?

Or could it be that there is an alternative – a side-stepping of fate and despair? A use of our forebears' tools combined with our own to split this path – to rupture and invert time, space and order? Are we dealing with an *excession* that is in fact not outside, but wholly within?

●●●●●●●●●●●●●●●●●●●●●●●●●●●●●●●

I defy any lover of painting to love a canvas as much as a fetishist loves a shoe.
Georges Bataille,
L'esprit moderne et le jeu des transpositions

Debates on 'use value' have swung to and fro since Marx published *Das Kapital*, yet it was the writer and thinker Georges Bataille who revealed the comparative paucity of these debates and injected into them a paradox: that the practices of sacrifice, potlatch and expenditure are more fundamentally crucial to the flow of energy in a system than acquisition or production. Walter Benjamin, too, addressed these issues with a notion of 'unproductive use', specifically in relation to art and cultural activity. At the beginning of the twenty first century, in the throes of astonishing economic growth in the West, we are still torn between rational expenditure, the gathering forces of conservativism and a more primal need to take risks, to squander, to gamble and commit the products of our efforts to a kind of conflagration, a consumption, to free us from the shackles of a mundane existence.

Ritual, religion, faith, culture – the 'invisible' commodities of our global economic society: as we seek to inflate our worth materially are we not in danger of upsetting a strategic balance by relegating them to minor roles in the structure of our civilization? In our fear of the unknown and the unquantifiable, of what we choose to ignore, are we not likely in the reckoning to discover a hole in the accounts?

I am intrigued by this "paradox of absolute utility", as Bataille would have it: that nourishment of the self can come as much (even more) from divestment of the products of labour. This form of consumption via destruction is the zenith to the nadir of consumption via consumerism or baseless acquisition. It insists upon a detachment from the value of commodity in favour of the ritual of sacrifice, of maintaining the flow of materials within the cycle of creation and destruction, of avoiding the entropy of acquisition, stagnation and death. Just as Kali destroys the universe to renew it, so there is a thread running through human history of reckless, profligate expenditure in the form of a sacred economy.

Classical theatre is generally perceived to have developed out of the ritual celebrations of the Bacchic mysteries in Ancient Attica – over time it became partly secularised within Athenian society, caught up in the radical developments of science, philosophy and politics. Maintaining its relevance to mainstream Athenian culture via its popularity, its religious context and its engagement with developments in knowledge and learning, this art form provided a crucial environment for bridging politics and culture. Art, in its wider sense, has also traversed the centuries, struggling to keep its place as a significant arena in the development of our society. And yet its vibrancy continues to contribute some of the hardest and most important questions we bear to face reality with. It exposes the essential banalities, the voids, the lack and emptiness of meaning so prevalent in contemporary life; it flirts with danger, with excess, even grappling with insanity, illness and death. It marshals enormous expenditures of time, materials, energy in the production of useless ephemera only to be recuperated in museums, collections and the trade of artifacts through the agency of *meaning*. And yet even so, there are moments when artworks, the products of kinds of personal ritual, manage to undermine the 'values' placed upon them by commodification in the museum and the academy. One such artist whose work remains, for me, on the brink of cultural value and reckless expenditure, is Gordon Matta-Clark.

•••••••••••••••••••••••••••••••

...the sacred is only a privileged moment of communal unity, a moment of the convulsive communication of what is ordinarily stifled.
Georges Bataille, *The Sacred*

Looking back more than twenty years and seen as a whole, Gordon Matta-Clark's work effects a collapse of external order into itself, an internalisation or inversion along a meridian, a degree zero. His cut is not just through the physical but the symbolic – unfolding the complex relationship of the domestic or small scale to the wider social space. Each cut is like a symbolic wound – a *vulnus*, an orifice, a Delphic oracle – the locus of a sublime communication or communion. He exposes the transmissible through a *punctum* in the skin of a system of logic and order which delineates and contains our space of representation, of property and hierarchy within society. Mankind is conceived and born into this world through a bloody orifice, a kind of wound, but not a site of damage. In Christian mythology, Christ's wounds are not just the evidence of his physical suffering, but are themselves the interface between his passion and his disciples' faith. Thus it was not just rational or logical that Saint Thomas had his faith renewed by touching Christ's body, entering through his wounds, it mirrored his rebirth into the world as a believer, a disciple.

That Matta-Clark chose to work with condemned buildings and often inaccessible spaces makes his legacy all the more powerful: he left no scars in the urban environment, a few *Building Cuts* are all that remain, absurd fragments of long since disappeared buildings which have no meaning in themselves, no value, but as loci of memory pointing to that which has vanished, been excised through humanity's remorseless

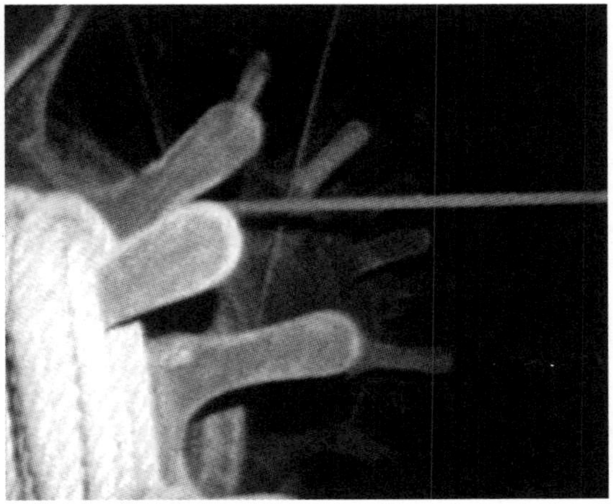

Gordon Matta-Clark, *Sous-Sols de Paris*, 1977. Courtesy of Electronic Arts Intermix, New York

drive for progress. Matta-Clark's films and photographic images of his projects, too, function as a horizon which flattens experience. The performances are oddly unmoving – their sense of danger and excess and the limits of endurance are faintly ridiculous. What they do achieve is the opposite of an experience: everything is reduced to the ephemeral, to the absent, the void, and in this lack we are faced with only ourselves, with what we can draw out from within through this puncture. It is a sublime communication precisely because it cannot simply be reduced to an experience, it refuses definition, representation. At the same time the concept of Matta-Clark's oeuvre can also be seen within the register of what Walter Benjamin styled *Profane Illumination* – a revolutionary force deriving from Matta-Clark's transfiguration of debris, or the abandoned. In a perverse twist, it corresponds to the idea of the Sacred as was being explored by Georges Bataille, Roger Callois and other members of the College of Sociology contemporaneously with Benjamin's own investigations into cultural production and revolution. What Matta-Clark's work deals with is the *trope* of experience rather than experience per se – this is why the force of his ideas remains powerful and transgressive even though it is no longer possible to physically experience the works themselves.

The energy released by Matta-Clark's work appears in his almost ritualistic attempts to transcend the sacred object of art – his work is figurative of contemporary practices that seek to break through the barrier that has kept the conception of the work of art chained to the *substantial*. Just as Benjamin had foreseen with the loss of *aura*, and Duchamp prefigured in both the concept of the *Ready-made* and his gender inversions in the guise of *Rrose Selavy*, the radical emptiness of Matta-Clark's oeuvre became the site of an epiphany that evades reification. Matta-Clark confronts us with an inversion – the cuts spilled forth an interiority to architecture that had not previously been considered; Matta-Clark unfolds the unspeakable, the guts, the very stuff of materiality. And it is no wonder that, just as his investigations and experiments trigger a dizzying vertigo propelling one from the rigid order of everyday life into the excess of the void, so he descended from the terrestrial to the cthonian world. Matta-Clark attempted the same unfolding, the same transfiguration of the earth, of the dirt and filth, as he had of architecture and the urban fabric.

There's moonlight at midday
There's sunshine at midnight
Light's beaming from above
No-one knows, no-one knows
No-one knows what really shines...
Goran Bregovic, *Mesecina* [Moonlight]

The constant thread weaving itself through Matta-Clark's work, through

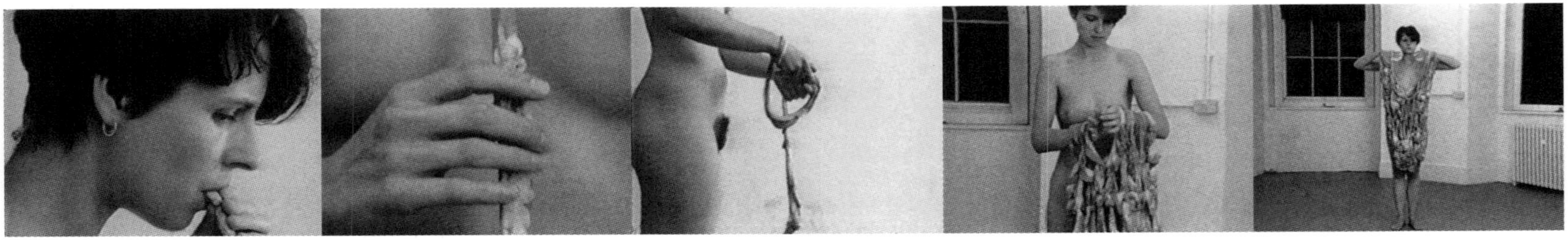

Jayne Parker, *K* (16mm, b&w 12mins, 1989)

all his experiments and investigations is the alchemy of transformation. He strove to transform base matter, detritus and dejecta, abandoned buildings and the debased through a process of uncovering, of revealing the nature of human relationships to space and matter. He privileged insight over vision, creating spaces that did not so much show the audience what he intended to evoke, as create the environment for feeling. This thread of transformation can be seen in his films, *Sous-Sols de Paris* and *Substrait*, as well as in the works *Descending Steps for Batan*, *Cherry Tree* and *Time Well*. His desire to knit communities together via a process of shared excess and consumption is again visible in his actions *Pig Roast* and *Cuisse de Boeuf*, both of which invoke the image of the carnevalesque – of the fool who becomes king for a day, and the king who gives away his wealth: a potlatch. Matta-Clark's fundamental need to pour out his energy into the world, to expend his worth is itself fundamentally at odds with the drift of mainstream culture towards ever more tightly-held property and a more rigidly stratified social structure. His work typifies that of someone for whom the blandishments of fame, money and peer acknowledgement are as nothing to the belief that no matter what one does, it is always in relation to a social ecology for which it should shine as a beacon of hope in a world abundant not just with food and goods, but also with misery and darkness.

Perhaps more significant than his role as an artist within the artworld, Gordon Matta-Clark's life was symbolic of the anguish – a passion – that so often drives creative production. His was not the work of someone who felt comfortably contained within a register or boundary, but that of someone who sought to smash the artifice of academicised and institutionalised disciplines, to break away and out from under the shadows of great men (and most importantly that cast by his father). His struggle was not with his own psychological image so much as with the ties of inherited social position, wealth, education and opportunity, inverting the emphasis on individual self-aggrandisement in favour of a practice that sought to foster community, to create communion with others. By refocussing attention on the overlooked, by rupturing the coherent fabric of representation, Matta-Clark injected into reality moments of vertigo primed for epiphany.

•••••••••••••••••••••••••••••••

Most of the obsessions I use are either my own or prevalent in society. Particularly the pain of self-destruction, the deluded arrogance of being chosen by God, and the craving for meaningful ritual amongst my own people.

Ron Athey, foreword to *Deliverance*

As a counterpoint to Matta-Clark, I would like to hint at another relationship to the sacred: the wild irreverence of Ron Athey. Brought up as a child within a tradition of inspired

Pentecostalists, Athey has vividly described his world of family members speaking in tongues, channelling spirits, prophecy and visions of the Virgin Mary, and of being the chosen of God, called to a ministry. As a performance artist Athey has since created a body of works that themselves are the sites of rupture, of transgressing the sanctity and integrity of the body. Tattooed, pierced and bound, Athey's performances reach beyond the spectacle of violence directed against the self, taking on the modes of ritual without valorising the endurance of pain or mysticizing the tribal neo-paganism of punk. In addition, Athey's HIV-positive status continually makes the attendance of his performances subtly unnerving – opening up a space of insecurity caused by the dread of contamination. Athey's performances embody a frisson of danger – raising the spectre of irrational fear triggered by proximity to blood, lymph and other body fluids, all of which we fear might somehow come into contact with us. That danger is perhaps not unrelated to the fear and apprehension that some felt who attended Matta-Clark's building projects, notably the form of vertigo caused in the project *Days End*, where parts of the pier floor were removed and visitors reported feeling drawn to its void, whilst co-incidentally wracked with terror.

The *solar annulus* is the intact anus... to which nothing sufficiently blinding can be compared except the sun, even though the *anus* is the *night*.
Georges Bataille, *The Solar Anus*

In his recent performance, *Solar Anus*, Athey becomes a living figure for Bataille's famous text and its mantra of "I AM THE SUN". With an alchemical sun tattooed around his anus, Athey proceeds to turn his back on the audience and pull an Ariadne's thread of pearls from inside himself; a defecation of white globules which suggests how base matter digests the "luminous violence" of the sun through a "scandalous eruption". Mystic traditions such as alchemy and the Kabbalah identify the Sun with intellect and the Moon with inspiration. Athey's performance affirms and yet inverts this order. It is ridiculous: a parody of the world and of literary reference. Sovereign, and seated upon a throne, he then proceeds to attach the flesh of his face with hooks to a large golden crown, more reminiscent of a jester's hat than a symbol of authority or divine right, and to fix dildos to the heels of his shoes. Auto-sodomizing his solar anus with these absurd spurs, a dizzying vertigo propels us into the void of this threshold between interior and exterior, this permeable orifice for the seen and the unseen. Shocking and yet again familiar, Athey provides a pivot around which our conceptions of suffering pleasure and pain are reconfigured, made complex and human. Accompanied by a hypnotic soundtrack, it is a ritual of use and *misuse* of the body, but never abuse. It is a sacralisation of our desires and weaknesses, an open wound rupturing the taboo of infection and inviting communion.

    Whilst firmly rooted in a (sub)culture of subversion, Athey reminds us that *pathology* is derived from the same root word and conceptual framework as *passion*: that anguish is not just the inspiration of artists but exists within everyone. By pushing the

rituals of sacrifice and mutilation into a different context – that of a Christianity not so far removed from the mainstream – he shatters the complacency which shrouds religion, which gives rise to the lie that it nurtures and protects us, both as individuals and communities. And he does so without rancour, contempt or bile, in a spirit of celebration and gentle criticism. Athey has responded to his Calling, but not as a minister of ignorance, instead he has woven a ministry of faith that binds his companions, his co-performers and audiences in mutual trust, that shares through excess a knowledge of humanity not predicated on power but on vulnerability. In suffering the puncturing of his body and those of his companions by each other, in sharing the acts of joy and rapture, Athey jolts us into a profound relation with each other as members of an audience, and beyond that as members of a community and society. In our sanitised society the visceral has been banished, the relations between life and death, between human and animal rendered in plastic and subjected to a regime of antibiosis. Athey reminds us of our inherent baseness, and that redemption exists, if at all, not in isolation and remoteness but in engagement with the stuff of life.

> **If I'm wrong… I hope it means I have to appear before God wearing a cheap costume-jewelry crown upon my head, and half a double-headed dildo hanging out of my ass.**
> **Ron Athey, foreword to *Deliverance***

Unwinding COIL...

some personal notes on *COIL's Last Stand* – a screening programme at the LUX Cinema

A L Rees

Timed to auto-destruct after ten issues, COIL ends its run with a celebratory look back at some of the film, videos and digital artworks which inspired its vision of "moving image culture in the late 1990s." Giles Lane and I have selected work by artists who have been discussed, mentioned or featured in the journal, along with others who – it seemed to us – are in keeping with its spirit. There were far more of both kinds than we could include in one programme, and we offer only a passing glimpse of a much wider picture. We also chose some work we hadn't seen yet, but wanted to, just to add an extra element of surprise.

Punctuated by a series of one minute pieces mostly commissioned by the BBC's *Late Show*, we screen some older and newer work across COIL's spectrum of interests. Two classics of Surrealism are chosen from opposite ends of the movement. Maybe. Walerian Borowcyk's *Jeux des Anges* explores interior vision (Chris Marker is also credited), while Humphrey Jennings turns an ambiguous and vivid eye on English dailiness in *Spare Time*. Jayne Parker's *The Pool* merges the theme of inner and outer imaginations, while the artists' document(ary) is further explored by Patrick Keiller (in a rare early work, pre-*London* and *Robinson in Space*), Gordon Matta-Clark, Tacita Dean and – in an early version of her classic *Shadow of a Journey* – Tina Keane. By contrast, Steve Farrer's *Ten Drawings* is completely composed in graphic form, including a soundtrack in which lines and dots turn into film music.

Among the shorter but no less weighty films and tapes, Steve Hawley and Judith Goddard transform time and the image with edit-suite precision, while Nicky Hamlyn – like Rob Gawthrop – turns his camera in a more materialist direction to depict film space. The montage wit of Guy Sherwin parallels the in-camera magic of Tony Hill, while Sarah Miles and Gina Czarnecki explode the screen with visual delight. David Hall turns the baleful eye of John Logie Baird's dummy – the first successful TV image and its best emblem – on the shape of things televisual to come in *Stooky Bill TV*, "a work for television". We end with Beban and Horvatic's *The Lifeline Letter*, in brief homage to a much-missed friend and collaborator, Hrvoje Horvatic, who died in 1997.

It's an eclectic collection, a bit retro and perhaps a shade more historicist than I might have expected, though a live online link to Victoria Mapplebeck's webcam for her underground Channel 4 epic *Smart Hearts* (flip side of the yBA) will run throughout as a real-time reminder of the digital revolution. A lot has happened in the last five years (the LUX itself opened in 1997, coincident with COIL issue five), but not enough as far as the electronic arts are concerned. Galleries full of adapted games programmes and spurious forms of interaction are no substitute. Tellingly, Mapplebeck is rooted in the documentary tradition; hence her critical eye for the fantastic in the real. Much digital art is still awash in ill-digested symbolism and clappy-happy access, but where's the beef? Only a few vivid sparks are visible in a sky-full of homemade movie-clips, notably the similar sounding but unrelated pioneering groups, Audio-Rom and Anti-Rom, who have genuinely innovated in digital space.

It will be some time before the digital arts shuffle off their narrative and quasi-cinematic coil to pluck from the air a live tradition, a few samples of which are shown in this programme. Progress will be all the slower while artists are still mesmerised by the big screen, or remain victims of the small one. There may be some space between cinema and art, however narrow, or it may be an illusion into which most installation art falls headlong.

But beyond the special effects, the boxes of tricks and even the society of the spectacle, other lines of force continue to emanate – like early issues of COIL – up and down and across the page. The abstract cinema of Richter and Eggeling is part of this matrix, looking ahead to a programmed art based on form and pattern. The single-frame syntheses of Kubelka and Breer yield a vocabulary of vision. Brakhage and Deren evoke (in Maya Deren's own phrase) "the creative use of cinematography", while the overlaps of vision and music are traceable in the montage art of LeGrice, Rhodes and Larcher. It's not all been done before – that's the point. But it all has to be done over again. While Judith Goddard and Stephen Partridge have variously turned the screen saver into art, the dominant trend is the other way around. By mixing surrealism, materialism, animation, vérité, abstraction and intervention in COIL's last stand at the LUX, another lifeline for digital art is suggested, a road not yet taken, which should be as inclusive, diverse, maddening, engaging and surprising as COIL set out to be on its five-year march to countdown.

July 2000

Jeux des Anges

Shadow of a Journey

I Love You

COIL Screening Programme at the LUX Cinema, July 2000

Sarah Miles	One Minute TV: I Love You (1989, video 1 min)
Walerian Borowcyk	Jeux des Anges (1964, 16mm 12 mins)
Steve Hawley	Trout Descending a Staircase (1989, video 1 min)
Rob Gawthrop	Place on the Hill (1979, 16mm 6 mins)
Patrick Keiller	Valtos (1987, 16mm 6 mins)
Judith Goddard	One Minute TV: Luminous Portrait (1989, video 1 min)
Jayne Parker	The Pool (1990, 16mm 10 mins)
Nicky Hamlyn	One Minute TV: Minutiae (1989, 16mm 1 min)
Gordon Matta-Clark	Sous-Sols de Paris (1975, 16mm 19 mins)
Jaki Irvine	Sadman (1993, video 2 mins)
Tony Hill	One Minute TV: Short History of Wheel (1989, 16mm 1 min)
Tina Keane	Shadow of a Journey (1972, Super8 3 mins)
Guy Sherwin	One Minute TV: Mile End Purgatorio (1989, 16mm 1 min)
Tacita Dean	Structure of Ice (1997, 16mm 3 mins)
David Hall	Stooky Bill TV (1990, video 4 mins)
Humphrey Jennings	Spare Time (194 , 16mm 18 mins)
Gina Czarnecki	FACADE (1987, 16mm 3 mins)
Beban & Horvatic	One Minute TV: The Lifeline Letter (1989, video 1 min)
Steve Farrer	Ten Drawings (1976, 16mm 20 mins)

The Lifeline Letter

Mile End Purgatorio

Short History of the Wheel

Luminous Portrait

Trout Descending a Staircase

The Pool

Spare Time

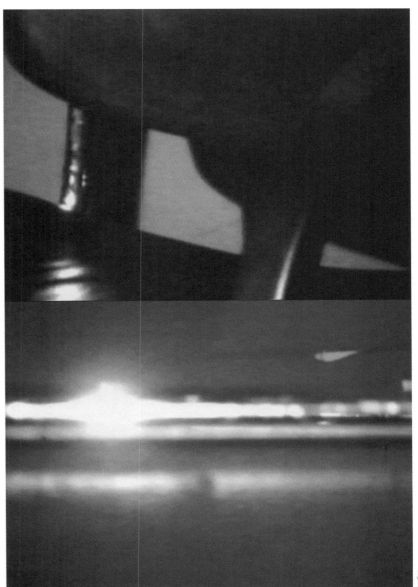

Minutiae

COIL ISSUE 1 (out of print)

TEXTS: Atif Ghani on Black and Asian British Film / Mark Cousins on Danger & Safety / Jamie Wagg on History Painting / Brandon LaBelle on Jarman's Blue / Eugene Finn on High Boot Benny / Kathleen Rogers on Psi-Net / Gina Czarnecki on the Authenticity of the Image / Wayne Sleeth on Rebecca Horn / Christopher Maris on Russian Filmmaking / Emina Kurtagic on Croatian filmmaking / Giles Lane on Walerian Borowcyk and John Hedjuk.

ARTISTS PROJECTS: Jayne Parker / Victoria Mapplebeck / Simon Lewandowski / Stef Zelynskij / Marion Reichert

COIL ISSUE 2 ISBN 1 90154O O9 X

TEXTS: Stuart Morgan on Bill Viola / Kathleen Pirrie-Adams on Tanya Syed / Anna Maris on Bristol Animators / William Firebrace — architecture & film / Gad Hollander — experimental film script / Laura Hudson on Super8 film revival / Marina Grzinic on East European art practice & philosophy / Clement Page on Matthew Barney.

ARTISTS PROJECTS: Anne Tallentire / Helen Sear & Mark Lythgoe / Rita Keegan / Andrew Kötting

COIL ISSUE 3 ISBN 1 90154O 1O 3

TEXTS: Sean Cubitt on CD-ROM art practice / Marcelyn Gow on architecture and the image / Rob Gawthrop on esperimental media festivals / Lowena Faull on Mnemoteknics / Steve Hawley on John Logie Baird's first TV transmission / Glyn Davis on the Ethnograhic Gaze / Denise Robinson & Susan Hiller in conversation / Brandon LaBelle on Phantom Memory.

ARTISTS PROJECTS: Marion Kalmus / Simon Robertshaw / Sharon Morris

COIL ISSUE 4 (out of print)

TEXTS:Pavel Büchler on the Shadow of the Crowd / Lisa Blackman on Harwood's Rehearsal of Memory / Declan Sheehan on Orson Welles & Voudoun / Stuart Morgan on Steve Farrer / Douglas Ord on David Rokeby / Jon Wagner on Tragic Realism / Lily de Rais on Jayne Parker & Georges Bataille.

ARTISTS PROJECTS: Clio Barnard / Graham ellard & Stephen Johnstone / Critical Art Ensemble / Judith Goddard / Steve Farrer

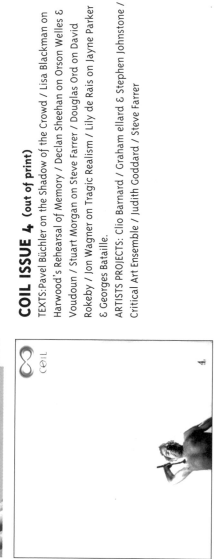

COLLECT THE BACK ISSUES

SINGLE BACK ISSUES

UK: £8, EUROPE: euro12 or WORLD AIRMAIL: US$12.95 (INC P+P)

SPECIAL OFFER - ISSUES 2, 3, 5, 6, 7 & 8

UK: £30, EUROPE: euro45 or WORLD AIRMAIL: US$50 (INC P+P)

COIL ISSUE 5 ISBN 1 901540 01 4

TEXTS: Ian Hunt on Chris Marker's LEVEL 5 / Charles Esche on Roderick Buchanan / Nicola Coutts on insects in art / Claire Lofting on Michal Rovner / Mark Lewis on Part Cinema / Rob Stone on Adorno, Benjamin & Performance Art / Virginie Dupray on Lydie Jean-dit-Pannell / Gilles Lazare on Tarkovskij, Benjamin & Humphrey Jennings.

ARTISTS PROJECTS: John Stezaker / Jon Thomson & Alison Craighead / Lyndal Jones / Breda Beban & Hrvoje Horvatic

COIL ISSUE 6 ISBN 1 901540 02 2

TEXTS: Kevin Henderson on performance and memory / Maria Walsh on Tacita Dean / Andrew Poppy — experimental sound and text project / Sean Cubitt — abandoned projects / Katrina McPherson dance for camera / Anna Maris on Swedish filmmaker Pelle Wichamn / Francis Mckee on Valerie Mrejen.

ARTISTS PROJECTS: Jaki Irvine / Marcelyn Gow / Pervaiz Khan & Felix de Rooy / Andrew Stones

COIL ISSUE 7 ISBN 1 901540 03 0

TEXTS: Regina Cornwell on The Computer & Art Making / Chris Darke on John Searjeant's The Blue Summer / Keith Griffiths on Petit & Sinclair's The Falconer / Nelly Voorhuis on Art Film & Video in the Arena of art exhibitions / Sandra Lahire on Sarah Pucill's Swollen Stigma / Sally Stafford on 1940s Women's Film / Sue Golding on Blood Poetics.

ARTISTS PROJECTS: Dalziell & Scullion / Sera Furneaux / Willie Doherty / Rory Hamilton / Damien Smith&ISO

COIL ISSUE 8 ISBN 1 901540 04 9

TEXTS: Joshua Oppenheimer & Christine Cynn on People who die in closets / Jesse Lerner & Rita Gonzalez on Mexican experimental Film & Video / Winfried Pauleit (German w/trans)on the Film Still / Sarah Turner — CUT (filmscript) / Emina Kurtagic on Lisl Ponger / Chris Byrne on Video Art & the Web / Laura Malacart on Ulrike Ottinger / Naomi Salaman on Duane Hanson.

ARTISTS PROJECTS: Brigid McLeer / Susan Collins / Dryden Goodwin / Hans Schierl

SEND A CHEQUE OR POSTAL ORDER TO:

PROBOSCIS

2 ORMONDE MANSIONS, 100A SOUTHAMPTON ROW
LONDON WC1B 4BJ, UNITED KINGDOM
EMAIL: info@proboscis.org.uk

Books Received

A History of Experimental Film and Video
A.L. Rees
BFI Publishing 1999
152pp 56 b&w illustrations
Hbk & Pbk £15.00 ISBN 0 851706 81 9
Landmark critical survey of twentieth century
experimental practices in moving image media.

Robinson in Space
Patrick Keiller
Reaktion Books 1999
256pp b&w illustrations
Pbk £16.95 ISBN 1 861890 28 1
A print translation of Keiller's eponymous
literary film.

Tokyo
Donald Ritchie
Reaktion Books 1999
143pp b&w illustrations
Pbk £16.95 ISBN 1 86189 034 6
Elegant and reverent investigation into space
and social mores of the Japanese city.

Strange and Charmed:
Science and the Contemporary Visual Arts
Edited by Siân Ede
Calouste Gulbenkian Foundation London 2000
200pp col/b&w illustrations,
Pbk £10.99 ISBN 0 903319 87 X
Preface by A.S. Byatt. Chapters by: Ken Arnold,
Richard Bright, Andrea Duncan, Siân Ede, Martin
Kemp, Mike Page & Deborah Schultz.
Very-readable and Illuminating overview of the
growing phenomenon of science-art collaborations.

Object to be Destroyed:
The Work of Gordon Matta-Cark
Pamela M. Lee
MIT Press 2000
280pp b&w illustrations,
Hbk £21.95 ISBN 0 262 12220 0
Doctoral thesis with literary pretensions. Well illustrated.

Site of Sound: of architecture and the ear
Edited by Brandon LaBelle and Steve Roden
Errant Bodies Press in association with Smart Arts
Press, Los Angeles 1999
178pp b&w illustrations + Audio CD
Pbk £15.00 ISBN 0-9655570-2-2
Contributions by: Alison Knowles, Achim Wollsheid, Jalal
Toufic, Hildegard Westerkamp, Phillip Corner, Christina
Kubisch, Giancarlo Toniutti, Jake Tilson, Brandon LaBelle,
Rolf Julius, Leif Elggren & CM von Hausswolff, Steve Peters,
Ralf L. Wehowsky, David Dunn, Christof Migone, Loren
Chasse, Maniek Darge, Michael Brewster, Max Eastley,
Tim Robinson, Steve Roden, Rupert M. Loydell, Tom
Marrioni, Minoru Sato & Toshiya Tsunoda and Jio Shimizu.
CD tracks by: Achim Wollsheid, Hildegard Westerkamp,
John Hudak, Christof Migone, Ralf L. Wehowsky, Steve
Peters, Christina Kubisch, LaBelle/Roden, Minoru Sato
& Toshiya Tsunoda, Jio Shimizu and Richard Lerman.
Wide-ranging collection of writings and audio contri-
butions exploring the architectonics of sound from an
impressive international cast.

DIFFUSION

A NEW SERIES OF DOWNLOADABLE EBOOKS

DIFFUSION is a new publishing imprint from Proboscis which aims to utilise the specific advantages of digital media to create a new means of combining critical thinking and creativity.

The first series is **PERFORMANCE NOTATIONS**: 10 new texts exploring the intersection between live arts and digital and moving image practices available to download as free PDF files from September 2000. The files are designed to be printed out and made into booklets by readers in a matter of minutes.

Contributors:

Rob Gawthrop	Marcelyn Gow	Marina Grzinic	Kevin Henderson
Vit Hopley & Yve Lomax	Katharine Meynell	johnny de philo [Sue Golding]	
Monica Ross & Anne Tallentire	Declan Sheehan	Aaron Williamson	

Series Editors: Catherine Williams & Giles Lane
Print Design: Paul Farrington & Nima Falatoori   Interaction Design: Noel Douglas

www.diffusion.org.uk

Funded by the Arts Council of England with additional support from CRD RESEARCH at the Royal College of Art

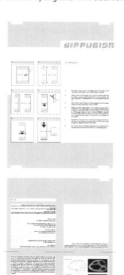

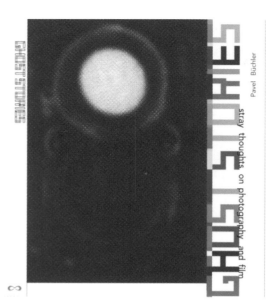

Ghost Stories
stray thoughts on photography & film
by Pavel Büchler

Edited by Giles Lane & Brandon LaBelle
Designed by Louise Sandhaus

A provocative collection of writings focusing on the magic, spectral, aspect of photography and the moving image. *Ghost Stories* presents original versions of texts published between 1983 and 1998, as well as some previously unpublished writings. The selection charts the development of Büchler's key critical approaches towards an unorthodox intellectual and aesthetic position. Stylistically diverse — from the journalistic, the academic and the critical to poetic speculation — the essays reflect the changing climates in which they were written.

"...storytelling, enthusiasm and flights of satiric fantasy expressive of a sceptic's love of the world... a constant duty of criticism and attention."

Art Monthly

"...richly metaphoric, open-ended critical/theoretical texts. ...his writing involves risky, gravity-defying 'intellectual leaps'..."

Creative Camera

paperback 132pp, 200 x 125mm portrait, b&w illustrations, ISBN 1 901540 07 3
Price £9.99 / US$ 16.95
available from good bookshops and by mail order from Proboscis: info@proboscis.org.uk

supported by the Arts Council of England

TOPOLOGIES
a public art for public libraries initiative

Curatorial Team: Alice Angus, Catherine Williams & Giles Lane

TOPOLOGIES is a new initiative breaking away from traditional manifestations of public art, and commissioning new works to be disseminated via the public library system.

By intervening within such public sites, TOPOLOGIES aims to introduce conceptual art practices (as distinct from public monuments and sculptures) to diverse and new audiences, attempting to widen the audience for contemporary art beyond the gallery experience.

Proboscis recently conducted a research and feasibility study supported by the Arts Council of England. A condensed report of the findings is available at:

www.topologies.org

TOPOLOGIES has 4 proposed components:

COMMISSIONS: new works (some derived from the residencies) which use distributable formats such as: visual (print-based or video); aural (audio CD); tactile (Braille, Moon or textile works); digital (CD-ROMs or online art). These artworks are designed to form part of public libraries' lending and reference collections, to be used, handled, read, touched or listened to rather than simply seen in a glass case.

ARTISTS RESIDENCIES: hosted by partner organizations such as Public Libraries, Local Authorities, Museum, Galleries, Art Centres and educational institutions.

www.topologies.org: a web portal with structured educational materials for schools, adult learning and academic uses, as well as directing users to other art-related websites. Integrated with the Peoples Network and the National Grid for Learning.

ARTISTS BOOKWORKS COLLECTIONS: selections of exemplary artists bookworks curated by Proboscis and sited as individual collections with all 209 UK library authorities.

MAPPING PERCEPTION

A collaboration between curator Giles Lane, Andrew Kötting, the acclaimed director of *Gallivant* and *Smart Alek*, and Dr Mark Lythgoe, neurophysiologist at the Institute of Child Health, London. Produced by Proboscis.

The project will look at the perceptions of impaired brain function to further understand the mind and body interaction and our relationship with its abnormality. It will aim to make visible the connections between the scientific and artistic explorations of the human condition, probing the thin membrane between the able and the disabled.

MAPPING PERCEPTION will result in two separate projects: an installation version and a short 16mm film. Both will be premiered at the Edinburgh International Film Festival (EIFF) in August 2001.

The Installation version is supported by a producton award from the sciart consortium, EIFF and the Institute of Child Health, London.
The Film version is funded by the National Lottery through the Film Council, London Production Fund, Institute of Child Health, London and South East Arts.

For further details on the project and associated events, please visit:

www.mappingperception.org.uk

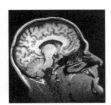

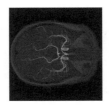

eden is cold and hungry

● COIL 9/10 | 2000

● **editor:** giles lane ┊┊┊ **contributing editor:** nicola coutts ┊┊┊ **associate editor:** brandon labelle ┊┊┊ **finance:** joan johnston ●

design: richard bonner-morgan Tel 020 7923 4040 ● **published in an edition of 1500 by proboscis** ┊┊┊ © 2000 proboscis and

contributors. all rights reserved ┊┊┊ the opinions expressed in COIL are not necessarily those of the editor and publisher ●

proboscis 2 ormonde mansions 100a southampton row london wc1b 4bj Tel 07711 069 569 Fax 020 7430 1147 Email

info@proboscis.org.uk Web www.proboscis.org.uk ● COIL is a unique 10 issue series published twice-yearly by proboscis

between 1995 and 2000. An interface between critical and creative texts and artists' projects within moving image media.

COIL promotes collaborations across diverse cultural disciplines. This is the final issue in the series ● **proboscis** is an

independent non-profit making organisation which researches, develops and facilitates innovation in creative practices ●

images courtesy of: Bill Viola; Electronic Arts Intermix; Museum of Modern Art, New York; Victoria Miro Gallery, London;

Marion Scemama; the artists and contributors ● **special thanks** to the Arts Council of England for their continuing support,

Easynet Group for Internet Service Provision and the Computer Related Design Research Studio, Royal College of Art.

Proboscis would also like to thank all of the contributors and volunteers without whose efforts COIL would not have been

possible ● COIL may be contacted in the usa via the associate editor, brandon labelle: po box 931124, los angeles, ca 90093

● barbies xr3i & barbies bauhaus typefaces created by jason rainbird ● **isbn** 1-901540-05-7 ┊┊┊ **issn** 1357-9207 ● **printed**

by geoff neal litho, middlesex, england ● **worldwide distribution:** art books international ltd. T (+44) 020 7720 1503 F (+44)

020 7720 3158 E sales@art-bks.com ● COIL is available by subscription for details on prices: email, fax or check the website

● **cover image:** Nick Norton